Karlheinz Kautz   Peter Axel Nielsen (Eds.)

Scandinavian Information Systems Research

First Scandinavian Conference
on Information Systems, SCIS 2010
Rebild, Denmark, August 20-22, 2010
Proceedings

Volume Editors

Karlheinz Kautz
Copenhagen Business School
Department of Informatics
Howitzvej 60, 2000 Frederiksberg, Denmark
E-mail: karl.kautz@cbs.dk

Peter Axel Nielsen
Aalborg University
Department of Computer Science
Selma Lagerlöfs Vej 300, 9220 Aalborg, Denmark
E-mail: pan@cs.aau.dk

Library of Congress Control Number: 2010931632

ACM Computing Classification (1998): J.1, H.4.1, H.3.5, K.6, D.2

ISSN   1865-1348
ISBN-10   3-642-14873-5 Springer Berlin Heidelberg New York
ISBN-13   978-3-642-14873-6 Springer Berlin Heidelberg New York

This work is subject to copyright. All rights are reserved, whether the whole or part of the material is concerned, specifically the rights of translation, reprinting, re-use of illustrations, recitation, broadcasting, reproduction on microfilms or in any other way, and storage in data banks. Duplication of this publication or parts thereof is permitted only under the provisions of the German Copyright Law of September 9, 1965, in its current version, and permission for use must always be obtained from Springer. Violations are liable to prosecution under the German Copyright Law.

springer.com

© Springer-Verlag Berlin Heidelberg 2010
Printed in Germany

Typesetting: Camera-ready by author, data conversion by Scientific Publishing Services, Chennai, India
Printed on acid-free paper   SPIN: 06/3180   5 4 3 2 1 0

Preface

The First Scandinavian Conference on Information Systems (SCIS 2010) took place during August 20–22, 2010 in Rebild, Denmark. The conference was held in conjunction with the traditional IRIS seminar for information systems research in Scandinavia. The IRIS seminar has a long-standing recognition for furthering information systems research. The objective of SCIS 2010 was to extend and formalize a part of the seminar to a full conference. The purpose of the conference was to exchange and publish high-quality research with a particular view on the Scandinavian research community.

The theme of the conference was "Engaged Scandinavian Information Systems Research." Scandinavian information systems research has for several decades been concerned with its relevance for practitioners of the field, for users, for industry, and for society at large. This concern for the usefulness outside the realms of research has shaped the Scandinavian researchers' awareness, attention, research conduct, and most importantly a focus on who we interact with on which issues, why we do this, and for whom we do it.

In his book *Engaged Scholarship* published in 2007, Van de Ven offered an enlightening view on organizational and social research that is highly relevant for Scandinavian information systems research. He suggests an interactional view in which professional and research practices contribute to each other through different types of activity. Embracing qualitative as well as quantitative methods and promoting process studies as well as variance studies, engaged scholarship offers opportunities to transcend the traditional dichotomies of rigor versus relevance, and positivist versus interpretive research. Van de Ven defined "engaged scholarship" as "a participative form of research for obtaining the different perspectives of key stakeholders (researchers, users, clients, sponsors, and practitioners) in studying complex problems." Much of the Scandinavian information systems research already followed this line of thinking as can be seen in a retrospective analysis which was presented in the *Scandinavian Journal of Information Systems*, Vol. 20, No. 2. The conference addressed and further promoted a view on Scandinavian information systems research with a particular focus on how "engaged" unfolds in different studies.

Altogether, a set of 10 scientific papers illustrating the conference theme was presented in a single track. A large Program Committee consisting of researchers from Finland, Norway, Sweden, Denmark as well as the USA and Australia carefully evaluated all submitted papers. Each submission was reviewed by three Program Committee members. Only the very best quality papers were selected, resulting in an acceptance rate of 25%.

During the conference we hosted three keynote speakers engaged in Scandinavian information systems research: Brian Fitzgerald, University of Limerick, Ireland; Jan Pries-Heje, Roskilde University, Denmark; and Suprateek Sarker, Copenhagen Business School, Denmark.

August 2010

Karlheinz Kautz
Peter Axel Nielsen

Organization

Program Co-chairs

Karlheinz Kautz   Denmark
Peter Axel Nielsen   Denmark

Program Committee

Kim Normann Andersen   Denmark
Karin Axelsson   Sweden
Jørgen Bansler   Denmark
Tone Bratteteig   Norway
Keld Bødker   Denmark
Susanne Bødker   Denmark
Jan Damsgaard   Denmark
Ole Hanseth   Norway
Liisa von Hellens   Australia
Ola Henfridsson   Sweden
Jonny Holmström   Sweden
Pertti Järvinen   Finland
Rikard Lindgren   Sweden
Kalle Lyytinen   USA
Lars Mathiassen   USA
Eric Monteiro   Norway
Bjørn Erik Munkvold   Norway
Markku Nurminen   Finland
Helena Holmström Olsson   Sweden
Samuli Pekkola   Finland
Matti Rossi   Finland
Maung K. Sein   Norway
Jesper Simonsen   Denmark
Erik Stolterman   USA
Reima Suomi   Finland
Carsten Sørensen   UK
Virpi Tuunainen   Finland
Margunn Aaenestad   Norway
Pär Ågerfalk   Sweden

Organizing Committee

Hanne Westh Nicolajsen	Aalborg University, Denmark
Lise Heeager	Aalborg University, Denmark
John Persson	Aalborg University, Denmark
Gitte Tjørnehøj	Aarhus School of Business, Denmark

Table of Contents

Relationship Management at the Operational Level in Outsourcing 1
  Sabine Madsen and Keld Bødker

User Experience: Consumer Understandings of Virtual Product
Prototypes 18
  Taina Kaapu and Tarja Tiainen

The Living Requirements Space: Towards the Collaborative
Development of Requirements for Future ERP Systems 34
  Femi Adisa, Petra Schubert, and Frantisek Sudzina

IT Governance through Regulatory Modalities. Health Care Information
Infrastructure and the "Blue Fox" Project 50
  Bendik Bygstad and Ole Hanseth

Boundaries between Participants in Outsourced Requirements
Construction 65
  Sari T. Salmela and Anna-Liisa Syrjänen

Is Standard Software Wiping Out Socio-Technical Design? - Engaging
in the Practice of Implementing Standard ERP Systems 79
  Lene Pries-Heje

Facing the Lernaean Hydra: The Nature of Large-Scale Integration
Projects in Healthcare 93
  Eli Larsen and Gunnar Ellingsen

Bootstrapping Revisited: Opening the Black Box of Organizational
Implementation 111
  Espen Skorve and Margunn Aanestad

Configuration Analysis of Inter-Organizational Information Systems
Adoption 127
  Kalle Lyytinen and Jan Damsgaard

An Analysis of Literature Reviews on IS Business Value: How
Deficiencies in Methodology and Theory Use Resulted in Limited
Effectiveness 139
  Guido Schryen

Author Index 157

Relationship Management at the Operational Level in Outsourcing

Sabine Madsen and Keld Bødker

Roskilde University, Department of Communication, Business and Information Technologies,
Universitetsvej 1, DK-4000 Roskilde, Denmark
{sabinem,keldb}@ruc.dk

Abstract. Research suggests that achievement of a successful outsourcing relationship requires a tremendous amount of detailed management. In this paper we draw on relationship theory to understand the management practices of a particular outsourcing setup. An empirical study of a Danish company operating an offshore development centre with 400 employees located in India identified a host of practices that form a seemingly complex and ambiguous picture. To make sense of the studied practice we develop a framework that consists of four relationship management strategies coined select-a-friend, develop-a-friend, control-a-person, and control-of-output. We provide illustrative examples of each strategy; reflect upon the alignment between the type of outsourcing setup and the identified portfolio of practices; and outline theoretical and practical implications. Key findings are that all four strategies are used, play an important role and that continuous improvement of the portfolio of relationship management practices is paramount to ensure effectiveness.

Keywords: Offshore outsourcing, relationship management, engaged research.

1 Introduction

Outsourcing is defined "as the handing over of assets, resources, activities and/or people to third party management to achieve agreed performance outcomes" (Lacity & Willcocks, 2006, p. 1). Outsourcing has been on the research agenda since the early 1990's and the literature on the topic is abundant. The extant literature has, e.g., addressed the *contract management* that is required when the service provider is completely in charge of a significant piece of work, i.e. when *total outsourcing* has been chosen (Dibbern et al., 2004). Moreover, a lot of research has looked at how to conduct *project management* when activities are jointly performed by an on- or offshore service provider and the client company, i.e. when a *cooperative outsourcing* strategy has been implemented (Dibbern et al., 2004). The term, onshore, refers to outsourced activities that are performed in the same country as the client company; offshore refers to outsourced work that is carried out in another country, and often at low-cost destinations such as India, China, and Russia; while the term, onsite, denotes the location of the client company's main operation (Holmström et al., 2008).

Despite the much literature that offers normative guidelines on how to perform outsourcing in practice, achieving success at the operational level remains a challenge (Willcocks & Lacity, 2006). This is, among other reasons, because it takes a tremendous amount of detailed management to ensure a successful outsourcing relationship (Lacity & Willcocks, 2006; Rustagi et al., 2008). Prior research suggests that managing the outsourcing effort on a daily basis represents the largest category of hidden costs, which however can be reduced by gaining practical experience with outsourcing and by cultivating a trust-based client-provider relationship as an antidote to opportunism (Barthélemy, 2001). There is increasing recognition of the importance of the client-provider relationship, but there is still a relative lack of empirical research on the topic (Holmström et al., 2008). And in general, the practicalities and required relationship management, particularly with regard to a cooperative, offshore outsourcing setup, are not yet well understood (Beck et al., 2008; King & Torkzadeh, 2008).

In this paper, we report from a case study of a specific company's chosen outsourcing strategy and its practical and managerial implications at the operational level. The case company is a major Danish organization (hereafter referred to as the CaseCompany) that has 3 years of operational experience with a cooperative outsourcing strategy implemented as an 'Offshore Development Center' (ODC) in India. The chosen strategy is such that approx. 400 Indians employed by an Indian service provider are 'hired' from the Indian company into the ODC. The Indians are considered a pool of resources to be allocated to IT development projects and/or system management areas (i.e. maintenance), just like other IT employees in the CaseCompany. The contract with the Indian service provider concerns the timely delivery of skilled personnel and billable hours rather than IT products or services. This outsourcing strategy has been chosen to ensure access to a cost-saving and scalable work force. 70% of the ODC resources are allocated to system management, while the remaining 30% work on development projects. Moreover, many ODC resources are allocated to tasks onsite, i.e. in Denmark; at any given time approx. 20-25% of the ODC resources are onsite. Another characteristic of the chosen outsourcing strategy is that five Danes are posted in India to oversee the daily operations.

Using the above company as our case we ask: *which practicalities and relationship management practices are key for ensuring the effectiveness of a cooperative, offshore outsourcing setup at the operational, day-to-day level?*

2 Research Approach

To answer the research question we present a practice study (Mathiassen, 2002) conducted for the purpose of understanding a particular cooperative, offshore outsourcing setup at the operational level. As we investigate offshore outsourcing in its natural surroundings, and as there still is a paucity of theory about this phenomenon, an in-depth case study has been conducted (Walsham, 1993; Yin, 2003). For interpreting our qualitative case study data we have gone through several rounds of analyses, and we have shared our empirical findings and theory-inspired conceptualizations with relevant stakeholders on an on-going basis. This explorative and engaged research approach has been chosen to overcome the lack of established theories about outsourcing as well as the research-practice divide; with the latter referring to research that overlooks the complexity of practice and research results that are either irrelevant or underused in practice (Van de Ven, 2007).

Below we describe the research setting as well as how data collection and analysis was conducted. To allow the reader to understand the explorative and engaged nature of the research as well as to make his/her own judgement about the reliability and validity hereof we go into some detail with the process whereby the research focus and findings have come about.

2.1 Research Setting

The study is part of a larger research project, which involves several companies and research organizations that work with both onshore and offshore outsourcing in various outsourcing setups. Inspired by Cullen et al.'s (2006) outsourcing life cycle model, at this stage of the research project we are concerned with the development of guidelines for managing outsourcing issues at the strategic, tactical, and operational level.

Our study focuses on the operational, day-to-day activities in a specific outsourcing setup, namely a cooperative, offshore outsourcing implemented as a dedicated development center (see, e.g., Villumsen, 2007; Rottman & Lacity, 2006 for an overview of different types of offshoring outsourcing setups). A dedicated development center is a facility *owned* by the service provider and *dedicated* to the specific client. It typically includes an IT infrastructure and branding of the facility targeted at the client. In the case under study, IT security is, e.g., extremely important. The service provider has therefore implemented the same technical solutions and IT security policies at the ODC as in the Danish headquarter. Moreover, the ODC is located in two adjacent buildings that bear the name of the CaseCompany and where only the employees working for the CaseCompany have access.

We had worked with the CaseCompany for about a year before embarking on this particular study. We therefore had a basic understanding of the company: its organization, IT development model, and outsourcing setup, including the goals, and operational challenges involved. Based on this, we developed a set of objectives and guidelines for the study that were negotiated and agreed with the Danish Manager of the ODC. In line with the managerial aspects suggested by Cullen et al. (2006), the focal points were organization of joint activities, communication and coordination, decision making, documentation, knowledge sharing, and relationship development between Danish and Indian employees.

2.2 Data Collection

In March 2009, we spent three weeks in India. At this time, the ODC had been in operation for 2.5 years and had 400 employees. We studied the activities of four teams and interviewed 18 people in total (see Table 1).

The Liaison officers (LO's) were all experienced Danish employees with a long term posting in India. Their tasks were to conduct screening interviews with all candidates from the Indian company, control and follow-up on the contract with the

Indian company, and to undertake process improvement. From the development project we talked to the task manager, the test manager, a solution architect and two developers. From the system management groups we talked to the task manager, IT-developers, and from one of the teams also an Indian employee posted in Denmark as onsite coordinator. In addition to interviewing we spent time with the participants at their desk studying use of IT tools, like development workbenches and error-reporting tools, and acquired and read documents mentioned during interviews. Each interview was recorded. After each interview we also went through our notes and jointly produced a note from the interview. For each team we developed a memo by gradually augmenting the memo with new information from each interview. Each memo was structured according to the themes of our interview guide. Altogether this gave us four memos of 7-9 pages.

Table 1. Interview activities

	# of interviews	total duration (hours)
India:		
Liaison officers	3	15
Development project	5	7.5
System mgt. P	6	6
System mgt. G	4	5
Denmark:		
Follow-up interviews	2	4
Liaison officers	2	3

At the end of our stay we presented and discussed our initial findings with the Danish LO's and the Indian task managers. The discussion contributed to our main impression, namely that an overwhelming set of activities and process improvement initiatives are undertaken to establish a smoothly operating offshore development centre.

Upon our return to Denmark, in April 2009, we did two follow-up interviews with a Danish employee and the Danish ODC manager participating on phone. Just before we arrived at the ODC, the employee had returned to Denmark from a short-term posting in India where she had completed a study of the support processes carried out at the ODC. This study, documented in a 50 page report, also confirmed our understanding that many managerial and administrative processes are necessary to establish and operate a cooperative, offshore outsourcing setup. At this point in time, we therefore felt comfortable formulating the research question (presented in the introduction) that was to drive our data analysis.

2.3 Data Analysis

The empirical data were analyzed by first mapping *all the employed practices* according to the themes in our interview guide as well as to emerging themes. Second, we identified higher level categories. The findings were further elaborated by discussing the process map and the high level categories with two Danish LO's in order to identify and place *the key relationship management practices* within an emerging framework.

During the first round of detailed data analysis, we found that two different, and somewhat competing, discourses were at play. One discourse was about providing the support that would put the ODC resources in a position to get the job done. This discourse reflected a perception of the ODC resources as colleagues with equal status, needs, and rights and as a part of the company. The other discourse concerned management control and follow-up on if the job was getting done, on time, within budget, and with the right quality. This discourse covered a view of the ODC resources as costs, and consultants, i.e. from outside the company, and contained elements of distrust due to (perceived) differences in the Danes and Indians' performance.

During the first round of data analysis, we also found that to understand the unique and practical implications of the chosen outsourcing strategy we had to take into account that there were ODC resources onsite and offshore. For understanding the applied practices this was important because onsite resources are co-located with their Danish colleagues, while the offshore resources are collaborating with the Danish organization in a distributed manner. Thus, based on the first thematic coding of the data, we developed a framework (see Appendix 1) that delineated the *support* and *control* processes that were key for making the particular outsourcing setup work both *onsite* and *offshore*. This framework was developed based on an inductive data analysis strategy.

Subsequently a second round of analysis was conducted. During this analysis we used our preliminary empirical findings - namely that many managerial and administrative practices were needed; that these practices reflected both support and control-oriented aspects; and that many process improvement initiatives were carried out in parallel - as our starting point for selecting relevant theoretical concepts and for developing a theoretical framework that could capture the complexity and nuances of the case. Second, we used the developed framework to re-interpret the intended effect and actual application of the identified key relationship management practices. The aim was to use theory to see 'more' in the data and to be able to reflect on the findings at a higher level of abstraction.

The findings and framework presented below are the product of a number of iterations between data collection at various empirical sites, data analysis, and presentations for the people involved in the studied activities, people with higher managerial positions in the CaseCompany, the other companies involved in the research project, as well as academic researchers.

3 Theoretical Background

Prior research about outsourcing has emphasized the importance of relationship management and in particular the need for techniques and procedures that impact the relationship in the desired way (Dibbern et al. 2004). Organizations and managers can e.g. use formal mechanisms concerned with output, behavior, and input control (Ouchi, 1979) to steer performance in the desired direction:

1. Output control. If it is easy to specify goals and measure the output in accordance with goals then output should be monitored and controlled. Incentives and penalties can be used to motivate the service provider to live up to expectations.

However, with regard to a cooperative outsourcing strategy, measuring the service provider's contribution is difficult because of the need for client – provider interaction and cooperation to produce the result. Instead trust in each other, commitment to the relationship, and investment of resources in the relationship is needed (Kishore et al., 2003).
2. Behavior control. If the task is well-understood it is possible to specify the behaviors to achieve the desired performance, e.g., in the form of standard operating procedures, codified processes, prescriptions for when to use which methods, techniques, templates, and tools, etc. In an outsourcing context, the standardization of processes for transferring work to the service provider and for getting the work done is emphasized (Beck et al., 2008; Dibbern et al., 2004; Sabherwal, 1999; Willcocks & Lacity, 2006).
3. Input control. If it is difficult to measure the output and/or the task is not well understood, input control is needed to ensure performance. Input control refers to selection, training, and socialization; i.e. to finding 'a good match' and the internalization of company values and behavioral norms. In line with this, in an outsourcing context it is recommended that the client oversees the allocation of human resources to the outsourced projects and areas (McFarlan & Nolan, 1995). It is also recommended that action should be taken to ensure that people can meet and interact. Interaction and especially formal and informal face-to-face meetings facilitate the building of trust, shared context, and cultural intelligence. A relationship based on these three aspects in turn makes knowledge sharing, communication, conflict resolution, and understanding of each other and each others' expectations, goals, requirements, etc., easier (Beck et al., 2008; Hinds & Bailey, 2003; Ngwenyama & Bjørn, 2008; Sabherwal, 1999; Siakas & Siakas, 2008).

Despite the existence of a vast amount of formal mechanisms and best practices for ensuring a successful outsourcing relationship, outsourcing continues to pose challenges in practice, even for experienced organizations (Cullen et al., 2006). Our reading of the literature as well as our empirical data suggest that this is because "best" practices are selected and implemented only to "…see that it does not work when working together with an Indian vendor. Then, you adapt your procedures as a consequence of your deeper understanding." (Beck et al., 2008, pp. 12). Thus, best practices are not really best practices, but merely a starting point. Also, smaller 'process improvement projects' to solve particular issues often take place simultaneously and while the 'normal' everyday activities are carried out by the client and the provider's employees. This makes it difficult to gain an overview of the improvement initiatives, and to evaluate each initiative's as well as the portfolio of practices' impact on performance. In the next section we develop a theoretical framework that helps us understand and evaluate the portfolio of relationship management practices applied in the case under study.

4 Theoretical Framework

Relationship theory has previously been used in the context of outsourcing due to its ability to help explain interaction and cooperation in inter-organizational relationships

(Dibbern et al., 2004). For understanding the practicalities and practices of cooperative outsourcing setups the theory seems particular relevant because a prerequisite for people to perform in such a setup is that they interact and are able to cooperate.

Relationship theory explains how and why different types of relationships begin, develop, maintain, and end. Research shows that for interpersonal relationships to form there has to be (spontaneous) opportunities to meet, and that proximity therefore greatly promotes the initiation of relationships (Rose & Serifica, 1986). Moreover, for relationships to develop frequent interaction between relationship partners is required (Rose & Serifica, 1986).

In a commercial setting it has also been found that sheer frequency of interaction, the need to cooperate to produce the result, and shared high-pressure experiences favour the formation of 'commercial friendships' (Price & Arnould, 1999). The more a (commercial) relationship resembles a friendship the more people feel comfortable around each other and able "to let their guards down". As a result, they also feel more able to ask for favors, fast approvals, flexibility in scheduling and to bring "thorny" issues up (Haytko, 2004). In contrast, it is not possible to ask someone who is "strictly business" for a favor or to ask a question that could be interpreted as incompetent (Haytko, 2004). Moreover, it has been found that clients and service providers who express positive feelings towards each other (such as "I know him well", and "he's more like a friend") also report a desire to work to maintain the relationship, and overcome misunderstandings and failures (Goodwin, 1996). The concept of commercial friendship is somewhat controversial as both theoretically and intuitively it is common to distinguish between communal (i.e. friends and family) and exchange (i.e. transactional) relationships (Clark, 1986; Clark & Mills, 1993). Yet, empirical research shows that development of interpersonal relationships characterized by trust, mutual knowledge, and affection in inter-organizational settings provides a number of benefits for the people and organizations involved.

Heide & Wathne (2006) delineate two prototypical types of business relationships, namely that of (1) 'a business person' who will either co-operate or not depending on what type of action that will be most opportune, and (2) 'a business friend' who follows the norm of "co-operation as a matter of principle". Heide & Wathne (2006) use the two terms to refer to the roles that companies and their employees can assume towards each other and the role-dependent norms that guide their interaction with each other. They also specify the mechanisms that can be used to create and develop a relationship in alignment with the desired partner role and interaction norms. To manage a 'business person' relationship output control, i.e. monitoring, measurement, incentives, and penalties, are emphasized as important to ensure that the partner behaves in the desired cooperative rather than opportunistic way. A 'business friend' relationship is primarily created and progressed through input controls such as careful selection, appropriate training, and continuous socialization (Heide & Wathne, 2006). Relationship strategies that work in both directions can and will often coexist in practice, but might lead to role switching and resource waste (Heide & Wathne, 2006; Price & Arnould, 1999). This suggests that socialization activities can be kept to a minimum if the tasks that the service provider undertakes are well suited for behavior and output control.

In delineating a framework for understanding and evaluating the practicalities and relationship management practices employed to support the CaseCompany's outsourcing setup we draw on the concepts of 'a business person' and 'a business friend' as well as the three formal mechanisms of output, behavior, and input control and the conditions under which they are applicable. This combination of concepts and mechanisms has been selected for two reasons, namely because (1) two different types of business relationships are delineated. The two types of relationships differ with regard to their view of and appropriate behavior towards the other. This fits well with the two discourses at play in the empirical case study; and because (2) different types of mechanisms for achieving the type of relationship that fits with the characteristics of the tasks are outlined. In this way some consideration for cost is included. These two elements allows for a nuanced understanding of our empirical material as they cover both aspects of trust and distrust as well as trade-offs between the needs for and costs of cooperation and control.

The framework is presented in Table 2. The framework is based on a number of theoretical assumptions, namely that (1) in a situation where much interaction and cooperation is needed to ensure high performance the business friend role is the most suitable, while (2) in a situation where goals can be measured and/or the task is well understood, the 'business person' perspective is the most appropriate, among other reasons, to avoid incurring costs on unnecessary interaction and relationship building activities. Based on these theoretical assumptions, the framework delineates four relationship management strategies coined select-a-friend, develop-a-friend, control-a-person, and control-of-output. All four strategies are instrumental in nature and aim to ensure and/or increase performance, albeit through different means. Importantly, the use of the two terms 'a friend' and 'a person' refer to the two prototypical types of business relationships (Heide & Wathne, 2006) and their inherent assumptions about trust and co-operation vs. distrust and control. Thus, the two concepts do not imply (but they also do not exclude) the existence of interpersonal relationships of a more communal nature. Instead the four strategies indicate the intended effect of one or more practices as seen from the client's perspective. For example a candidate that participates in a job interview might not perceive the situation as concerned with the 'selection of a friend', yet the intention might be to hire ODC resources that seem trust-worthy, able to adopt company values and behavioral norms, and willing to work closely together with both Indians and Danes.

Below, we apply the framework to the empirical case study. As the outsourcing setup under investigation has existed for some time we focus on the operational level. However, the framework could also, in this and perhaps in other cases, be applied to study the use of practices throughout the relationship management life cycle, i.e. for studying the selection of the service provider, the initial formation of the client-provider relationship, and the ongoing relationship management.

5 Case Study Analysis and Discussion

In this section we first use the four relationship management strategies (see Table 2) as a structure for presenting the practices that are paramount for making the particular outsourcing setup under study effective at the operational level. Then we summarize the employed practices in accordance with the framework of relationship management strategies. Based on this overview, we discuss the portfolio of practices and its alignment with and support for the chosen cooperative outsourcing strategy.

Table 2. Framework of relationship management strategies

Roles and Conditions (Theoretical assumptions)	Relationship management strategies (Intended effect)	
Business Friend: Suitable when much interaction and cooperation is needed	Develop-a-friend	Select-a-friend
Business Person: Suitable when goals can be measured and/or the task is well-understood	Control-a-person	Control-of-output

5.1 Select-a-Friend

In a situation where much interaction and cooperation is needed to ensure high performance selection of the 'right' resources' is important. We have identified two key processes of this type. As mentioned earlier, the ODC as a unit with 400 employees has been established in less than 2.5 years. This has been achieved through a time consuming process where a great number of candidates proposed by the Indian provider have been screened and interviewed by the LO's to check their qualifications and 'cultural fit'. By engaging with an established Indian service provider the CaseCompany was able to attract well qualified candidates. However, the CaseCompany was aware that the ODC resources further had to have the right personal style, coined a pro-active style (internally defined as an independent, questioning, and analytical way of working; proactivity is a core value in the CaseCompany, but less so in the Indian culture), and possess 'cultural intelligence' to enable constructive working relations with Danish employees.

The LO's also play a key role when new development projects or system management areas involving ODC resources are initiated. When a new project/area is being established the Danish project/system manager requests a number of resources with specific competencies. The LO enters into a dialogue with the project/system manager and the CaseCompany's project staffing unit to ensure the right mix of ODC and Danish resources. In sum, select-a-friend oriented processes have been very important in establishing the ODC and they continue to be important for the further consolidation process where recruitment and staffing continuous to be critical for the formation of a successful working relationship between the Danish IT organization and ODC resources.

5.2 Develop-a-Friend

After the right resources have been selected, training and socialization can be used to ensure that the employees align with and internalize the organization's values and behavioral norms. This type of indirect control can facilitate employee commitment and performance that is considered high by the organization and its members. In line with this, all new ODC resources receive a three-week training course that introduces them to the industry, and to the company, its business model, IT systems, an extensive CMMI-inspired development model, etc.

After end training, the LO's make allocation decisions. In particular decisions about who, when, and for how long ODC resources should be onsite are very important as experience and quarterly performance surveys show that ODC resources that have been onsite for three weeks or more perform much better. It is not possible, for the CaseCompany or us, to determine if the increase in the performance rating is due to an 'objectively' better performance, e.g. because of better understanding and a more shared context, or if it is mainly a result of a closer, more communal relationship with the Danish colleagues. Either way, onsite/offshore allocation decisions have much impact on the 'perceived' performance of ODC resources and the formation of relationships between Danish and ODC employees. In effect, when onsite allocation decisions are made the LO's are in many ways deciding who they trust and believe might become high performers. However, making the decisions is not enough of course. Many practicalities and practices – concerning visa, accommodation, access to IT systems, key cards, introduction and integration activities, and several settlement phone calls from the ODC to the onsite resource, etc. – are necessary to ensure that the onsite stay is successful, both while it lasts and to achieve a lasting effect with regard to relationship formation and performance.

The LO's have also implemented a process prescribing steps to be taken by the Danish project manager to set up an agreed upon communication and meeting structure in the beginning of all development projects involving ODC resources. The process does not state how the communication and meeting structure should be, merely that there should be one. For this reason we do not consider the process to be about behavior control. Instead we view it as an attempt to increase the interaction and cooperation that takes place between the Danish and the ODC employees on development projects.

In conclusion, the CaseCompany and in particular the Danish LO's have developed many practices and continuously carry out many daily activities that explicitly aim to develop the ODC resources into like-minded 'friends' via training, onsite allocation, and the formalization of a process that increases communication on development projects.

5.3 Control-of-Output

In situations where the outcome can be measured in accordance with goals, output control is suitable. The agreement with the Indian service provider delineates that the CaseCompany can request a certain number of resources with specific skills, e.g., in PL/1 programming, within a pre-determined deadline. Numbers, skills, and time limits are specified in the contract that constitutes the transactional foundation between the two outsourcing partners. The Danish LO's therefore check if all requests are met with regard to these three criteria. The LO's also check if the reported billable hours actually have been delivered to the projects and tasks in ODC. This entails a detailed walk-through of the billable hours reported from the service provider against the working hours that have been reported from the development projects and system management areas as well as "haggling" over mismatches and mistakes every month.

In sum, due to the CaseCompany's chosen outsourcing strategy and the type of contract, only a few output control processes has been identified. They deal with monitoring and measuring the deliverables as specified in the contract to determine the related payment and penalties. This monitoring is necessary to make sure that the overall goal of a cost-saving and scalable work-force is met, which in turn ensures continuous top management support for the setup.

5.4 Control-a-Person

If it is difficult to measure the outcome in accordance with goals, behavior control might be applicable instead. In this case the intended effect of all the practices mentioned in this category was to specify behavior and follow-up on progress in order to explicitly focus on and increase performance. This intended effect was articulated by both the interviewed Danes and Indians.

All system management areas were previously handled in Denmark and each area was handled differently. In the beginning the lack of a formalized system management process was not seen as problematic. However, after a while it was recognized that it took too long before a full transition of the technical aspects of a system management area to ODC was in place (a Danish system manager and a number of Danish business analysts remain in charge of the business aspects. Interpersonal relationships and cooperation therefore also continue to be important). Moreover, the ODC system management areas were performing very dissimilarly. Effort was therefore put into understanding and codifying the process for transferring a system management area from the Danish organization to ODC and for the daily handling and prioritizing of defects and change requests for system management areas. The codification of these two processes was performed jointly by Danish and ODC personnel. The formalization of the system management process reduces the interaction that has to take place between ODC personnel and the rest of the organization as more can be taken for granted with regard to roles, responsibilities (including the division of work between the two units) as well as ways of working. The formalized process for daily system management process has subsequently been implemented in both ODC and the Danish organization. Thus, this process was collaboratively developed to increase performance and minimize the need for and costs of interaction.

For development projects formalized processes and meeting structures for joint Danish – ODC estimation and detailed Danish project management follow-up on estimates and progress have also recently been implemented. The Danish ODC manager explains that the joint estimation process works well because it facilitates requirements clarification, allows for early detection of misunderstandings, and gives commitment. She further states that detailed management follow-up on individual and project progress in accordance with estimates is necessary as it, in an Indian context, signals interest and that the work is important. This is in stark contrast to how management follow-up would be interpreted in Denmark, where a CaseCompany employee most likely would view such behavior as unnecessary intrusion and distrust. The intended effect of this practice as seen from the Danish LO's perspective is to exercise control to increase performance, yet in an Indian context the practice might not be perceived negatively. This indicates that trust and distrust is created and maintained differently in the Danish and Indian culture, and that the practices intended to increase cooperation or exercise control therefore might not be perceived entirely in line with the intentions.

To further follow-up on behavior, a number of practices are employed. Danish project managers, who have onsite ODC resources, receive several phone calls from a LO to evaluate performance, make quick re-allocations if the relationship is not working, and provide mentoring, e.g., about cultural differences. Moreover, the

Danish managers rate their perceived satisfaction with all onsite and offshore ODC resources' performance each quarter. We characterize this practice as behavior control instead of output control as no attempt is made to relate the perceived performance to pre-specified goals. The Danish project managers are also encouraged to follow-up on the ODC resources' use of time to avoid idle time, and ensure correct time registration. In sum, a variety of practices have been implemented in order to reduce the need for Danish – ODC interaction with regard to system management, to increase the communication about estimates and progress on development projects, and to generally follow-up on the ODC resources' performance, and especially their use of time.

Table 3. Key relationship management strategies and practices in CaseCompany/ODC

<td colspan="2" align="center">**Relationship management strategies**</td>	
Develop-a-Friend • 3-week introductory training program for all ODC resources • Decisions about who, when, and for how long ODC resources should go onsite • Onsite placement of ODC resources for knowledge transfer (select phases for development projects and during start up of system mgt. areas) • Use of ODC resources as onsite coordinators • Practical arrangements: visa, accommodation, IT, key cards, etc. • (onsite) Introduction and integration • (onsite) Settlement phone call process (ODC to resource) • Formalized communication and meeting structures for development projects	*Select-a-Friend* • Interviews of all candidates for check of 'cultural fit' • Formalized process for allocation of ODC resources to new projects and system mgt. areas
Control-a-Person • Formalized process for transitioning a system mgt. area to ODC • Formalized process for handling and prioritizing defects and change requests for system mgt. areas • Formalized process and meeting structure for joint estimation and mgt. follow-up on estimates • Formalized process and meeting structure for detailed mgt. follow-up on progress • Individual performance measurement and oral mgt. feedback • Mgt. follow-up to avoid idle time and ensure proper time registration • Evaluation phone call process (ODC to Danish manager of onsite resources)	*Control-of-Output* • Detailed follow-up on agreements with Indian company (on resource requests and reported billable hours)

5.5 Discussion

Even though all the processes implemented by the Danish LO's aim to ensure and/or increase performance the actual work of conducting process improvements does not fit *within* the framework; rather it *encapsulates* the framework and the key practices within it. Thus, for the CaseCompany/ODC, the most important practice for ensuring an effective outsourcing setup is to continuously engage in the articulation, codification, implementation, and evaluation of relevant onsite and offshore relationship management processes (Zollo & Winter, 2002). We speculate that this might always be the case even though the prevailing relationship management strategies might differ from company to company depending on the chosen outsourcing setup.

Table 3 summarizes the key practices that the CaseCompany uses to manage the outsourcing relationship. As mentioned, an overwhelming amount of activities are undertaken to ensure a smoothly operating offshore development center; many more processes have been codified than we are able to present; and more new improvement initiatives are on their way. Thus, the identified key practices serve as illustrative examples that help (a) define each of the relationship management strategies and (b) provide overview of how the chosen outsourcing setup manifests itself at the operational level.

Table 3 shows that the two strategies concerned with the development of a friend and control of the ODC resources' behavior are the most prevailing. Even though this contrasts somewhat with the more either-or theoretical view on cooperation and control, this seems to fit well with the chosen cooperative outsourcing setup. This is because the process and product interdependent nature of such a setup means that management in the form of training, socialization, and process formalization is more attainable than output control. However, with this said, the CaseCompany/ODC do use all four relationship management strategies and all four strategies play an important role in supporting the outsourcing setup. Thus, in this case, it is not a question of cooperation *or* control, but of using managerial mechanisms that facilitate both cooperation *and* control, and to find the right balance between the two.

We speculate that all cooperative outsourcing setups will tend to be left-sided, i.e. to emphasize socialization and behavior control, just like it seems reasonable to assume that all total outsourcing setups will lean to the right by emphasizing service provider selection and output control (e.g., in accordance with requirement and service agreements). However, we also speculate that for both types of outsourcing setups and as learning takes place over time a variety of relationship management practices will be implemented leading to a more balanced portfolio of practices. In the case under study, initiatives are for example currently being taken to increase the level of output control.

6 Conclusion

This paper reports from an empirical case study of a Danish company operating a dedicated offshore development center in India. A field study at the service provider's facilities revealed that a huge amount of practices were used (a) to provide the support that put the ODC resources in a position to get the job done, and (b) to control if and how the job is getting done. Preliminary data analysis conducted to identify key practices showed that these practices all relate to relationship management. Therefore, we draw on relationship theory to develop and apply a framework of relationship management strategies to the case. Further data analysis showed that all four strategies are in use in the following way:

- Select-a-Friend: Much effort is put into screening, selecting, and staffing development projects and system management areas with the 'right' candidates, i.e. to ensure 'cultural fit'.
- Develop-a-Friend: Training, onsite allocation, and formalized processes that prescribe increased communication on development projects are used to align the ODC resources' ways of thinking and working with the rest of the organization's.
- Control-a-Person: Formalized processes that reduce the need for interaction with regard to system management, increase the communication about estimates and progress on development projects, and follow-up on the ODC resources' use of time are used to control the Danish project/area managers' and the ODC resources' behavior. The explicit aim is to increase performance.
- Control-of-Output: Detailed check of resource requests and reported billable hours is conducted to make sure that the overall goal of a cost-saving and scalable workforce is met, thereby also ensuring continuous top management support for the outsourcing setup.

This paper contributes to the outsourcing literature with empirical findings about relationship management as it is carried out at the operational level in a particular cooperative, offshore outsourcing setup. To make sense of the many identified relationship management practices we develop a theoretical framework that allows us to capture the complexity and nuances of the case. The framework helps us understand the intended effect of the applied key practices as seen from the client side, gain an overview of the portfolio of practices, and reflect upon the alignment between the chosen outsourcing setup and the identified portfolio of practices.

For practice, the main implications of this research are (a) that successful management of the outsourcing relationship requires a willingness to invest in the identification, articulation, codification, implementation, and evaluation of relevant processes, and (b) that it therefore takes time, and much activity and learning to establish an effective portfolio of relationship management practices. For research, our results indicate (a) that relationship theory is a relevant foundation for understanding the type and amount of management that is needed at the operational level, and (b) that more research should address the implementation and learning required to achieve the intended effect of the so-called 'best practices' that dominate the existing literature on outsourcing.

Currently the findings and framework are presented and developed in accordance with and to understand the specific case under study. Our next step is to continue to engage with relevant stakeholders to challenge, rethink, and strengthen our theoretical framework and empirical findings about relationship management concepts, techniques, and dilemmas. The aim is to arrive at potentially transferable research results in the form of theoretical abstractions that are motivated and explained by empirically grounded examples.

References

1. Barthélemy, J.: The Hidden Costs of IT Outsourcing. MIT Sloan Management Review 42(3), 60–69 (2001)
2. Beck, R., Gregory, R., Prifling, M.: Cultural Intelligence and Project Management Interplay in IT Offshore Outsourcing Projects. In: Proceedings of the International Conference on Information S ystems (ICIS), Paris, France (2008)
3. Clark, M.S.: Evidence for the Effectiveness of Manipulations of Communal and Exchange Relationships. Personality and Social Psychology Bulletin 12(4), 414–425 (1986)
4. Clark, M.S., Mills, J.: The Difference between Communal and Exchange Relationships: What it is and is Not. Personality and Social Psychology Bulletin (19), 684–691 (1993)
5. Cullen, S., Seddon, P., Willcocks, L.P.: Managing the Outsourcing Process: A Life Cycle Perspective. In: Willcocks, L.P., Lacity, M.C. (eds.) Global Sourcing of Business & IT Services. Palgrave Macmillan, New York (2006)
6. Dibbern, J., Goles, T., Hirschheim, R., Jayatilaka, B.: Information Systems Outsourcing: A Survey and Analysis of the Literature. The DATA BASE for Advances in Information Systems 35(4), 6–102 (2004)
7. Goodwin, C.: Communality as a Dimension of Service Relationships. Journal of Consumer Psychology 5(4), 387–415 (1996)
8. Haytko, D.: Firm-to-Firm and Interpersonal Relationships: Perspectives from Advertising Agency Account Managers. Journal of the Academy of Marketing Science 32(3), 312–328 (2004)
9. Heide, J.B., Wathne, K.H.: Friends, Businesspeople, and Relationship Roles: A Conceptual Framework and a Research Agenda. Journal of Marketing (70), 90–103 (2006)
10. Holmström, H.O., Conchúir, E.Ó., Ågerfalk, P.J., Fitzgerald, B.: Two-Stage Offshoring: An Investigation of the Irish Bridge. MIS Quarterly 32(2), 257–279 (2008)
11. Hinds, P.J., Bailey, D.E.: Out of Sight, Out of Sync: Understanding Conflict in Distributed Teams. Organization Science 14(6), 615–632 (2003)
12. King, W.R., Torkzadeh, G.: Information Systems Offshoring: Research Status and Issues. MIS Quarterly 32(2), 205–225 (2008)
13. Kishore, R., Rao, H.R., Nam, K., Rajagopalan, S., Chaudhury, A.: A Relationship Perspective on IT Outsourcing. Communications of the ACM 46(12), 86–92 (2003)
14. Lacity, M.C., Willcocks, L.P.: Transforming Back Offices through Outsourcing: Approaches and lessons. In: Willcocks, L.P., Lacity, M.C. (eds.) Global Sourcing of Business & IT Services. Palgrave Macmillan, New York (2006)
15. Mathiassen, L.: Collaborative Practice Research. Information Technology &People 15(4), 321–345 (2002)
16. McFarlan, F.W., Nolan, R.L.: How to manage an IT Outsourcing Alliance. Sloan Management Review 36(2), 9–23 (1995)
17. Ngwenyama, O., Bjørn, P.: Interrogating the Dynamics of Distributed Collaboration: Findings from Four Field Studies on CSCW Use. Journal of Information Technology, 1–13 (2008)
18. Ouchi, W.G.: A Conceptual Framework for the Design of Organizational Control Mechanisms. Management Science 25(9), 833–848 (1979)
19. Price, L.L., Arnould, E.J.: Commercial Friendships: Service Provider-Client Relationships in Context. Journal of Marketing (63), 38–56 (1999)
20. Rose, S., Serafica, F.C.: Keeping and Ending Casual, Close and Best Friendships. Journal of Social and Personal Relationships (3), 275–288 (1986)

21. Rottman, J., Lacity, M.C.: Offshoring IT Work: 29 Practices. In: Willcocks, L.P., Lacity, M.C. (eds.) Global Sourcing of Business & IT Services. Palgrave Macmillan, New York (2006)
22. Rustagi, S., King, W.R., Kirsch, L.J.: Predictors of Formal Control Usage in IT Outsourcing Partnerships. Information Systems Research 19(2), 126–143 (2008)
23. Sabherwal, R.: The Role of Trust in Outsourced IS Development Projects. Communications of the ACM 42(2), 80–86 (1999)
24. Siakas, K., Siakas, E.: The Need for Trust Relationships to enable Successful Virtual Team Collaboration in Software Outsourcing. International Journal of Technology, Policy and Management 8(1), 59–75 (2008)
25. Zollo, M., Winter, S.G.: Deliberate Learning and the Evolution of Dynamic Capabilities. Organization Science 13(3), 339–351 (2002)
26. Van de Ven, A.H.: Engaged Schorlarship, A guide for Organizational and Social Research. Oxford University Press, Oxford (2007)
27. Villumsen, J.: Managing Offshore Outsourced Software Development. Pharmaceutical Engineering 27(4), 34–45 (2007)
28. Walsham, G.: Interpreting Information Systems in Organizations. John Wiley & Sons, Inc., Chichester (1993)
29. Willcocks, L.P., Lacity, M.C.: Global Sourcing of Business & IT Services. Palgrave Macmillan, New York (2006)
30. Yin, R.: Case Study Research - Design and Methods. Sage Publications, Thousand Oaks (2003)

Appendix 1

Practicalities and key processes for making the chosen outsourcing strategy work in practice.

	Onsite (and co-located)	**Offshore (and distributed)**
Support	• Practical arrangements: visa, accommodation, IT, key cards, etc. • Introduction and integration • Settlement phone call process (ODC to resource) • Onsite placement of ODC resources for knowledge transfer (select phases for development projects and during start up of system mgt. areas) • Use of ODC resources as onsite coordinators • Translation of documentation to English	• Interviews with all candidates for check of 'cultural fit' • Decisions about who, when, and for how long ODC resources should go onsite • 3-week introductory training program for all ODC resources • Formalized process for allocation of ODC resources to new projects and system mgt. areas • Formalized communication and meeting structures for development projects • Formalized process for transitioning a system mgt. area to ODC • Formalized process for handling and prioritizing defects and change requests for system mgt. areas • Process improvement initiatives, e.g., for learning how to transfer knowledge and coordinate without sending too many resources onsite
Control	• Mgt. follow-up to avoid idle time and ensure proper time registration • Individual performance measurement and oral mgt. feedback • Evaluation phone call process (ODC to Danish manager)	• Detailed follow-up on agreements with Indian company • Formalized process and meeting structure for joint estimation and mgt. follow-up on estimates • Formalized process and meeting structure for detailed mgt. follow-up on progress • Individual performance measurement and oral mgt. feedback

User Experience:
Consumer Understandings of Virtual Product Prototypes

Taina Kaapu and Tarja Tiainen

University of Tampere, Department of Computer Sciences,
Kanslerinrinne 1, FIN-33014 University of Tampere, Finland
taina.kaapu@uta.fi, tarja@cs.uta.fi

Abstract. In this paper, we focus on users' evaluations of virtual product prototypes designed by furniture companies. Our study is the first step towards design research in the context of physical products. We study virtual prototypes of physical products via the concept of user experience as a subjective issue, not technology-driven as in most user experience studies. To get an idea of users' subjective experience, we conducted an empirical study using, as our research approach, phenomenography, which allows outlining the differences in users' technological understandings. In our results, the user experience of virtual product prototypes is understood as a unique combination of various elements, the focus varying from technology to the user's taste and from a part of a product to a product in its environment.

Keywords: User Experience, Virtual Environment, Product Design, Consumers, Interpretative Research Methods, Phenomenography.

1 Introduction

The starting point of product design process is to respond to customers' needs and wishes [1]. Co-operation between designers and customers is challenging, since their concepts of products are different [2]. In the negotiation process it is critical that clients get correct and exact information about the product without misinterpretations [3]. With more complex presentation formats, consumers perceive the products better than they would with stable pictures [4]. These experiences can also be referred to as virtual product experiences (VPEs). Three-dimensional (3D) virtual technology, such as immersive projection technology (IPT), provides a promising opportunity for presenting designers' plans with virtual prototypes (VPs) to clients and supporting negotiation over them. However, acting in a virtual environment (VE) is not an easy task for an occasional user [5].

In this paper, occasional users' VE visits are studied in the context of user experience (UX). Our aim is to support customers' participation in product design process. For this reason, we have created an application for VE, which is a prototype of our Furniture Fitting-Room. In it, 3D virtual prototypes can be presented to customers and customer feedback about them obtained. This paper reports on the study which analyses how customers experience the VE visit and the evaluation of VPs.

Our study belongs to the *engaged scholarship*. The concept, according to Van de Ven, means close connection between practice and research [6]. These kinds of studies have a strong tradition among Scandinavian information systems (IS) research, and are based on researchers' commitments to labour union, work design and information technology (IT) users' perspective [7]. Our study follows this tradition, as our aim is to empower non-professionals in their roles in product design process.

Mathiassen classifies the forms of engaged scholarship within IS research based on their underlying knowledge interests: 1) Practice research, 2) Design research, and 3) Action research [8]. We present a case the aim of which is to take a first step towards design research in the context of physical product design. Our study includes two steps: First, we create a tool (i.e., Furniture Fitting-Room) with practitioners for supporting consumers' participation in product design process. Second, we make visible the variation among consumers' experience in a VE visit for evaluating VPs. In this study, we aim to answer to the question:

How do consumers understand 3D product VPs?

We study this by using the concept of UX, as it gives space for users' (i.e. consumers') subjective interpretations. To study the interpretations, we use phenomenography, which is a qualitative method focusing on a second-order perspective. With the phenomenographical approach, it is possible to understand the variety of conceptions of VPs. When the nature of the interpretations is understood, it offers building blocks for further UX research and for the use of 3D VPs in design.

First in this paper we describe what is meant by UX and, second, the practical background of this study (a business related project) and the technical case situation (Furniture Fitting-Room as a virtual space for evaluation of 3D VPs of furniture). Third, we outline the phenomenographical research approach and our research process in practice (test setup, test users, and interviews). Fourth, we describe the results of this study: i.e., the variation in consumers' interpretations of 3D VPs in virtual reality (VR). We found twelve conceptions which the consumers use when talking about virtual products. These conceptions can be categorized further to three *forms of thought* which describe the alternative collections of conceptions. The forms of thought illustrate how to understand VPs. Finally, we discuss the UX results in the context of VPE and the methodological challenges that we encountered during the study process.

2 User Experience (UX)

When one talks about UX, the user concept connects the context to technology related situations. A widely accepted definition of UX [9] is that UX means "a consequence of a user's internal state (predispositions, expectations, needs, motivation, mood, etc.), the characteristics of the designed system (e.g., complexity, purpose, usability, functionality, etc.) and the context (or the environment) within which the interaction occurs (e.g., organisational/social setting, meaningfullness of the activity, voluntariness of use, etc.)" [10].

A survey among human-computer interaction (HCI) researchers and practitioners about their views of UX has shown that the respondents tend to agree on a concept of

UX as dynamic, context-dependent and subjective, which stems from a broad range of potential benefits users may derive from a product [9, 11]. The term UX is scoped to products, systems, services, and objects that a person interacts with through a user interface. In this context the UX can be studied [10]:

- *beyond the instrumental*, which includes traditional usability testing and beauty (or harmony) as a quality aspect of technology
- *emotion and affect*, especially focusing on positive emotions such as joy, fun and pride.
- *the experiential*, which emphasizes two aspects of technology use, namely its situatedness and it being temporally-bounded.

Besides of the above artifact-centered UX concept, which is used in the HCI community, also a psychology-based UX concept is used in studying persons and information and communication technology (ICT). In this case, the concept *Flow* is used to mean an optimal experience that stems from people's perceptions of challenges and skills in given situations. The dimensions of *Flow* are: (1) clear goals; (2) immediate feedback; (3) personal skills well suited to given challenges; (4) merger of action and awareness; (5) concentration on the task at hand; (6) a sense of potential control; (7) a loss of self-consciousness; (8) an altered sense of time; and (9) an experience which becomes autotelic, i.e., requires no goals or rewards for the self [12, 13]. The concept of *Flow* has been used in studying Web use [13], e-Commerce [14], and virtual environments [15], for example.

The difference between the two above views of UX is that whereas the artifact-centered UX concept focuses on the artifact and its features, *Flow* focuses on the balance of users' skills, the task situation, and the ICT artifact used.

3 Practical and Technical Background

A traditional way to make the designers' ideas concrete to the customers is to use physical prototypes, although these are often expensive and time-consuming to make [16]. By using VPs the above problems can be avoided. In our case, we studied UX with VPs with the help of furniture VPs: a piece of furniture usually embodies many meanings as a member of a design-intensive product category [17], consequently, consumers have different desires and expectations concerning this type of product (e.g. [18, 19]). This provides promising research situations for studying subjective interpretations without being limited to just one normative concept that all test users describe.

Our study is a part of a larger research project investigating alternative ways to present furniture prototypes to customers. One of the sub-projects studied the traditional way in which physical prototypes are presented, while our sub-project focused on the use of VPs. Twenty small and medium-sized local furniture companies (in Finland) participated in the project.

VR was chosen as the alternative presentation environment, as only a minimum change is needed to the traditional setup for this. The traditional way is to present physical prototypes in a room, and a similar environment can be created in virtual reality: a virtual room with prototypes of their normal size. In the case of furniture and interior, the feeling of space is important and can be created better with immersive VR than with alternative display technologies (e.g. [20]).

For presenting 3D VPs we used a Cave-like environment in a VR laboratory. (As CAVE is a registered trademark, the term Cave-like environment is used of other cubic, walk-in virtual environments.) The space has five rear projection surfaces: three walls, a floor and a ceiling (see Figures 1 and 2). The user's view is rendered, according to his/her position and orientation, with the help of a magnetic tracking system. An active 3D stereo image is produced and a conventional Wand input device is used for the controlling movements.

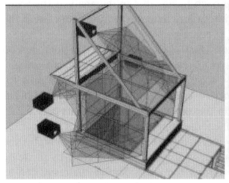 

Fig. 1. The architecture of VR laboratory   **Fig. 2.** The Cave-like VE inside

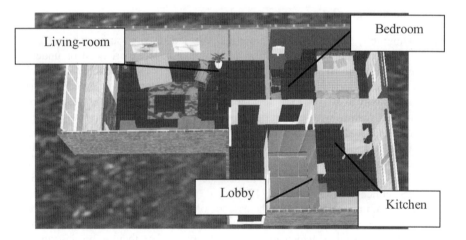

Fig. 3. The apartment in the Furniture Fitting-Room used to present the VPs of furniture

In our case, the test users evaluated 3D VPs presented in the prototype of the Furniture Fitting-Room. The virtual space there consists of virtual furniture (3D VPs) and a virtual apartment with a living room, bedroom, and kitchen (see Figure 3). All the rooms are furnished with some common furniture such as a sofa in the living room and a bed in the bedroom. The prototype of the Furniture Fitting-Room was done in our research project.

4 Methodology

Theoretical definitions about UX state that UX is subjective and situated [10]. Studying an issue such as this requires a method which gives space to informants. Such methods are qualitative methods focusing on the empirical material without any a priory expectation. So the starting point is that we let some test users tell us about their experience. However, this kind of approach means that in the analysis the focus is on the test users' own interpretations, without any theoretical framework (as is the case with UX in HCI studies [10] or Flow [8] being employed for the task).

One part of deciding whose concepts are used is to decide whether to focus on individuals' or groups' interpretations. Our research question deals with individuals' ways to understand VPs. Also the technical solution which we use was designed for one user at a time mainly. In addition, we wanted to avoid the problem that could occur if the process were dominated by the views of one or two of the participants only.

Among the possible methods we chose phenomenography, since it aims to describe, analyse and understand conceptions held by informants [21]. In phenomenography, the aim is to create a categorization in which the views differ from each other by the level of abstraction or the diversity and the extension of the views, so that the result can be presented as a hierarchy. In the following sections, we outline the method of phenomenography, and then we describe the procedure used in this study in practice.

4.1 Phenomenography

Phenomenography is a qualitative, empirically based research approach that aims to interpret, describe, and categorise how a phenomenon is experienced or understood within a group of informants [21]. The roots of the phenomenographical approach are strongly connected to empirical studies of learning. Marton [22] adopted the term of phenomenography as a label for a new idea in educational research. Phenomenography has been used mainly with educational focus. This has been its focus also in the IS field and related disciplines: for example, students' conceptions about programming [23] and educators' conceptions about teaching IS [24] have both been studied with phenomenography. Furthermore, the approach has been employed to some other cases in the IS field, for example, to study IS designers' conceptions on IS design [25] and consumers' conceptions on e-privacy [26].

Most research methods focus on the essence of a phenomenon, which means the use of the first-order perspective. Phenomenography, on the other hand, focuses on the second-order perspective, which means that the researcher focuses on describing the phenomenon studied as others (than the researcher) see it [21]. In this sense, second-order perspective means that the objective of the study is to reveal the inherent variation in people's views. More studies which present multiple voices and interpretations are needed, but few methods support this [27]. However, phenomenography is a method for making the variation of conceptions visible (i.e., intentionality), so its aim is to present alternative views.

People's views are studied with empirical material in which people describe how they view the world (or phenomenon). The empirical material is generally collected by interviewing informants [28]. Interviewees describe their views by using some conceptions. People create conceptions with respect to the external and internal horizons of the structural (what) aspect of a phenomenon dialectically merged with the referential (how) aspect of that particular phenomenon [29].

The aim of a phenomenographical study is to create a categorization which presents the different ways to view the phenomenon. In the analysis of interviewees' descriptions, the focus is on *what* and on *how* aspect, which the interviewees use when describing the phenomenon. Since the categories illustrate different aspects of the same phenomenon, they are logically related to each other. In general, some categories offer a wider or richer perspective and often come to embrace others in an inclusive structure [30]. It tends also to be the case that, for a given phenomenon, the categories of description are hierarchical. Based on the categories of conceptions, it is also possible to compile *forms of thought* [29], which are on an even more general level than categorization.

4.2 Test Users

The empirical material of phenomenographical studies is typically gathered with open-ended interviews. Due to the richness of the data, the number of interviews is usually restricted [29]. Selecting interviewees so that they represent a wide range of variation concerning the relevant characteristics is one way of ensuring unbiased and unrestricted results [31]. We asked volunteers to fill in a web form with some background information. After a month (February 2007), 68 consumers had filled in the form.

In the selection of test users we were careful about the demographical features involved. First, we selected test users from different age groups (as presented in Table 1) to avoid bias found in many studies where the focus is often on younger users [32]. The other feature with which we were careful was sex. Earlier studies show gender differences in IT use and in consumption (e.g. [33, 34]), so we decided to make the number of male and female test users as equal as possible.

A brief description of the test subjects' backgrounds is shown in Table 1. This may help the reader better understand the empirical base of this study. In prior phenomenographic studies, twenty informants have been found to be a sufficient number for theoretical saturation [35, 36]. We followed this guidance. After twenty user tests and the related interview analyses, we agreed that we had reached the saturation point, since the last informants did not contribute any new elements to the categorization.

Table 1. The test users

Participants	Age (years)						
	20-29	30-39	40-49	50-59	60-69	70-79	Total
Male	2	2	3	3	-	1	11
Female	2	1	1	1	4	-	9
Total	4	3	4	4	4	1	20

4.3 Test Situation and Interviews

As VE was usually unfamiliar for test users and as during the first VE experience the use of technology can dominate the user's attention, we planned the test situation carefully by following general user test rules (37). A research group worked together with each individual test user. A research assistant accompanied the user, conversed with him/her and guided in the use of the control unit. There was also an operator who was responsible for the equipment, and a researcher who observed the test and interviewed the test user afterwards.

Each test took about an hour and included an introduction, a VE visit and an interview – not forgetting short breaks between the three parts. In the introduction, the first part dealt with the research process and the second part was a short practical session on how to use a VE. The video-taped test consisted of a visit to the Furniture Fitting-Room. We asked the participant to think aloud and see if there were something interesting available. In each room, the test users needed to evaluate some variation of the furniture, for example, the sofa in the living-room in different materials. The visit to the Furniture Fitting-Room lasted from 15 up to 30 minutes.

We collected our empirical material using individual theme interviews (conducted in 2007). The interviewer observed the test situation, so that she knew how the interviewee's visit to the Furniture Fitting-Room had proceeded. The interview took place immediately after the user test. The interviews included three themes: 1) the interviewees' background in relation to their e-commerce related consumption and home interior; 2) the understanding of 3D VPs: what they thought about the Furniture Fitting-Room and how easy they found it to evaluate the VPs; 3) the interviewee's experience of visiting VE. The progress of the interviews was quite similar in all of the interviews, although the duration varied from 20 to 45 minutes. The interviewer's role was to follow the interviewees' ideas and explore their narration. The atmosphere in the user tests and interviews was pleasant and friendly, which became evident from the participants' comments: many of them spontaneously expressed their willingness to return, were similar user tests to be arranged in the future.

4.4 Analysis

In the interview analysis, we followed the norms used in phenomenographical studies. In phenomenography, the categorizations are made from utterances by which informants describe their perceptions, experiences and concepts. These utterances result from a process by which an individual gives meaning to a certain phenomenon. There are no right or wrong conceptions in phenomenography: so all the expressions were incorporated into a pool of meanings formed by the data [29].

We started the analysis by reading through all transcribed interviews (the whole material totalled 157 pages) in order to find all the aspects of the informants' conceptualizations. At first, the focus in phenomenographical analysis is on the referential component, which describes what the phenomenon means in everyday language [31]. In our case, the first analysis focus was on what the interviewees meant with 3D VPs of furniture on the level of everyday language. The interview texts were split in small items, and the texts were categorized in order to obtain a single dimension of the categorization.

In the second analysis phase, the focus is on the structural component, which refers to a deeper level of the phenomenal meaning of how [29]. The analysis continues by focusing on the structural component of VPs. The structure is constructed by analysing the target of the referential component. An example of this is what the interviewee is talking about, as he/she describes the textile fabrics of a chair or colors of a sofa or a living-room.

However, by creating a framework, it is possible to use phenomenography in order to reach a more common view. A framework is made up of combinations of the presented categories comprising thought forms or higher levels of understandings [30]. The frameworks can also be referred to as forms of thought.

Conducting the data analysis was iterative work that consisted of reading and re-reading of empirical materials collected. During the process we made comparisons between meanings of single statements and the surrounding statements, and the data as a whole. We also analysed the interdependencies of these meanings. During the analysis, we formed the categorizations and the forms of thoughts to describe informants' conceptions as precisely as possible. The results, thus, were made up of parts and their interrelationships. We conducted six analysis rounds including comparisons and cross-checkings with the whole material so that, finally, our categorization represented the interviewees' views. The result is presented next in Subsection 5.1 in the form of a categorization of the concepts that consumers use.

Having found the conceptions to describe the VPs, we analysed which of them each test user used in their description. The analysis reveals the set of conceptions employed, giving an idea about the wideness or scope of thinking, and about alternative perspectives that were used. There were variations among those conceptions: we identified three forms, which are described in Subsection 5.2.

5 Results

The results show how consumers interpret VPs of products. This can be described by two layers. The first layer includes twelve different conceptions by which consumers talk about VPs. The second one includes three thought models, which are combinations of conceptions. Consumers use them when describing VPs.

5.1 First Layer: Conceptions

We identified twelve different conceptions by focusing on referential and structural aspects (Table 2). The referential aspect is a combination of three objects comprising selected descriptions which emphasize the interviewees' focus of reflections when conceptualizing 3D VPs of furniture. The structural aspect highlights four distinctive but hierarchical dimensions within the interviewees' conceptions. To illustrate the contents of the conceptions further, we use examples from the interviews (Table 3).

The referential aspect includes three alternative objects, which differ by their scope. The most narrow scope is possessed by Object A (One part of a product): for example, the interviewee describes whether the backrest of the rocking chair is high enough. Object B (One product) describes a piece of furniture, for example, a table

Table 2. Summary of the categorization of consumers' conceptions on 3D prototypes of furniture presented in the Furniture Fitting-Room

C	One product in an environment	Conception 1C	Conception 2C	Conception 3C	Conception 4C
B	One product	Conception 1B	Conception 2B	Conception 3B	Conception 4B
A	One part of a product	Conception 1A	Conception 2A	Conception 3A	Conception 4A
↑ Referential aspect Structural aspect →		As a technical implementation	As a photograph of a product	As a concrete product	As a desired or disliked product
		1	2	3	4

and whether it seems steady. The third object, C (One product in an environment), describes a piece of furniture as a part of interior. It deals with, for example, judgments about whether some wallpaper colors play well together with other colours in the room.

In the structural aspect, there are four levels of 3D VPs of furniture: (1) a technical implementation, (2) a photograph of a product, (3) a concrete product, and (4) a desired or disliked product. The first hierarchical level is about advantages and disadvantages of graphical implementation. The interviewees often use words like "model" or "texture", which belong to the context of technology. The interviewee might focus, for example, on how it is possible to walk through VPs or what kinds of programs were used.

On the second level, the model of a product is discussed as a traditional photograph or a picture in a catalog. The interviewees compare the image in VE to a picture; they might say, for example, that the quality of the virtual model does not reach that of photographs. The two first levels (1: as a technical implementation and 2: as a photograph of a product) are close to each other; the difference is that on the first level the interviewee describes the implementation and, on the second level, the product. On the third level, the focus is on the 3D product. The interviewee sees a piece of furniture in a concrete form. On this level, a piece of furniture is evaluated as a physical piece of furniture (as a concrete product).

The fourth level consists of evaluation of the product or interior based on personal taste. Sometimes the interviewee, disliking some models, might claim being unable to evaluate that piece of furniture at all or might just ignore it. However, this kind of statement nevertheless reveals that the person is interpreting the image as a furniture or room and thus did evaluate it. This level differs from others in that a lack of comments can be regarded as negative. When the test user did not like something, he/she might not comment on anything about it.

Table 3. The contents of the conceptions illustrated with examples from the interviews

	Conception	Content illustrated with an example from the interview
A: One part of a product	1A (technology)	Consumer 15: When I looked at the textile fabrics on the chair, the model vibrated so much that I didn't get a proper idea of shapes or threads.
	2A (photograph)	Consumer 8: The general picture is very accurate. When I try to focus on details of a piece of furniture I need more sharpness to the picture.
	3A (product)	Consumer 19: In the bedroom, it was easy to see how different colours and materials in bedstead work. It is a very different experience if you see only a piece of something and somebody says that also this colour is possible.
	4A (taste)	Consumer 17: The sofa in the living-room was such a cube. Maybe it was the idea. However, I didn't evaluate that sofa at all because it didn't appeal to me. It was so featureless.
B: One product	1B (technology)	Consumer 5: It was easy when I didn't have to move by myself. At some point, I could see through a piece of furniture.
	2B (photograph)	Consumer 11: I think that this virtual picture should be like a photograph. Then it would give a more realistic sense of a piece of furniture.
	3B (product)	Consumer 2: There were two chairs. I had a realistic feeling that I could sit down on the first chair but not on the second one. It was uncomfortable to sit because it didn't have any support for my lumbar region.
	4B (taste)	Consumer 4: Because I think that the rocking chair doesn't fit in my home I didn't look at it such a way.
C: One product in an environment	1C (technology)	Consumer 7: I would like to evaluate a piece of furniture in a room where I were to place it - and I'd hope that the texture of the model were more realistic.
	2C (photograph)	Consumer 2: Maybe I can interpret these pictures given more time. I would like to have a real photograph in here. I could then see the bookshelf and outline the space needed in the living room.
	3C (product)	Consumer 1: I think that there were many corners in the bedroom and the bed didn't fit in the interior. The bed isn't bad as such, and I think it is a nice bed to sleep.
	4C (taste)	Consumer 4: In the living-room, the interior design was gaudy and the curtains and carpet were really disturbing for the evaluation of any of the furniture.

5.2 Second Layer: Forms of Thought

On the second layer, we describe the interviewees' conceptions as different levels of understanding the phenomena (which in this case is VPs). This is in accordance with the primary idea of intentionality in phenomenography: some conceptions form more comprehensive understandings than others [29]. A hierarchical categorization can be presented, the higher level including the lower levels. A person is located to one level, reflecting the form of thought he/she has.

We identified three forms of thought about 3D VPs of furniture: (1) a picture of a product via new technology; (2) a separate product; and (3) a product in its context. Table 4 illustrates the three forms. They are presented based on the first layer (i.e., referential and structural aspects), since their construction is based on that layer.

Table 4. The hierarchy of the interviewees' individualised forms of thought

C: One product in an environment			FORM III: context	
B: One product	FORM I: picture		FORM II: product	
A: One part of a product				
	1: As a technical implementation	2: As a photograph of a product	3: As a concrete product	4: As a desired or disliked product

Form I focuses on technology development, as in it the interviewees concentrate on the quality of presentation technology and other technology-centered issues. The persons of this level talk only about technology when describing VPs. Form II focuses on separate products, and also includes Form I thought models. The thought model of Form II means that a person thinks of and evaluates separate products when seeing virtual prototypes, ignoring technological issues as well as the room space and its interior. Form III is the highest form as it connects the products to their context – in our case furniture to an interior. However, the use of this form is connected to the interviewees' taste. This means that when the product of the interior of the room did not agree with the test users' taste, they refused to discuss anything else than the clash between the room's (or product's) appearance and the test users' view of a pleasant interior (or product).

6 Discussion

Our paper describes the differences in consumers' understanding of VPs of products. Twenty test users evaluated furniture VPs in a virtual apartment. We observed the test situation and interviewed the test users. In the analysis, we identified different ways to view VPs. Our results will contribute for further UX research that is discussed in the following.

6.1 Consumer Understandings on Virtual Prototypes

We studied consumer understandings as UX in the context of Furniture Fitting-Room. Among researchers there are at least two views about UX: 1) the artifact-centered UX which is used especially among HCI researchers, and 2) psychology-based Flow. Common to both of these views is that the UX is understood as a subjective experience.

The existing interest in UX among academia and industry is the result of researchers and practitioners becoming aware of the limitations of the traditional usability frameworks, which usually focus primarily on user cognition and user performance in human-technology interactions [12]. In contrast, UX highlights non-utilitarian aspects of such interactions, shifting the focus to user affect and sensation. So we decided to challenge the researchers' taken-for-granted interpretations and to study UX from the user's point of view.

Phenomenograhy as a research approach allowed us to conduct this in a multilevel fashion (see Figure 4). The researcher examines informants' understandings of a certain phenomenon and then takes steps from the informant's personal perspective towards informants' collective view. The researcher has to take all the steps: it is not possible to start other way than from the bottom.

We started with consumers' conceptions 1A - 4C (see Table 2). The second step is where the researcher presents classifications of individuals' conceptions. These were presented in referential and structural aspects of conceptions by us. The categories are presented in a hierarchical manner, some describing a more advanced or complex understanding than others. The variations between the categories present the critical points in understanding and are highlighted in the analysis [29].

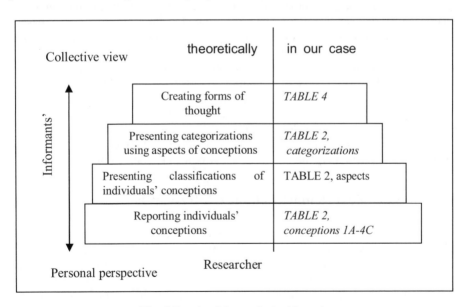

Fig. 4. Levels of the results in this study

The final step is to create the forms of thought (Renström's framework) [30]. In our case, we created the forms of thought by constituting first the understandings of interviewed individuals. These were then outlined by those individuals to different forms of thought. It is easier to accept it as a research outcome; it is a step in theory building. According to March and Smith, one possible research output is to create a model (of the studied phenomena) [38]. A model can be viewed as a set of propositions or statements expressing relationships among constructs. The forms of thought represent this kind of result. Our result consists of three forms of thought: Form I: A picture of a product via new technology, Form II: A separate product, and Form III: A product in its context. Form I is connected to artifact-centered UX, Form III to Flow and Form II somewhere between them.

The results of our empirical study can be attached also to the context of engaged scholarship [6]: the research of UX was conducted with local furniture companies, and we provided them with information on how new technologies can be used in the product design from their customers' perspective. Understanding the variation of users' views will help in the future when taking deeper steps in design research.

6.2 Limitations and Future Research

We aimed to describe users' understandings rather than evaluate them, so we selected phenomenography as our research approach. This kind of theory-building approach is needed in the context of VPs since we need to create new conceptualizations and test prevailing assumptions about how informants' view them. Thus, our solution opens a new perspective for UX studies: giving space to informants' subjective experience.

The target of our study was an occasional VE users' experience. Still, further studies from different perspectives are needed. We focused on identifying how users' experience VE, but we did not investigate any casual relationships. Further studies are needed in this respect: connecting both personal backgrounds to the UX and situational and temporal issues to it. For these kinds of studies, our results offer building blocks on how consumers' interpretations of VPs differ from each other.

We studied UX with one case: evaluation of VPs with one technical environment. Alternative situations (e.g., a larger apartment) with an alternative presentation technology (e.g., with a better 3D image) could give more versatile UX. This could give the test users a better understanding of their own experience by changing their expectations of a VE visit and VP evaluation situation. Furthermore, this kind of research situation could provide an opportunity for a comparative research.

7 Methodological Remarks about UX Research

The results of our study provide methodological insights for the study of UX as a subjective phenomenon. Hassenzahl and Tractinsky note that "the absence of empirical research – whether qualitative or quantitative – impedes theoretical advancement and restricts our understanding of UX as concept and its further development" [10].

Based on our study, the phenomenographical approach is found promising for studying UX for the following reasons. UX consists of smaller experiences and the UX is in each use case unique, because the user's internal state, the use context, and the system are dynamic [10]. In our study, the reference period included one visit in a

VR laboratory. It should be kept in mind, however, that the previous use cases in similar situations clearly affect the user's expectations for the examined UX, and, together with information and perceptions received from other sources, build up an attitude towards virtual product presentations in general. Phenomenography allows informants to tell about their experiences in their own words, and it is possible to spot informants' expectations in their descriptions [28].

The phenomenographical method places researchers in a "learning role" viz-a-viz the informants and their context. This means that the researcher has to be humble to understand how the interviewee sees the phenomenon under study in reality. Like an apprentice and independent craftsman, the interviewer has to learn from the interviewee. The researcher has to listen and accept understandings different to her/his own without trying to correct the interviewee's conceptions [29]. A researcher who takes this approach wishes to get a deep understanding about how people view things, about the underlying causes, nuances and details. In this way, phenomenography merges research and praxis, and thus the informants' answers are not disconnected from the context.

Another kind of benefit is the opportunity that this approach offers for studying IS use in a multilevel fashion, keeping an eye on the whole as well as its parts. Phenomenography can focus to multilevel issues starting from the bottom (individual users' interpretations) and continue to creating collective levels of understandings (see Figure 4). When phenomenography is used in this way, it gives space to informants' own interpretations and also enables forming informants' collective view [30].

One challenge in conducting a multilevel phenomenographical study is how to move from one analysis level to another. The researcher should avoid studying levels too far apart because that may lead to discontinuity between individual and collective levels. This is a complicated question since informants naturally have several approaches, although some approaches are preferred to others. Furthermore, the literature of phenomographical approach gives little guidance on the analysis in practice. For example, there are no agreed principles for testing the validity of formed categorizations.

While we acknowledge these challenges, we believe that they represent research opportunities rather than problems to be avoided. The results of our study show how, with the phenomenographical approach, users' technological understandings, which are constantly under construction, can be studied, as the user gets new information or experiences. Thus, in our study, phenomenography offers a way to do research that leads to a more multifaceted view to users' understandings (see Figure 4). This kind of approach is needed in design research to understand stakeholders' views about future development.

Acknowledgments

The authors acknowledge three anonymous reviewers for their suggestions to improve the paper. We also thank Prof. Asko Ellman, Dr. Vuokko Takala-Schreib, Tarja Katajamäki, Joonas Laitinen, and Harri Mähönen for their comments during the research process. We are grateful to Steve Legrand for making our English more readable.

References

1. Crilly, N., Moultrie, J., Clarkson, P.J.: Shaping things: intended consumer response and the other determinants of product form. Design Studies 30(3), 244–254 (2009)
2. Chamorro-Koc, M., Popovic, V., Emmison, M.: Using visual representation of concepts to explore users and designers' concepts of everyday products. Design Studies 29(2), 142–159 (2008)
3. Meyer, C., Schwager, A.: Understanding Customer Experience. Harvard Business Review, 117–126 (February 2007)
4. Jiang, Z., Benbasat, I.: The Effects of Presentation Formats and Task Complexity on Online Consumers' Product Understanding. MIS Quarterly 31(3), 475–500 (2007)
5. Tiainen, T., Ellman, A., Katajamäki, T., Kaapu, T.: Occasional Users' Experience on Visiting in a Virtual Environment. In: Proceedings of Tenth IEEE / ACM DS-RT, pp. 63–69 (2006)
6. Van de Ven, A.H.: Engaged Scholarship: A Guide for Organizational and Social Research. Oxford University Press, Oxford (2007)
7. Mathiassen, L., Nielsen, P.A.: Engaged Scholarship in IS Research: The Scandinavian Case. Scandinavian Journal of Information Systems 20(2), 3–20 (2008)
8. Mathiassen, L.: Collaborative Practice Research. Information Technology & People 15(4), 321–345 (2002)
9. Law, E.L.-C., Roto, V., Hassenzahl, M., Vermeeren, A.P.O.S., Kort, J.: Understanding, Scoping and Defining User eXperience: A Survey Approach. In: Proceedings of Human Factors in Computing Systems, CHI'09, pp. 719–728 (2009)
10. Hassenzahl, M., Tractinsky, N.: User Experience – a research agenda (Editorial). Behavior & Information Technology 25(2), 91–97 (2007)
11. Parés, N., Parés, R.: Towards a Model for a Virtual Reality Experience: The Virtual Subjectiveness. Presence: Teleoperators & Virtual Environments 15(5), 524–538 (2006)
12. Csikszentmihalyi, M.: Beyond Boredom and Anxiety: Experiencing Flow in Work and Play. Jossey-Bass, San Francisco (1975)
13. Chen, H., Wigand, R.T., Nilan, M.S.: Optimal experience of Web activities. Computers in Human Behavior 15(5), 585–608 (1999)
14. Novak, T.P., Hoffman, D.L., Yung, Y.F.: Measuring the customer experience in online environments: a structural modelling approach. Marketing Science 19(1), 22–42 (2002)
15. Särkelä, H., Takatalo, J., May, P., Laakso, M., Nyman, G.: The movement patterns and the experiential components of virtual environments. International Journal of Human-Computer Studies 67, 787–799 (2009)
16. Tseng, M.M., Jiao, J., Su, C.J.: Virtual prototyping for customized product development. Integrated Manufacturing Systems 9(6), 334–343 (1998)
17. Luomala, H.T., Lindman, M.T.: A Quasi-experimental Exploration of Consumers' Furniture Product Experiences in Different Store Environments. In: The proceedings of 35th EMAC-conference (2006)
18. Hart, C.W.: Made to Order. Marketing Management 5(2), 10–23 (1996)
19. Gilmore, J.H., Pine II, B.J.: The Four Faces of Customization. Harvard Business Review, 91–101 (January-February 1997)
20. Gomez, A., Figueroa, P.: Size Estimation in Product Visualization using Augmented Reality. In: The proceedings of VRST'08, Bordeaux, France (2008)
21. Marton, F.: Towards phenomenography of learning, Integratial experiments aspects. University of Gothenburg Dept. Education, Gothenburg (1982)

22. Marton, F.: Phenomenography – descriping conceptions of the world around us. Instructional Science 10, 177–200 (1981)
23. Boustedt, J.: Students' understanding of the concept of interface in a situated context. Computer Science Education 19(1), 15–36 (2009)
24. Tutty, J., Sheard, J., Avram, C.: Teaching in the current higher education environment: perceptions of IT academics. Computer Science Education 18(3), 171–185 (2008)
25. Box, I.: Toward an understanding of the variation in approaches to analysis and design. Computer Science Education 19(2), 93–109 (2009)
26. Kaapu, T., Tiainen, T.: Consumers' Views on Privacy in E-Commerce. Scandinavian Journal of Information Systems 21(1), 3–22 (2009)
27. Buchanan, D.A.: Getting the story straight: Illusions and delusions in the organizational change process. Tamara Journal of Critical Postmodern Organization Science 2(4), 7–21 (2003)
28. Marton, F.: Phenomenography: Exploring different conceptions of reality. In: Fetterman, D.M. (ed.) Qualitative approaches to evaluation in education: The silent scientific revolution, pp. 176–205. Praeger, New York (1988)
29. Marton, F., Booth, S.: Learning and awareness. Lawrence Erlbaum, Mahwah (1997)
30. Renström, L.: Conceptions of matter. A phenomenographic approach. Acta Universitatis Gothoburgensis. Göteborg studies in educational sciences, vol. 69. University of Göteborg (1988)
31. Pang, M.F.: Two Faces of Variation: on continuity in the phenomenographic movement. Scandinavian Journal of Educational Research 47(2), 145–155 (2003)
32. Tatnall, A., Lepa, J.: The Internet, e-commerce and older people. Logistics Information Management 16(1), 56–63 (2003)
33. Dholakia, R.R.: Gender and IT in the Household: Evolving Patterns of Internet Use in the United States. The Information Society 22, 231–240 (2006)
34. Rodgers, S., Harris, M.A.: Gender and e-commerce: An exploratory study. Journal of Advertising Research 43(3), 322–329 (2003)
35. Alexandersson, M.: Metod och medvetende [Method and consciousness]. Acta Universitatis Gothoburgensis. Göteborg studies in educational sciences, Göteborg (1994)
36. Sandberg, J.: Understanding human competence at work: An interpretative approach. Academy of Management Journal 43(1), 9–25 (2000)
37. Rubin, J.: Handbook of Usability Testing. John Wiley, New York (1994)
38. March, S., Smith, G.: Design and natural science research on information technology. Decision Support Systems 15(4), 251–266 (1995)

The Living Requirements Space: Towards the Collaborative Development of Requirements for Future ERP Systems

Femi Adisa, Petra Schubert, and Frantisek Sudzina

Copenhagen Business School, Denmark
{fa.caict,psc.caict,fs.caict}@cbs.dk

Abstract. Companies worldwide are faced with an increasingly volatile business environment. This leads to frequent changes in business requirements. The research described in this paper looks at the software development process for the supporting ERP System, standard software, which is generally available through specialised ERP software vendors. We argue that the cycle from gathering requirements to actually implementing them in the software has to be shortened and made more efficient. We propose the Living Requirements Space (LRS), a Web platform for the distributed gathering, storing and discussion of business requirements. Knowledge about business processes is often distributed among different experts. While most existing tools for requirements management are localized and often limited to a particular project or organization there is an increasing need for distributed heterogeneous collaboration. The proposed solution combines aspects from social software as well as from traditional business requirements modelling.

Keywords: Enterprise Systems, ERP systems, software development, requirements, Web 2.0, social software.

1 Introduction and Research Objectives

There has been much discussion in recent years about whether a company should be required to adapt to the inherent (standard) processes of software or whether the software should provide enough flexibility for highly customized processes. In 1998, Davenport described the situation as follows: "most companies installing enterprise systems will need to adapt or even completely rework their processes to fit the requirements of the system." [1]. The term *Enterprise System* is a meta-concept for all kinds of software systems that support the activities of a company. Enterprise systems comprise hardware, software, databases, and the necessary networks to link different software systems. *ERP Systems* are a specific kind of enterprise system, which puts an emphasis on the management of resources (information, financial and human) of a company. In this paper we focus specifically on the further development of standard business software, which is generally available through specialised ERP software vendors such as SAP, Microsoft, Oracle, and Sage. The work presented here is part of an international research project to investigate the *"next generation of ERP systems"*.

One of the objectives of the project is to improve the adaptability of software to the needs of the user company.

The current expectation is that future generations of ERP systems will be much more flexible and more easily adaptable to the needs of an individual company (similar to individual software) but should retain the advantages of a standard ERP solution. One of the big challenges presented by this scenario is the identification and documentation of requirements at the source: that is from the users who are dependent on the software to support their specific tasks.

According to [2], the process of identifying, gathering, and specifying requirements is the most difficult aspect in information systems development. Identifying requirement for enterprise resource planning systems (ERP Systems) is considered especially difficult due to the fact that ERP Systems address all the concerned functions of an organization [3]. A basic problem is the fact that the developers of such software struggle to gather, document, and manage the requirements for their products [4].

[5] sees the challenge in the requirement collection process between the method for *problem structure* on one hand and the *description per se* on the other. The same is described by [6], who speaks about *"requirements as needs"* and *"requirements as text"*. The two authors express that there are two different types of requirement specifications. They describe the challenge of transforming requirements from text into a formal description, which can be used to programme a software feature. ERP Systems operate in the business applications domain, an environment that is complex, uncertain, and volatile. Constantly evolving business needs require that information systems take into account not only current business requirements but also *future* requirements.

In order to address the challenge of constantly changing requirements we coined the term *"living requirements"*. The concept of living requirements is a reference to the volatile nature of business requirements. Our solution to this challenge is the *"living requirements space (LRS)"*, a platform that supports an online community of stakeholders in the ERP domain. Members of this Web-based community include requirements engineers, domain experts, business analysts, software users, ERP providers and other stakeholders who are collaborating on the development of business requirements for future third generation ERP Systems. The platform aims to support the information flow from users to software developers. The concept of the LRS platform is described in this paper which provides a framework that fosters the collaborative collection and development of business requirements for ERP Systems. We use a combination of empirical research, hermeneutics and design research. In the first step (*empirical research*), we conducted interviews with a large ERP software vendor (industry partner) and learned about the internal process of requests for change. The ERP vendor is selling the software through a network of independent implementation partners. As a consequence, the ERP vendor cannot "learn" directly from implementation projects and is dependent on the feedback from business analysts in the partner companies. We performed an analysis of pain points (reference deleted for blind review) and learned that the indirect sales channel poses a great challenge and that it is currently difficult to request and receive user requirements in a form that can be interpreted by a programmer. The works demonstrated in this paper represents ongoing research exploring new ways for better and more efficient requirements specifications methods for future ERP systems, that will take into account the volatile nature of business requirements. A part of our solution is a collaborative Web platform that is built on principles from Social Software and Web 2.0 (*the LRS platform*). The last step (*design research*), which is still ongoing, involves the programming of the prototype which will later be tested (validated) with the ERP vendor's implementation partners (business analysts) in the field.

The research question that is addressed in this paper is thus the following: *To what extent can business requirements for ERP systems be collected and discussed collaboratively in a worldwide community of business process experts?*

The remainder of this paper is structured as follows: The next chapter presents the literature review on requirements and an explanation of the basic terms and definitions used in this paper. The process of collecting requirements is described. The following chapter describes the proposed solution with its technical components. The last section concludes the findings and gives an outlook into future work in this area.

2 Literature Review and Definition of Terms

2.1 Requirements

A *requirement* is a specification of what should be implemented. It is a description of how the system should behave, including application domain information, constraints on the system's operation, or specification of a system property or attributes [7]. According to [8], a *System Requirement* is a system capability needed by the user to solve a problem or achieve an objective, and/or a system capability that must be met or possessed by a system or system component, to satisfy a contract, standard, specification or other formally imposed document. Thayer's definition underscores the importance of the user focus when dealing with requirements. Understanding user requirements is crucial to the planning and success of a project and the subsequent acceptance of the new system. According to [9], requirements provide the basis for project planning, risk management, acceptance testing, trade-off, and change control.

A *requirement* describes what is needed in order to achieve something. [10] state that "a requirement is something that the product must do or a quality that the product must have". Further refining this definition, it can be suggested that requirements could be referred to as statements of needs. In this article we focus on two different kinds of requirements: business and system requirements. We use the term *business requirement* when we speak about the needs of a user. We speak about *system requirements* when we define what is needed to generate a software code (software programme).

2.2 Domain

[9] emphasize the importance of making a clear distinction between the "*problem domain*" and the "*solution domain*" from an engineering and management perspective when dealing with requirements. They state that *requirements in the problem domain* are stakeholder requirements that describe the capabilities which users expect from the new system (these are addressed in subsection 2.3), while *requirements in the*

solution domain represent system features, which engineers implement to solve stakeholder requirements (these are addressed in subsection 2.4). [6] adopts the same definition on requirements but also says that what people talk about when they talk about requirements depends on the situation. Requirements in the context of system development may be defined as: 1) a function, capability, or property required of a proposed system and/or it is 2) the statement of such a function, capability or property.

Requirements engineering (RE) is often described as the process of closing the gap between a specific problem and the solution for that problem. Having a process view of RE means that RE consists of a set of activities which cover the discovering, documenting, and maintaining a set of requirements for a computer-based system. The activities in requirements engineering process include requirements elicitation, requirements analysis and negotiation, requirements documentation, and requirements validation, all running in parallel with the requirements management process which is intended to monitor and control changes to the requirements document [7].

Requirements Management (RM) is described as the requirements engineering activities concerned with finding, organising, documenting and tracking requirements for software systems [11]. [12] state that the *requirements management process* should deal with requirements as they evolve through the system lifecycle. So, the primary focus of RM is maintaining traceability, "the ability to describe and follow the life of a requirement, in both forwards and backwards direction (i.e. from its origin, through its development and specification, to its subsequent deployment and use, and through all periods of on-going refinement and iteration in any of these phases)" [13].

Requirements are specified in a *system requirements specification* (SRS) document or requirements document (see Fig. 3). This is a document consisting of a textual description of the requirement in natural language supplemented by diagrams, process diagrams, system models, etc.

The *quality of requirements* collected has been linked to the tools utilized and RE tools are said to provide better support for the RE process than general office and modelling tools, resulting in higher quality requirements documents [14] and this has informed our decision to focus on the requirement tool as a means to overcoming the challenges posed by the difficulty to request and receive user requirements in a form that can be easily interpreted by programmers. However, according to [11], a dominant issue with current RM tools is *distribution*; they claim that most of the existing RM tools are localized (in a sense that they are meant for a particular project/organization) and are, therefore, not suitable for highly distributed heterogeneous collaboration. The ability to collaborate on the development of business requirements is highly desirable, especially because expert knowledge on business requirements that shape ERPs is scarce and typically thinly distributed. Therefore there is a need for tools, which foster distributed collaboration in the development of requirements on a global scale. This is also supported by [15], who found that "distance has a significant impact on the collaboration between geographically distributed functional groups involved in the negotiation of requirements from a diverse customer market". Subsection 2.7 addresses the concept of mass collaboration.

Stakeholder requirements, also known as *user requirements* or *business requirements*, are requirements written from the point of view of system stakeholders [16]. They are an initial statement of capability that defines the problem and standard practices within the particular industry that an organization operates in [17]. They belong to the stages of development associated with the highest levels of system description and together with statement of need and usage modelling should be firmly rooted in the problem domain [9]. Stakeholder requirements are not usually expressed in great detail and should state no more than is necessary to define the problem at a level of abstraction that avoids referencing any particular solution. On the other hand, as described by [18], it would be useful to have stakeholder requirements not only for ordinary but also for critical and disaster situations.

Systems requirements are derived by modelling business requirements. They should be aligned with business requirements and focus on possible solutions to help the business get its job done more effectively [17]. [8] defines a system requirement as "a system capability needed by the user to solve a problem or achieve an objective". System requirements are more detailed specifications of requirements that should be expressed as an abstract model of the system [16]. According to Hull [9], systems engineers should refrain from inappropriate bias for a certain software product and avoid encroaching into the solution domain space of designers by making sure the elements of solution introduced through functional modelling remain at a high level, allowing designers the freedom of designing an abstract solution. System requirements are used to create system models of the proposed systems that are abstracted from the final solution. They serve as a basis for discussion and understanding what characteristics the system must have irrespective of the final detailed design [9]. Figure 1 shows an overview of the requirements process.

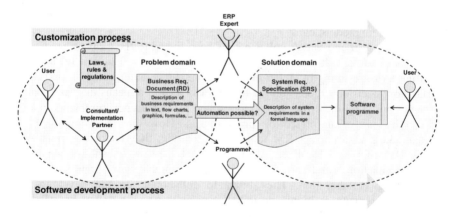

Fig. 1. The process from requirements gathering to programming the software

2.3 Requirements in the Problem Domain (User Perspective)

The *problem domain* represents the business environment where a system will be used (see fig. 1). It is the starting point of any systems engineering project. It is here that the capabilities required from the new system are established. The end product of the RE process in the problem domain is a requirements document that is a structured set of stakeholder requirements.

Requirement engineering in the problem domain is primarily about eliciting capabilities. In order to be able to do this, it is important to establish what people want to be able to do with the system. This leads to an important question and the first aspect of RE in the problem domain: "who should be asked?"

2.4 Requirements in the Solution Domain (Programmer Perspective)

The solution domain is the domain of engineers (programmers). This is where problems outlined in the problem domain are solved. The refined and structured set of business requirements that were the output of the problem domain, provide the input and serve as the basis for the development efforts in the solution domain. Once the stakeholder requirements are well understood and documented, it is time to think of potential solutions in terms of the characteristics that the new system must have irrespective of the final detailed design. This process is known as establishing the system requirements [9].

An abstract model of the proposed system is developed to provide a basis for discussion and establishing a common understanding of the proposed solution among the development team. The model provides a structure for documenting the system requirements and may also be used to explain the solution concept to stakeholders. The produced document serves as an aid to reviewing the complete requirements set from a consistency and completeness perspective.

The next phase is to develop architectural designs based on the set of system requirements. The design architecture is expressed as a set of interacting components that collectively exhibit the desired properties. It defines what each system component must do and how the system components interact with each other to produce the overall effects specified in the system requirements [9].

2.5 The Concept of Living Requirements

Requirements changes are inevitable and do not necessarily point to bad RE practices. They occur while requirements are being elicited, analysed and after the system has gone into service. Such changes occur as a result of stakeholders developing a better understanding of the application domain or due to external circumstances e.g. legal, social etc. [7]. In the ERP application domain requirements management is not about keeping these changes under control. RM is about creating an environment where ERP providers can keep abreast with changing business requirements and hopefully be able to gain an insight into how such trends develop over time, so that they can be in a position to better predict requirements. The concept of living requirement stems from the volatility and constantly evolving nature of business requirements in the ERP domain. The *Living Requirements Space (LRS)* is our proposed solution to the constantly changing nature of requirements – a platform where domain experts, business analysts and stakeholders can collaborate in every stage of the requirements lifecycle, from the identification, to the analysis, through to the management of business requirement for ERP systems.

In classic software development, the requirements development phase of RE ends as soon as documented requirements are passed on to developers. RM then tries to keep changes under control during the rest of the software development cycle [7][4]. ERP providers have no such luxury. They must avail themselves to the changes in the application domain, if their products are to continue to offer "best practice" solutions. Requirement development and management in the ERP domain are parallel, intertwined, and overlapping continuous activities.

In a volatile business environment, which frequently characterizes the ERP application domain of the vendor the ideal situation is one in which the software developer is able to involve the various stakeholders from across multiple organizations and regions in the requirements engineering process. Such collaboration could lead to a better understanding of how business requirements are evolving in various regions across the globe and the ability to predict future requirements and implement them as system features prior to their next release. The LRS platform provides such an environment.

2.6 Requirements Template

The end product of the requirements documenting activity is the requirements document. This is a formal document used to communicate the system requirements to customers, end-users, software developers and managers of the software engineering process [16] using different software development models [19]. Different organizations have different names for it including: "Requirements Document (RD)" [20], "functional specification", "the requirement definition", "the software requirements specification (SRS)" (ANSI/IEEE Standard 830 1998) and there is no universal standard template. Depending on the target audience a requirements document can be either customer or developer oriented. The RD plays an important role in the requirements specification process. It serves as the basis for software development contracting [10]; proving a means for external reviews [21], for reuse in other projects [22], as well as a standard medium to communicate requirements between customers [16], users, managers and developers.

An important characteristic of requirement documentation is that it should not have a definite end. The information about a requirement is typically illustrated with various process and system model diagrams and can also be supplemented with other detailed documentation files. This multi-document nature of a requirements document requires a template that makes it easy to link all these documents together and maintain traceability.

[6] states that the documentation is often regarded as the end goal itself but it can be said that, since an information system needs to change and often does, the requirements document should work as a supporting tool in this process. Changes to requirements are inevitable due to changes in the problem domain or external (social, legal, political) factors [7]. This requires that RM practices and tools for ERP systems must provide the flexibility, adaptability and agility to support the volatile and constantly evolving environment in which ERP systems operate.

2.7 Mass Collaboration and Open Source Development

Sound requirements processes emphasize a collaborative approach to product development that involves multiple stakeholders in a partnership throughout the project (Wiegers 2003). In their book "Wikinomics: How Mass Collaboration

Changes everything". [23] base their concept of mass collaboration on four ideas 1) *openness*, 2) *peering*, 3) *sharing* and 4) *acting globally* leading to what they call an economic democracy based on business strategies as "models where stakeholders and even competitors co-create value in the absence of direct managerial control". Mass collaboration relies on free individual agents to come together and cooperate to improve a given operation or solve a problem. However, this type of coming together neither requires participants to be physically present in one location, nor participate at the same time. Such collaboration is usually Web-based and employing the use of social software and computer-supported collaboration tools such as Wiki technologies. This decentralized model of mass collaboration is the source of success and uniqueness over the traditional collaboration paradigm, where central control is applied [24]. Mass collaboration differs from traditional forms of collaboration in that the collaborative process is mediated by the content being created and not by direct social interaction.

Although the term mass collaboration is relatively new, the concept has been around for some time. The Open Source community has been enjoying the benefits of mass collaboration. Linux owes its success to the collaborative efforts of open source enthusiasts, scattered around the globe. Wikipedia, a popular online resource, owes its contents to the efforts of about "10 million volunteers who collaborate over the web to create a worldwide encyclopaedia" [25].

It is our belief that active user engagement is the new way for organizations to improve the quality and capability of their products. The *LRS platform* described in this paper is based on the concept of mass collaboration combining elements from open source software development (requirements description) and Wikipedia (for the development of a joint understanding of terms in the ERP area).

[26] refer to open source software development as a somewhat orthogonal approach where much of the activity is openly visible and where there is no formal project management, regime, budget or schedule, mainly oriented towards the joint development of a community of developers and users concomitant with the software system of interest.

3 Process of Requirements Collection

Requirements elicitation is a set of activities aimed at discovering the requirements of a proposed system. They are usually done by interacting with stakeholders to establish what they want to be able to do with the system, as well as identifying any constraints that might affect the goal of the new system. [9] describe the first aspect of requirements elicitation process as establishing "who should be asked". According to [7] this not only involves asking people what they want but also requires a careful domain analysis of the organization where the system will run and a thorough understanding of their business processes.

3.1 The Generic Process of Requirements Collection

Once the stakeholders have been identified, the process of discovering the requirements can begin. However, the overriding sentiment is that stakeholders rarely have a clear picture of what they want and their initial statements of needs are rather vague at best. The process of understanding what they want becomes a series of analysis and negotiations. This would imply that the processes of requirements elicitation, analysis and modelling are intertwined, parallel and iterative. The analysis process employs modelling techniques to develop various use scenarios and process models, as a tool for understanding and communicating requirements. The analyst depicts his understanding of the operations of the users in several hierarchical and sequential use scenario models and shows it off to the users. This then serves as a basis for the analysis process including checks for incomplete, inconsistent and missing requirements and further negotiation of requirements, discussion, prioritization and agreement. The aim is to transform the initial statement of needs into capabilities requirements for the proposed system and to produce a clear set of unambiguous high level statements of stakeholder requirements. This will be included in the requirements document that will serve as a basis for system development.

[7] outlined four dimensions to requirements elicitation: 1) application domain understanding, 2) problem understanding, 3) business understanding, and 4) understanding stakeholder needs and constraints. They, however, outlined the following obstacles to understanding system requirement:

- *Application domain knowledge* not being collected neatly in one place but existing in a variety of different sources such as: textbooks, operating manuals, in the heads of practitioners and usually involves specialist jargons.
- *Accessibility of people* who understand the problem to be solved. They are either too busy or unconvinced of the necessity for a new system.
- *Organizational issues*, political factors and other mutually exclusive factors may influence the system requirements.
- *Stakeholders not knowing* what they want or not being able to articulate their requirements from the computer system and making unrealistic demands.

The LRS platform is designed to incorporate requirements from multiple sources. Allowing common methods for requirements elicitation - interviews with stakeholders, scenario exploration (in conjunction with interviews), studies or market research, existing systems, problems and change requests from existing systems, prototyping, questionnaires - to be documented and connected to each requirement.

In the ERP domain a distributed collaborative process for collecting requirements is the method of choice as some ERP providers depend on their network of implementation partners for the implementation of their systems and do not have direct access to the users (customers). There must be a mechanism for partners to communicate those requirements that do not exist in current systems back to the ERP vendors with a view to having those requirements implemented in future ERP releases.

The large ERP system providers, such as SAP, Microsoft, Oracle and Baan, offer their own software specific methods for undertaking a complete requirement specification [27]. However, vendor-specific methods are software specific and most support the implementation process but do not support the requirement specification or the change management adopted before the implementation process [28].

The LRS is designed to be an open, vendor-independent platform for the elicitation and engineering of business requirements that is also independent of any particular implementation or development project for ERP systems.

3.2 Requirements Tools Survey

Before indulging into the process of developing a new tool for the gathering of requirements we performed an analysis of existing tools for RE. The base for our investigation was the INCOSE requirements management tools survey [29].

One conclusion that can be suggested from the investigation is that software management tools work under the assumption that, new as well as old, requirements must be connected to a project. This is a problem in the ERP System context since the development of an ERP system is not a single project. An implementation of an ERP system can be seen as a project – in fact it is probably the biggest and most problematic IT project most organizations can conduct, however, since the development of ERP Systems represents the development of a standard software package a specific requirement cannot be connected to a single instance in the form of a project. Another limitation of the existing software management tools is that they do not support a distributed, collaborative collection and analysis of requirements, so they are not able to support different stakeholders in a distributed environment.

A crucial functionality of ERP systems requirements management software tools is to support an efficient communication as well as fast response to changes on requirements. In that way it can be claimed that the tool needs to support agile development methods by delivering software in small and frequent increments. However, from our investigation of software requirements management tools existing on the market that was conducted from the perspective of a distributed requirements management view, the main conclusion is that existing tools do not support requirements management in the ERP system context. The *LRS platform* is meant to fill this gap and support requirements from a disparate environment consisting of many independent stakeholders, creating a repository that will serve as a one-stop shop for ERP systems requirement that will be useful and beneficial to the business and academic communities.

4 Proposed Solution: A Platform for Requirements Collection

The LRS platform is a Web-based, OS and project independent, requirements development and management tool designed to support the collaborative discovery of business requirements and support the analysis, linkability and traceability management of the discovered requirements for ERP systems. The use of the Web as a platform for the collection of business requirements offers a strategic positioning advantage. Unlike current RM tools that are localized and project centric, the *LRS platform* is an architecture that is based on participation and it aims to harness collective intelligence by providing an avenue for practitioners and stakeholders in the ERP domain with shared and /or similar interests and tasks to generate knowledge about business requirements for ERP systems collaboratively, irrespective of locale. The goal is to create an online community of ERP stakeholders, who will not only participate in the elicitation of business requirements but will further contribute to the development of such requirements by collaborating in the further analysis and negotiation process of the collected requirements.

The adoption of Web 2.0 technologies and particularly the Wiki approach and the social software aspect to requirements management is based on several implicit and inherent technology features that make it ideal for collecting and managing business requirements. Furthermore, with the generation of users who have grown up with the Web as a technology coming into the workforce, they expect the tools that allow things they are used to - collaboration, immediate ubiquitous access, and so on - will be there for them.

4.1 Motivation and Participation

Why would the target audience want to take part in such an endeavour? The current dominant trend in systems engineering is towards global organizations, partnerships and inter-organizational working, distribution therefore requires serious attention. However, we do not take it for granted that the desired audience will be attracted by default to the proposed platform. [30] talked about developers in the open source community for example finding that the greatest benefit from participation is the opportunity to learn and to share what they know. Others [31][32], have stated that participation is an avenue for individuals, project groups, and organizations to continuously improve or adapt their processes and practices. Peer recognition and to be seen as trustworthy and reputable contributors is also recognized as a factor [33].

We acknowledge existence of lurkers – visitors who take a back seat approach and just want to observe - who will not contribute. But as [34] discovered, contributors are more satisfied with their online community experience than lurkers. This should motivate contributors to continue to contribute and it may also stimulate lurkers to become more active.

A global repository on business requirements might be attractive to stakeholders in the ERP domain because it will harness the collective intelligence on universal ERP implementations, and centralize it by making it available through a single unified portal. It is a known fact that even within an organization, it is quite difficult to capture and structure internal organizational knowledge that is held in the heads of individuals.

4.2 The Database

The structure of the requirement object as an entity made up of several entities of different structures with direct links between them makes them better suited to object-oriented databases, as opposed to relational databases that perform best when records are of the same structure with minimal links [7]. OO databases are better suited for RM because they intrinsically handle complex data types like video, audio, graphs and photos, all which can be attributes of the requirements object and which traditional RDBMS were not natively designed to handle. Furthermore, OODBMS excel when a huge amount of diverse and related data about one item is to be stored as in the case with requirements. The number of actual requirements that will be stored in an RM database may number in the few thousands but the links to its corresponding attributes like documents, images, text file, model diagrams and other related requirements will be exponential.

A requirement is a complex entity that needs to be pre-defined when used by a community of users. We developed a special hierarchy of elements which is displayed in *Figure* 2. We combined different existing methods for the abstract representation of requirements, e.g. the ProZoom and eXperience methods [35] and Event-Driven Process Chains [36]. The elements of the resulting requirement hierarchy are connected through hyperlinks. This design means that requirements can be traced upwards to their highest level of abstraction and the purpose of a requirement being to support upper level business goals is realized. A business use scenario can also be drilled down to its most granular level to view the set of requirements that supports its processes. Figure 2 shows a schematic overview of the requirement hierarchy.

Examples for instantiations of the elements are the following:

- Business Scenario (e.g. procurement process in the wholesale industry, business partners: manufacturer and customer)
- Process (e.g. order process of a wholesaler, customer view)
- Sub-process (e.g. call order process, collection of necessary data)
- Process step (e.g. generate call order in ERP system)
- Task (e.g. key in order quantity)
- Details of task (e.g. a formula for calculating a special discount)

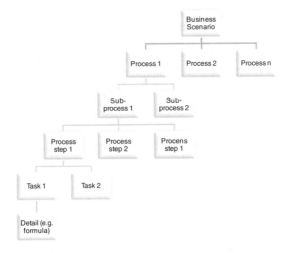

Fig. 2. The decomposition of a requirement (hierarchy)

4.3 The Software Architecture

The LRS RM tool architecture is based on Semantic Web 2.0 technologies. It leverages the knowledge management ability of Wiki technologies which natively supports collaboration and several intrinsic Wiki features to support the requirements development and management processes. Key components include: Open Source Wiki system, with key functionalities which support RM; History and versioning; Traceability; User authentication; Updating capabilities; Linkability; Flexibility of a Web browser interface which supports the embedding of all media types. The core is an enterprise Web application backed by an object oriented database, which implicitly provides versioning of content and meta-data, linkability between objects, knowledge spaces for users/groups, and a freely configurable interface. The Wiki software sits on top of the database and provides the interface for interacting with the database objects through a Web browser. It is easy to set up Wiki pages to represent the various objects in the database. The Wiki software not only provides the electronic interface to collect requirements, it also allows for the easy creation of interlinked Web pages using a simplified mark-up language or a WYSIWYG text editor.

Links to images, use case diagrams, use scenarios and process models are displayed on the base RD as thumbnail images which on clicking, opens the full image in a new browser window. Links are also placed in the document template to point to current research, references and literature that support the requirement. Sections and subsections can be rolled up to show only headers and hide details or drilled down to display greater levels of details in the requirement hierarchy. The LRS RD supports the multiple roles that a requirements document must play in the requirements lifecycle. The LRS RD facilitates the registering of new requirements, searching and viewing of registered requirements and associated attributes and appendices, communication of requirements, easy editing and updating of requirements attributes, reviewing of requirement, as well as easy management of the complex documents that supports a requirement. Requirements change during their lifecycle and in the situation where we are trying to promote collaboration, it is imperative that the volatility of requirements is supported. The document template also needs to make it easy to have an overview of requirements and its supplementary attributes. These make the electronic template ideal.

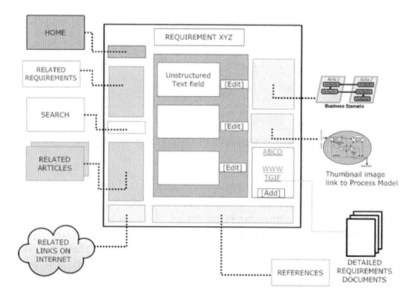

Fig. 3. The requirement template

5 Conclusion and Future Research

In a large scale research project with interdisciplinary partners from business schools and computer sciences faculties (reference deleted for blind review) we designed a prototype for a *Living Requirements Space (LRS)*, a platform that can be used to collect, store and display requirements from an international community of independent stakeholders. We extend the traditional concept of requirements engineering by applying collaborative aspects to it. There are several aspects where our platform goes beyond the traditional RE paradigm. The *LRS platform*

- follows the Web 2.0 approach of sharing and free access to information
- addresses a world-wide community of users and business analyst
- does not belong to a single company but is run by a team of researchers
- is independent of a specific ERP System (vendor)

Challenges that need to be addressed are the different cultural backgrounds, languages, and experiences of the users [15]. The LRS platform will harness the potential of its users to collaboratively develop definition of terms and thus a joint understanding of the underlying vocabulary (Folksonomy or social tagging). Internet users are increasingly willing to contribute to the global knowledge base. The LRS platform makes use of this global movement by combining advantages of social software with the fixed structure (hierarchy) provided by the requirements template. We do not brand the community as a community of practice nor of interest. [37] described the advantages and disadvantages of both but because of the peculiarity of our approach; the LRS puts the community in between the two extreme positions.

Once the platform is operational, one direction of research will be to find ways to use the collected business requirements to (automatically or semi-automatically) transform them into formal descriptions which can be used to generate code. This by far will pose the most significant challenge as converting business requirements collected as free text into formal specs with formal language support borders on the line of formal specifications methods which is currently a major research area.

It will be interesting to see how the different paradigms in ERP software development will evolve in the next ten years. Today, ERP software companies are collecting "their own requirements". Most of them are learning through implementation projects. The ones with indirect sales channels are dependent on their implementation partners. With software getting more and more modularized (thinking of SOA) it is likely that customers will require increasingly more individualized solutions. This makes the process of requirements collection even more challenging. The LRS platform has the potential of becoming a valuable source for ERP developers.

References

1. Davenport, T.: Putting the Enterprise into the Enterprise System. Harvard Business Review 76(4), 121–131 (1998)
2. Alvarez, R.: Confessions of an information worker: a critical analysis of information requirements discourse. Information and Organization 12(2), 85–107 (2002)

3. Worley, J.H., Chatha, K.A., et al.: Implementation and optimisation of ERP systems: A better integration of processes, roles, knowledge and user competencies. Computers in Industry 56(6), 620–638 (2005)
4. Wiegers, K.E.: Software Requirements. Microsoft Press, Redmond (2003)
5. Jackson, M.: Software requirements & Specifications: a lexicon of practice, principles and prejudices. ACM Press, London (1995)
6. Power, N.M.: A grounded theory of requirements documentation in the practice of software development. School Dublin, Dublin City University. Ph.D: 223 (2002)
7. Kotonya, G., Sommerville, I.: Requirements Engineering: Processes and Techniques. Wiley, Chichester (1998)
8. Thayer, R.H.: Software Systems Engineering: An Engineering process. IEEE Computer Society Press, Los Alamitos (1997)
9. Hull, E., Jackson, K., Dick, J.: Requirements Engineering. Springer, London (2005)
10. Robertson, S., Robertson, J.: Mastering the Requirements Process. Addison-Wesley, Reading (1999)
11. Finkelstein, A., Emmerich, W.: The future of requirements management tools. In: Quirchmayr, G., Wagner, R., Wimmer, M. (eds.) Information Systems in Public Administration and Law (2000)
12. Cant, T., McCarhty, J.: Tools for requirements management: a comparison of Telelogic DOORS and the HiVe. D.o.Defence. Edinburgh, Defence Science and Technology Organisation (2006)
13. Gotel, O.C.Z., Finkelstein, A.C.W.: An Analysis of the Requirements Traceability Problem. In: 1st International Conference on Requirements Engineering. IEE Computer Society Press (1994)
14. Matulevicius, R.: How requirements specification quality depends on tools: A case study. In: Persson, A., Stirna, J. (eds.) CAiSE 2004. LNCS, vol. 3084, pp. 353–367. Springer, Heidelberg (2004)
15. Damian, D.E., Zowghi, D.: The impact of stakeholders' geographical distribution on managing requirements in a multi-site organization. In: Proceedings of the IEEE Joint International Conference on Requirements Engineering (RE'02), pp. 1–10 (2002)
16. Sommerville, I., Sawyer, P.: Requirements Engineering: A good practice guide. John Wiley and Sons, Chichester (1997)
17. Krebs, J.: Dissecting Business from Software Requirements (August 15, 2005), http://www.ibm.com/developerworks/rational/library/aug05/krebs/index.html (accessed September 14, 2005)
18. Ministr, J., Stevko, M., Fiala, J.: The IT Service Continuity Management Principles Implementation by Method A2. In: IDIMT- 2009 Systems and Humans – A Complex Relationship – 17th Interdisciplinary Information Management Talks Preceedings, Linz, Trauner Druck, pp. 131–139 (2009)
19. Doucek, P.: Dynamic modeling of the software development process. Cybernetics and Systems 27(4), 403–410 (1996)
20. Kovitz, B.M.: Practical Software Requirements: A Manual of Content and Style, Greenwich, Connecticut (1998)
21. Boehm, B.: Get ready for agile methods with care. Computer 35(1), 64–69 (2002)
22. Czarnecki, K.: Domain Engineering. Encyclopedia of Software Engineering. Wiley, Chichester (2002)
23. Tapscott, D., Williams, A.D.: Wikinomics: How Mass Collaboration Changes Everything Portfolio Hardcover (2006)

24. Braffman, O., Beckstrom, R.: The Starfish and the Spider: The Unstoppable Power of Leaderless Organizations, Penguin Group (2006)
25. Panchal, J., Fathianathan, M.: Product realization in the age of mass collaboration. In: ASME Design Automation Conference, DET2008-49865 (2008)
26. Scacchi, W., Feller, J., Fitzgerald, B., Hissam, S., Lakhani, K.: Understanding free/open source software developement processes. Software Process - Improvement and Practice 11(2), 95–105 (2006)
27. Soffer, P., Golany, B., Dor, D.: ERP modeling: a comprehensive approach. Information Systems 28(9), 673–690 (2003)
28. Vilpola, I., Kouri, I.: Improving ERP requirement specification process of SMEs with a customer-centered analysis method. In: Proceedings of the Frontiers of e-Business Research (FeBR 2005), pp. 140–151. Tampere University of Technology and University of Tampere, Tampere (2005)
29. INCOSE, INCOSE Requirement Management Survey (2009), http://www.paper-review.com/tools/rms/vencon.php?vendor=CASE%20Spec%208.0 (accessed September 14, 2009)
30. Lakhani, K.R., von Hippel, E.: How open source software works: 'free' user-to-user assistance. Research Policy 32(6), 923–943 (2002)
31. Nakakoji, K., Ye, Y., Yamamoto, Y., Kishida, K.: The co-evolution of systems and communities in free and open source software development. In: Free/Open Source Software Development Processes, pp. 59–82. IGI Publishing, Hershey (2004)
32. Huntley, C.I.: Organizational learning in open-source software projects: An analysis of debugging data. IEEE Transactions on Engineering Management 50(4), 485–493 (2003)
33. Stewart, K.J., Gosain, S.: An exploratory study of ideology and trust in open source development groups. In: Proceedings of the 22nd International Conference Information Systems (ICIS-2001), New Orleans, LA (2001)
34. Nonnecke, B., Andrews, D., Preece, J.: Non-public and public online community participation: Needs, attitudes and behaviour. Electronic Commerce Research 6(1), 7–20 (2006)
35. Schubert, P., Wölfle, R.: The eXperience Methodology for Writing IS Case Studies. In: Proceedings of the Thirteenth Americas Conference on Information Systems, AMCIS (2007)
36. Scheer, A.-W.: ARIS – Business Process Modeling, 3rd edn. Springer, Heidelberg (2000)
37. Jones, A., Preece, J.: Online communities for teachers and lifelong learners: A framework for comparing similarities and identifying differences in communities of practice and communities of interest. International Journal of Learning Technology 2(2/3), 112–137 (2006)

IT Governance through Regulatory Modalities. Health Care Information Infrastructure and the "Blue Fox" Project

Bendik Bygstad[1] and Ole Hanseth[2]

[1] Norwegian School of IT
[2] Institute of Informatics, University of Oslo

Abstract. The purpose of this paper is to discuss a framework for governance of information infrastructures. While most research in IT governance suggests top-down governance frameworks, we argue that a more viable approach is to explore a broader set of more indirect measures of control.

One excellent area in which to study this is IT in health, because the high political expectations to health information systems exert an immense pressure on the health sector and the IT solution vendors. Our case evidence is a project called the "Blue Fox".

Building on Lessig's four modalities of regulation, we suggest an alternative set of governance principles for information infrastructures. Our conclusion is: in certain contexts it is possible to extend national information infrastructures by a regulatory approach, a deliberate combination of legal, technical, social and economic measures, which reinforce each other. We argue that this approach also may lead to simpler projects.

Keywords: IT governance, information infrastructures, regulatory modalities.

1 Introduction

IT governance has become a prominent field the past decade, partly because of the increasing pressures on CIOs to provide both stable and agile IT infrastructures, and partly because of macro regulations such as the Sarbanes-Oxley Act in the USA and Basel II in Europe. The ISO 38500 offers a standard for "guiding principles for directors of organizations (including owners, board members, directors, partners, senior executives, or similar) on the effective, efficient, and acceptable use of Information Technology within their organizations" [22].

Most of the IT governance research has addressed the internal needs of the typical corporation [28,35]. One of the most cited frameworks were suggested by Weill and Ross, in which they identify five areas for IT decisions; IT principles, IT Architecture, IT Infrastructure Strategies, Business Application Needs, and IT investment and prioritization. In order to manage these areas they suggest six basic IT governance forms; business monarchy, IT monarchy, feudal, federal, IT duopoly and anarchy [35]. The main objective of the framework is to ensure the alignment with business goals, while also safeguarding the continuous IT operations.

These approaches emphasize that in order to manage an increasingly complex IT portfolio it is necessary to establish governing systems that reflect this complexity, in line with the Ross Ashby Law of Requisite Variety. But is this an effective approach in the context of large information infrastructures, with many stakeholders and various technologies? Building on a number of studies [5,8,16,34] we find that the evidence rather indicates that such approaches often fail. The main reason is that information infrastructures are heterogeneous networks without central control. In such structures more management control is not only ineffective, but also tends to hinder innovation of local solutions.

The issue, then, is how to ensure sensible overall solutions, while at the same time allow for local adaptation and flexibility? As a point of departure, we think there is a need to understand and manage the use of more indirect measures than management directives. There is also a need for smaller and simpler projects, in contrast to the mega-programmes that dominate in particular the public sector.

One excellent area in which to study this is IT in health. Our example is from the Norwegian health sector, which (together with most other developed countries) is characterized by three classes of problems. First, the political and organisational environment is both complex and unstable. The sector is a labyrinth of three administrative levels, two main levels of services (specialist and primary care), regional and local hospitals, 450 municipality health services, and a network of laboratories, pharmacy chains and other private actors. Most of these units have their own ICT solutions, some partly shared and some integrated with others. There is no national infrastructure, except for a VPN service (Helsenett), but a number of large initiatives are ongoing, such as regional EPR systems and a national E-Prescription project. The political pressure to standardize and integrate the solutions is increasing, and new politically driven initiatives are expected.

Second, the technical complexities are formidable. To support a single hospital unit with IT solutions is in itself quite challenging, as documented in many cases. To give integrated support to a whole hospital is so challenging that there are today very few, if any, successful examples. And to integrate hospitals and primary care, at a national level, into one streamlined and controlled "supply chain" is at the moment only a vision. Several authors have shown that "integration" is a deceptive term in the health sector; it tends to hide the socio-technical complexities of inter-organisational solutions [13].

Third, one may question whether the system of knowledge creation in the sector is viable. In an article of *Journal of Information Technology,* Sauer and Willcocks write that the enormous expectations to the British national program "Connecting for Health" are unrealistic. The three key stakeholder groups have become engaged in a "game of dishonesty": the government authorities expect that ICT should contribute heavily to increase efficiency in the sector, and thereby curbing the growth of national health costs. The health sector itself has, increasingly, realized that fulfilling these expectations is much more difficult and time-consuming than assumed. The third stakeholder group, the media and the "professional critics", are cheering the political initiatives, but also criticizing harshly projects that are not completely successful [29]. The problem is that in this game of high expectations, the question is too often; who is to blame? However, a more fundamental question is; how is the production of knowledge organised in this sector? How do we frame our understanding, and to which degree do we learn systematically from experience?

This situation calls for caution in advocating quick solutions. It also, however, calls for new perspectives on IT governance in health. The current knowledge regime mainly builds on "best practice" from the computer science field (i.e. distributed SOA architectures), and IT management literature (in particular strategic planning and project management). While these approaches might have worked reasonably well in limited business organisation contexts, their transferability to the much more complex health sector is questionable, considering the challenges described above.

In this paper we will discuss an alternative and more organic strategy for IT governance in health. Our main argument is that the main challenge is not really to build "IT systems", but to extend a heterogeneous existing information infrastructure (II) in the health sector, consisting of people, technology and organisations. Thus, a viable strategy should build on two knowledge premises; we need to understand the dynamics of infrastructure growth, and we need to broaden our repertoire of measures in order to influence on this dynamics. Such analysis should be theoretically informed, in order to understand the underlying mechanisms of successful infrastructures.

We proceed in section 2 by outlining related research on information infrastructures and IT governance. In section 3 we briefly describe our method, while presenting the case study, the Blue Fox project, in section 4. Drawing on Lessig's four modalities of regulation, we discuss the implications in section 5, before we conclude and point to further research in the last section.

2 Related Research

Most II research has aimed at identifying the main features and characteristics of IIs - their "nature" as they evolve and developers and users are struggling to make them work [7,8,9,11,23,31].

Standards are core elements of IIs; hence standards research constitutes a major part of II research [11,31]. A large part of this research has focused on and disclosed a very dense and complex web of relations between technical and social (or non-technical) issues and elements of the standards [4,17,26]. Another key part of the research has focused on the creation and role of network effects, i.e. self-reinforcing processes leading to lock-ins [14,30].

A few researchers have addressed design strategies for infrastructure development. Hanseth et al. [18] recognize the need to manage the tension between standardization and flexibility. (See also Egyedi [12].) Hanseth and Aanestad [19] argue, using telemedicine as an illustration, that II design needs to be seen as a bootstrapping process, which utilizes network effects and spill-overs within a growing user base by using simple solutions as a sort of "stunts", which offer "detours" on the road towards infrastructures [1]. Hanseth also demonstrates the importance of gateways in flexible II design by reviewing the history of the Internet design in Scandinavia [15]. Hanseth and Lyytinen [20] have synthesized much of this research into a design theory.

Mechanisms and structures supporting the successful coordination and control – or *governance* - of the development, evolution and use of II's have not been the target for much research. There may be one exception to this; standards have been widely assumed to be the key to successful establishment and use of infrastructures. Accordingly, standards and standardization bodies have been (implicitly) assumed to be the key institutions for II governance. But recent research on IIs and their standards, mentioned above, demonstrates clearly that just knowing that we need standards to develop infrastructures is not of much help. *How* to successfully develop and implement standards is the tricky question. And a part of this question is how to govern these processes.

IT governance has emerged the last decade or so as a major IS research area. This research, however, has focused mostly on how to govern IT inside the borders of ordinary business corporations. And, further, it has also focused almost exclusively on identifying the levels and domains where various decisions regarding IT should be made [6,28], Weil and Ross 2004, Xue et al. 2008). For this reason, this research does not provide much help for those struggling with the governance if IIs being shared by a huge number of independent organizations. Fortunately, some research addressing some of the issues involved is emerging. There is, for instance, a growing body of research on Internet governance [10, 27]. Much of this research, and the related discussion, are, however, centred on whether ICANN should be a part of the UN (and ITU) system.

Another emerging field of research is related to the control, or governance, of user behaviours on the Internet (to avoid distribution of spam and child pornography, copyright infringement, etc.). This has partly been a discussion about IP legislation on the one hand and the use of Digital Rights Management technologies on the other. But this has also triggered a broader discussion about regulation and governance in the modern globalized high-tech society. Julia Black [2,3] for instance, argued that we need to move away from the traditional "command-and-control" paradigm of regulation and towards one more based on self-regulation and the idea of cultivation.

Along similar lines Lawrence Lessig [24,25] has developed a more sophisticated theory saying that behaviour is regulated by four kinds of constraints: *Law* regulates by telling people how to behave in certain situations, or else being punished. Social norms do much of the same, but they are enforced not by the government, but by community. Third, *markets* regulate behaviour by price; the price of a good will influence on how much we will use it. And fourth, we are regulated by the constraints of the designed physical environment, what Lessig calls *architecture*. The four modes of regulation influence on each other, both in constraining and enabling them. For example, law will constrain the design of IT solutions and economic incentives, but an information infrastructure will also constrain what is possible to enforce by law. The four modes may be implemented directly, as directives, or indirectly, as constraining and enabling mechanisms [24]. Thus, particularly as a self-reinforcing ensamble, the regulatory modalities constitute a powerful alternative to traditional IT governance. Lessig's ideas have been used in research on the governance of inter-organizational activities or what is called architectures of participation.

3 Method

Our research approach was a multilevel case study [21]. We conducted the study in the Norwegian health sector during a period of 12 months in 2008 and 2009, focusing on organisational and management issues. Interviews were conducted with key actors at the Ministry of Health and the Directorate of Health, with managers at the Regional Health Authorities, and with IT personnel and doctors in several public and private health organisations. We also tried to get an overview of the somewhat overwhelming amount of both official and internal documents. Our aim was to analyse the governance of eHealth in Norway, in particular the interplay of macro and micro initiatives. The study was conducted during a period of turbulence, as key actors in the sector competed on positions and premises in the future Norwegian eHealth infrastructure.

The Blue Fox project was a part of the investigation, one of several past and ongoing IT related projects in the sector. Data specifically collected for this case was mainly collected from the Norwegian Medicines Agency, including interviews with the two project managers and a review of the available documentation. The use of Blue Prescription was demonstrated and commented by a specialist doctor at a hospital (using DIPS), while a GP in a municipal health centre demonstrated and commented the solution in WinMed. We also reviewed the audit reports on blue prescription from NAV (the Norwegian Labour and Welfare Administration).

The analysis was done in the following steps. We started by identifying the more general challenges of IT in the health sector, building on the experiences of some of the large projects, such as EPR systems and E-Prescription, and also the research from other European countries. Then we analysed the Blue Fox a process in detail, focusing on the interplay of stakeholders and the linking of events. In particular, we tried to understand the dynamics between the different stakeholders and levels of the sector, for example the means and ways that central authorities attempted to influence of the behaviours of GPs and pharmacies.

The result of this analysis was some possible patterns of successful implementation, in the context of an information infrastructure without a clear chain of command. We reframed the analysis of these patterns by using Lessig's four primary modes of regulation, allowing for a more general discussion on the implications of the Blue Fox case.

Findings were discussed with various informants. The paper was also sent to key stakeholders in NoMa for comments and corrections.

4 The Blue Fox Case

The Blue Fox project was run from 2005 to 2008 by the Norwegian Medicines Agency (NoMA), which is the national, regulatory authority for new and existing medicines and the supply chain. The agency is responsible for supervising the production, trials and marketing of medicines, and is a central actor in the Norwegian health sector.

The background was a government report [33] raising concerns that the subsidized medicine routine ("blue prescriptions") was out of control. The costs of blue prescriptions were high (10 bns NOK per year) and rising. The report documented that the regulation was too complicated, resulting in different practices from doctors and concerns on accountability of refunds. In 2005 the Ministry of Health asked NoMA to suggest a new set of regulations, and a plan for implementation. NoMA consented to this, but also argued that a successful change of doctors' (and pharmacies) prescription practices demanded not only new regulations but also support of a new IT solution.

IT Governance through Regulatory Modalities 55

NoMA organized the Blue Fox project in the autumn of 2005. The time line of the project is described below.

Oct 2005-July 2006   : Legal regulation is drafted
Aug 2006- June 2007   : Ministry sends the draft regulation on a public hearing
June 28th 2007   : Regulation is approved
Jan 2007-Dec 2008   : Awareness campaign
June 2007 – March 08: Development of ICT solution
March 3rd 2008   : Regulation is implemented
March – Sept 08   : Transition period
Oct 2008 →   : Regular operations

Legal regulation is drafted (Oct 005-July 2006)
The top management group of NoMA was the steering group, and the Ministry of Health and the Norwegian Labour and Welfare Administration (NAV) constituted the Project Board. A number of actors were invited to participate in an Advisory Board; The Norwegian Medical Association, Norwegian Association of Physiotherapists, Norwegian Association for Critical Care Nurses, The Association of the Pharmaceutical Industry in Norway, Norwegian Pharmacy Association, Association of Disabled, the five Regional Health Authorities, Norwegian Directorate of Health, The Norwegian Institute of Public Health, Norwegian Knowledge Centre for the Health Services and NAF Data. The vendors of Electronic Patient Record systems and the National E-Prescription project were also involved in the process.

The project group consisted of six employees of NoMA: An economist as the project manager, and one lawyer, one GP and three pharmacists. There were no IT people in the project, but a consultant was hired to develop a prototype of the solution.

The aims of the new regulation were:

- To clarify and ensure the compliance with regulations
- To ensure a cost effective practice
- To provide software support to the GPs for prescription practice

The project group started to work late autumn 2005. The core task was to specify a prescription solution through the use of codes. The key elements were:

- The ICD and ICPC international codes of diseases. The IDC code specifies a disease in three digits, for example J45 *Asthma*. (In ICPC it is *R96 Asthma*). The Norwegian version of these codes are maintained by KITH.
- The register of active medical substances, and the corresponding brand pharmaceuticals. For Asthma this is for example the substance *Salbutamol*. These codes (both the substances and the brand medicines) are maintained by NoMA.
- A condition for the refund of expenses ("blue prescription"). For asthma this is *condition 92*: "The asthma diagnosis must be verified by spirometri by children over 8 years and adults." These condition codes are maintained by NoMA.

Thus, the basic mechanism of the solution is that combining these three elements will determine the prescription and refund of a medicine, with a high degree of medical accuracy, transparency and accountability.

These principles were described in a report with a draft regulation, and submitted to the Ministry of Health in July 2006 [32]. The report also discussed the implementation, focusing on a number of elements; the dependencies of other public and private actors, the technical solutions, the relationship to vendors, information activities among doctors and pharmacists.

Regulation draft on public hearing (Aug 2006- June 2007)
The draft was sent on a public hearing at various agencies and stakeholders. Some stakeholders were critical. For example, the association of doctors was concerned, for privacy reasons, that the Refund Code would be visible for pharmacy personnel. After some minor adjustments is was approved in June 2007.

Awareness campaign (2007)
The project group conducted an extensive awareness campaign during 2007, aimed at all involved stakeholders. In addition to the aim of implementing the regulation, the campaign also sought to influence the culture of medical personnel, to ensure commitment to the reform. The Blue Fox project executed a number of country-wide activities, in order to inform and promote the regulation. The materials argued that the Blue Fox would ensure uniform and accountable prescription, and also enable the doctors to explain to the patients why (or why not) a blue prescription was granted.

Development of ICT solution (June 2007 – March 08)
The Blue Fox project decided that the ICT solution that should support and help implement the new prescription practices should be designed as a tool both doctors, pharmacies and patients. The solution should provide information about drugs and the regulation. It should primarily be designed as a decision support tool for doctors. The solution consisted of two main (logical) parts: the FEST register containing information about the regulations and drugs, and a module used by doctors when prescribing and pharmacists when handing out drugs. The FEST register would be provided and maintained by NoMA. The register was primarily developed as a part of another large health IT initiative, i.e. the E-Prescription project. The Refund List (substances and conditions) were however not dependent on the E-Prescription project, and could be downloaded by anyone in XML format (or bought as a booklet).

The Blue Fox project decided that they would develop one single common module for all users. This module would then be integrated with the systems used by the users. In the case of general practitioners and hospitals this meant their Electrondic Patient Record systems and in the case of pharmacists the systems used in the pharmacies. In total this included six different systems.

The basic functionality had been prototyped by a consultant in 2006, and discussed with various EPR vendors during the project. The solution was implemented by all the EPR vendors, both in the GP and the specialist segments. In most cases the solution was pretty simple; the whole Refund Register is downloaded to the system (web service 1). It is maintained by a (web service 2) call for regular updates.

The implementation was done as a relatively minor extension of the EPR. For example, in the hospital system DIPS, the medicine catalogue was presented as a web page with a link to the Refund Code. Clicking this link would present the user with the medicines and the conditions for Blue Prescription. The EPR systems present the user with a GUI for diagnosis and prescription, based on ICD/ICPC codes or medical substance. The system will then return the associated pharmaceutical brands, and the conditions for blue prescription. The printout prescription will include the ICD/ICPC code.

For pharmacies, the refund code (the ICPC or ICD code) is registered by the pharmacy at the point of sale. The PharmPro system was extended to receive the code. This transaction also serves at documentation for the refund from NAV to the pharmacy. In addition, in order to survey the use of medicines in the population, the Norwegian Prescription Database (administered by The Norwegian Institute of Public Health) receives a copy of the transaction.

A web based service was established in order to allow all patients access to the same information. The service is illustrated in figure 1 below. The example is the substance Salbutamol, which is used for R96 Asthma, with the condition 92. One brand pharmaceutical with this substance is Ventoline from GlaxoSmithKline.

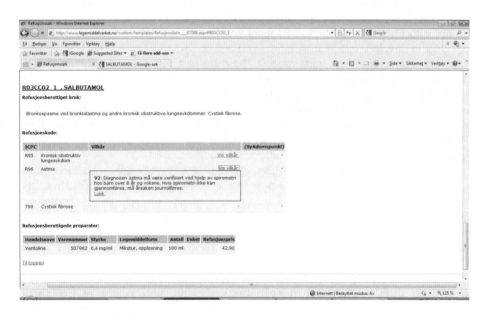

Fig. 1. The public web page of Blue Prescription (NoMA)

Implementation (March 3rd 2008)

The new regulation was legally valid from March 3rd 2008. Prior to this date, the Blue Fox team had conducted a full professional marketing campaign, including the use of a market intelligence bureau. The activities included e-mails to all doctors and pharmacies, a web portal, an e-learning application for health personnel and a number of presentations and journal articles.

There was some negative press, and some of the stakeholders were critical. For example, the association of doctors was concerned that the preparations were insufficient. Some doctors were also critical that the regulation removed their options for individual judgements of granting blue prescriptions.

However, after six months, almost 90% of the blue prescriptions were issued according to the new regulation. This included all the doctors of Norway, and all pharmacies. For the project costs of a modest 5 mill NOK per year, this was a rather outstanding result.

5 Discussion

In this section we discuss the results of Blue Fox, and then frame our interpretation of the case in terms of how it was governed by means of a regulatory approach composed of Lessig's four modalities [24,25].

5.1 The Results of Blue Fox

The lessons of the Blue Fox may be summarized this way. First, it was an undramatic project, with an atmosphere of small scale and low tech. It was run by a small project group, with little IT competence. Its main vehicle was a regulation, which they spent one year to develop, one year to approve (!) and one year to implement. The software which was developed was quite modest, the main part being a register of medicines and the associated conditions for blue prescription. The solution in relation to the EPR vendors was a simple batch routine. In principle, it would have been possible to use the Blue Fox functionally without integrating it into the EPR at all. Also, for the pharmacies the solution was pretty simple, based only on manual entering of the Refund Code on the prescription. The solution was simple to develop, simple to integrate with the users' other applications and simple to use!

Second, it was a successful project, by almost any measure, with large scale effects. It involved almost all the actors in the Norwegian health system, from the Ministry of Health to the doctors in the remotest villages on the coast of the Barents Sea. It involved the selection, purchase, distribution and refund of medicines at a yearly total of 8 billion NOK. It gave both prescription support to the doctors, and the necessary accounting data to the Norwegian Labour and Welfare Administration (NAV).

Summing-up, the project extended a complex national infrastructure, with small means and little conflict. The project was successful, not because of one single success factor, but because of a deliberate combination of measures. To discuss these measures, we draw on Lessig's theory of regulation.

5.2 Four Modalities of Regulation

As briefly reviewed in section 2, Lessig's [25] four modalities for regulating behaviour are; *law, norms, markets and architecture*. Architecture refers to the designed physical environment, in particular to the software of the internet.

The four modalities have in particular been used to understand behaviour in "cyberspace", and the strongest regulator will be architecture. In the context of ICT, we relate to the hardware and software of cyberspace, which to a great extent enable and constrain our behaviour. In Lessig's poignant language; "code is law". The four modalities often also work together, reinforcing each other. For example, the technical architecture will influence which norms are acceptable and which economic mechanisms are possible.

Reframing the Blue Fox case with this framework, we illustrate our argument in table 1 below.

Table 1. Four governance mechanisms in the Blue Fox project

Modality	Mechanism	Outcome	Overall outcome
Law	Blue Fox Regulation	All actors prepare in order to comply with the regulation	Extending the national health infrastructure
Code	Refund register	Extending EPR systems	
Norm	Equal and just prescription	Most actors agree on the need for better practice	
Incentive	Prescription support	Doctors use the solution during patient consultation	

Law: Blue Fox Regulation

The project was initiated and driven by the need for a new regulation of the practice of blue prescriptions. The work in the project group was very much focused on the political and economic call for the regulation, and the need for uniform and accountable prescription practice.

The result of the (slow) legislative process was that the regulation became a strong foundation for the project. Another result was that all actors in the sector starting preparing for the change.

Code: Refund Register and Decision Support System

The core of the regulation was implemented in the client and server modules of the Refund register, as described in section 4. The register, together with the disease codes, was relatively easily integrated in EPR systems, and was in use from March 3rd 2008. It was also taken into use by the pharmacies, requiring only minor changes in their systems. The effects of this was certainly to amplify the force of the regulation; it made it quite visible at the point of medical decision (i.e. prescription of medicine), and it also made the decision transparent for the patient.

We would also like to highlight a more subtle aspect of the software and the impact this had on the overall governance of the project. The architecture of the solution differs from the large majority of project aiming at developing infrastructural solutions for health care. Typical examples are projects aiming at developing solutions for exchange of information like lab orders and reports, submission and discharge letter, prescriptions, etc. The solutions include modules for a number of different users like general practitioners, hospital doctors, pharmacists, lab personnel, etc. Further, the solutions need to be integrated with applications already used by the different user groups. And the standard project model and system architecture is based on an approach where the new functions are implemented as extensions of existing systems (like the medical doctors EPR systems) and the development work is then supposed to be taken care of by the vendors of these systems. This implies that different actors need to be involved in the projects and each of them need to do a substantial amount of work, the actors need to reach agreement on the systems' design and the interfaces, and their work need to be coordinated. This leads to rather complex technological solutions, but more important, complex project organizations with a high number of independent actors with competing and conflicting interests. In total this means a complexity beyond what can be managed or governed. The Blue Fox project decided to develop the whole solution as far as possible within the core project team at NoMA, putting the interfaces between the modules developed by the vendors of the users' ordinary applications at a different place compared to other projects. This reduced dramatically the amount of work need to be carried out by the vendors and accordingly the complexity of the project was dramatically reduced, and its governability and chances of success equally increased.

Norm: Equal and Just Prescription

The Blue Fox regulation emphasized, in addition to the need for accountability, the need for a uniform and fair prescription practice. The same applies to the awareness campaign that the Blue Fox project ran during 2006-2008, emphasizing that the regulation benefited all stakeholder groups.

The outcome of these messages and activities is difficult to assess precisely. However, it is hard to argue, at the level of principle, against a "uniform and fair prescription practice". Thus, the fact that some doctors did not agree to a more controlled (with less room for the GPs discretion) practice, was not picked up by the doctors' association.

Incentive: Prescription Support

A challenge in many IT initiatives is the incentive for the end user. Often, the end user is simply told to use the system, regardless of his or her perception of the usefulness of the solution in relation to the work routine. In the Blue Fox case an important objective was to support the doctor (and patient) in the prescription process. This was implemented in the EPR systems, and also made transparent through the public web access, as shown in figure 1.

At the last stage of the prescription chain, the pharmacies, the printed Refund code on the prescription (in contrast to the often unintelligible scribbling of the doctor) obviously saved time and prevented errors. Thus, the pharmacists were generally quite positive to the Blue Fox.

Mutual Influence

The four mechanisms contributed to the outcome of the project, as illustrated in table 1. In addition, they interfere and influence each other. They may reinforce as well as weaken each other's impact. The most prominent mechanisms were the regulation and the code. The regulation, of course, shaped the basic logic of the code, but also the norms and incentives. And the code (i.e. the Refund register and the associated web services) influenced on the incentives (the prescription support), by supporting the prescription process.

We would also argue that the code, at the stage of being only a possibility, influenced on the regulation. Drafting the regulation, the Blue Fox group identified the potential role of the code as an amplifier; it would make the regulation *formative* at the prescription moment and *visible* through the prescription chain.

5.3 The Regulatory Approach: Implications

One might object to this story that the Blue Fox was a small and relatively trivial project, and therefore not very relevant in an IT governance context. We think that this misses the point. We argue that the success of the Blue Fox can be explained by two main reasons:

- The regulatory approach allowed for a small and simple project
- The regulatory approach combined a set of indirect but effective measures

It is easy to forget that there are *two options* at the start of most current IS initiatives; namely the choice between a software engineering project (based on a comprehensive requirements specification) *or* improving on the current solution with simpler (and not integrated) extensions. Often, the first option is chosen, because it is the preferred solution by IT professionals: a new, fully integrated and tidy system based on new technology is expected to solve many problems.

The initiators of the Blue Fox project could have chosen this option, but they did not. One reason was probably that there were no IS people among them, another was that the regulatory approach had been used successfully by the project manager in a previous project. The difference between the two approaches is illustrated in table 2.

Table 2. IT governance approaches

	Traditional IT governance	**Regulatory approach**
Context	Single organisation	Information infrastructure
Control	Strategic planning, project management	Law, norm, incentives and architecture
Solutions	Integrated solutions, focusing on requirements	Extension of existing structures, focusing on installed base

Good governance of infrastructures is a combination of central and local action, allowing for decentralized initiatives and local appropriation. The focus of the Blue Fox project was on user behaviour in the existing infrastructure of systems, networks and practices. The pressure for change was indirect; a regulation grants you a space of action, as long as you do not break it. In the same sense, code will constrain your actions, but the technical solution of Blue Fox was rather flexible. Norms are constraining, but are also plastic in the sense that they will be discussed and maybe modified. And incentives are certainly constraining, but users will make their choices according to their overall interests. The mild, but deliberate combination of these measures ensured the success of the Blue Fox.

Summing-up our point: the regulatory governance principles constitute an alternative approach to ICT governance in information infrastructures. The approach represents a broader portfolio of measures compared to traditional top-down directives, in the sense that it combines four very different but mutually reinforcing measures. The Blue Fox case illustrates neatly how they influence on each other. Used carefully, the approach may lead to simpler and less risky projects. It might also, we admit, over time contribute to a more heterogeneous (and less integrated) environment.

Finally, we should acknowledge that this overall picture does not imply that this framework solves all problems related to IT development and implementation. Rather, they highlight that successful IT projects is demanding and difficult, requiring a broad set of measures. It also implies that extending information infrastructures through the regulatory framework may be take longer time than a tightly controlled project. In our opinion this is justified by a larger probability of success.

6 Concluding Remarks

The purpose of this study was to discuss a framework for governance of information infrastructures. Our approach was to understand the mechanisms and structures supporting the successful governance of the development, implementation and use of large scale distributed ICT solutions in general, and information infrastructures in health care in particular. Our key premise was that health information systems are infrastructures that resist being designed top-down by management directives and implemented by large-scale projects.

Building on Lessig's four modalities of regulation, and a case study in Norway, we suggest an alternative set of governance principles for information infrastructures. Our conclusion is: in certain contexts it is possible to extend national information infrastructures by a regulatory approach, a deliberate combination of legal, technical, social and economic measures, which reinforce each other. We also argue that this approach may lead to simpler projects and a more effective implementation.

References

1. Aanestad, M., Hanseth, O.: Growing Networks: Detours, Stunts and Spillovers. In: Fifth International Conference on the Design of Cooperative Systems. St. Raphael, France (2002)
2. Black, J.: Proceduralising Regulation: Part I. Oxford Journal of Legal Studies 20(4), 597–614 (2000)
3. Black, J.: Proceduralising Regulation: Part Ii. Oxford Journal of Legal Studies 21(1), 33–58 (2001)
4. Bowker, G.C., Star, S.L.: Sorting things out. Classification and its consequences. MIT Press, Cambridge (1999)
5. Braa, J., Hanseth, O., Mohammed, W., Heywood, A., Shaw, V.: Developing Health Information Systems in Developing Countries. The Flexible Standards Strategy. MIS Quarterly 31(2), 381–402 (2007)

6. Brown, C.V.: Examining the Emergence of Hybrid IS Governance Solutions: Evidence from a Single Case Site. Information Systems Research 8(1), 69–94 (1997)
7. Bygstad, B.: Information Infrastructure as Organization. A Critical Realist View. In: International Conference of Information Systems (ICIS), Paris, AIS (2008)
8. Ciborra, C., Braa, K., Cordella, A., Dahlbom, B., Failla, A., Hanseth, O., Hepsø, V., Ljungberg, J., Monteiro, E., Simon, K.: From Control to Drift. The Dynamics of Corporate Information Infrastructures. Oxford University Press, Oxford (2000)
9. Contini, F., Lanzara, F.G.: ICT and Innovation in the Public Sector – European Studies in the Making of e-government. Palgrave Macmillan, Basingstoke (2009)
10. Dutton, W.H., Palfrey, J.G., Peltu, M.: Deciphering the Codes of Internet Governance: Understanding the Hard Issues at Stake. OII Forum Discussion Paper No. 8. SSRN (2007), http://ssrn.com/abstract=1325234
11. Edwards, P.N., Jackson, S.J., Bowker, G.C., Knobel, C.P.: Understanding Infrastructure: Dynamics, Tensions, and Design. In: Report of a Workshop on History & Theory of Infrastructure: Lessons for New Scientific Cyberinfrastructures, pp. 1–50 (2007)
12. Egyedi, T.M.: Standards Enhance System Flexibility? Mapping Compatibility Strategies Onto Flexibility Objectives. In: EASST 2002 Conference. University of York, UK (2002)
13. Ellingsen, G., Monteiro, E.: The organizing vision of integrated health information systems. Health Informatics Journal 14(3), 223–236 (2008)
14. Hanseth, O.: The Economics of Standards. In: Ciborra, et al. (eds.) pp. 56–70 (2000)
15. Hanseth, O.: Gateways - just as important as standards. How the Internet won the "religious war" about standards in Scandinavia. Knowledge, Technology and Policy 14(3), 71–89 (2001)
16. Hanseth, O.: Complexity and Risk. In: Hanseth, O., Ciborra, C. (eds.) Risk, Complexity and ICT, pp. 75–93. Edward Elgar, Cheltenham (2007)
17. Hanseth, O., Monteiro, E.: Inscribing Behaviour in Information Infrastructure Standards. Accounting, Management and Information Systems 7(4), 183–211 (1997)
18. Hanseth, O., Monteiro, E., Hatling, M.: Developing information infrastructure: The tension between standardization and flexibility. Science, Technology and Human Values 21(4), 407–426 (1996)
19. Hanseth, O., Aanestad, M.: Design as Bootstrapping. On the Evolution of ICT Networks in Health care. Methods of Information in Medicine 42, 385–391 (2003)
20. Hanseth, O., Lyytinen, K.: Design Theory for Dynamic Complexity in Information Infrastructures: The Case of building Internet. Journal of Information Technology (2010)
21. Hitt, M.A., Beamish, P.W., Jackson, S.E., Mathieu, J.E.: Building Theoretical and Empirical Bridges Across Levels: Multilevel Research in Management. Academy of Management Journal 50(6), 1385–1399 (2007)
22. ISO: ISO/IEC 38500:2008 Corporate governance of information technology (2008)
23. Kallinikos, J.: The Consequences of Information. Edward Elgar Publishing, Cheltenham (2006)
24. Lessig, L.: Code and Other Laws of Cyberspace. Basic Books, New York (1999)
25. Lessig, L.: The Law of the Horse: What Cyberlaw Might Teach. Harvard Law Review 113, 501–546 (2001)
26. Lyytinen, K., Fomin, V.: Achieving high momentum in the evolution of wireless infrastructures: the battle over the 1G solutions. Telecommunications Policy 26(3-4), 149–170 (2002)
27. Rasmussen, T.: Techno-Politics, Internet Governance and Some Challenges Facing the Internet. OII Working Paper No. 15. SSRN (2007), http://ssrn.com/abstract=1326428

28. Sambamurthy, V., Zmud, R.W.: Arrangements for Information Technology Governance: A Theory of Multiple contingencies. MIS Quarterly 23(2), 261–290 (1999)
29. Sauer, C., Willcocks, L.P.: Unreasonable expectations – NHS IT, Greek choruses and the games institutions play around mega-programmes. Journal of Information Technology 22, 195–201 (2007)
30. Shapiro, C., Varian, H.R.: Information Rules: A Strategic Guide to the Network Economy. Harvard Business School Press, Boston (1999)
31. Star, S.L., Ruhleder, K.: Steps Toward an Ecology of Infrastructure: Design and Access for Large Information Spaces. Information Systems Research 7(1), 111–134 (1996)
32. Statens_Legemiddelverk: Revisjon av blåreseptordningen. Forslag til ny blåreseptforskrift og endringer i legemiddelforskriften m.v., Høringsnotat (2006)
33. Statskonsult: Informasjon og kontroll i blåreseptordningen. Oslo, Statskonsult (2004)
34. Sun, V., Aanestad, M., Skorve, E., Miscione, G.: Information infrastructure governance and windows of opportunity. In: Proceedings of the European Conference on Information Systems, Verona, Italy (2009)
35. Weill, P., Ross, J.W.: IT Governance. Harvard Business School Press, Boston (2004)

Boundaries between Participants in Outsourced Requirements Construction

Sari T. Salmela and Anna-Liisa Syrjänen

Department of Information Processing Science, University of Oulu, P.O. Box 3000,
FIN-90014 Oulun Yliopisto, Finland
{sari.t.salmela,anna-liisa.syrjanen}@oulu.fi

Abstract. The concept of the boundary is a powerful analytic tool for analyzing the challenges in collaboration between participants in outsourced requirements construction. Through an ethnographic study in a requirements construction project, where participants came from the client and vendor organizations, and represented varying expertises and organizational positions, we found professional boundaries between users and external software developers, and between external software experts and in-house information system (IS) experts. The authority boundary between the client's manager and operatives was evident. Findings were discussed within the knowledge areas that are needed in the professional IS development. In order to help IS experts, participatory design (PD) practitioners and IS researchers in their attempts to develop the user-designer and client-vendor relationships, PD for outsourced IS development should be developed and further researched.

Keywords: Boundary, IS profession, requirements construction, outsourced information systems development, user participation, client-vendor relationship, user-designer relationship, ethnographic field study.

1 Introduction

Information system development (ISD) is a collective labour process involving multiple participants with varying backgrounds, experiences, authority levels, and sources of expertise and knowledge [1], [2], and having varying motivations to participate in. Therefore, heterogeneity with boundaries is an intricate part of the ISD practice [3]. There is a long tradition of research on user participation and collaboration between the users and designers of information systems (IS) in the context of in-house development. The need for bridging the gap between users and designers has been recognized [4] [5], [6], [7], [8]. However, user participation in outsourced ISD comprises clear challenges and needs to be revisited [9].

Today less and less information and software systems are developed in-house. In addition to application package-based IS development, outsourced IS development has become common [10], [11], [9], [12], [13]. Outsourced or subcontracted ISD brings along a client-vendor boundary [13], involving a third side, the vendor or supplier, whose application domain and especially organizational work domain knowledge [14] is often thin. All this makes user-developer collaboration and knowledge sharing between participants even more complicated than in the context of in-house ISD. Even though global distributed work [15] and distributed participative design [16] have also become common, this paper focuses on outsourced ISD, in particular on requirements construction. Comparing the nature of boundaries in distributed and outsourced ISD contexts would be one interesting research topic in the future.

In the requirement construction phase of outsourced ISD, the client and the vendor attempt to achieve a mutual agreement about the requirements that would serve as the basis for the development of a new system. Requirements construction is also called 'requirements determination', 'requirements elicitation', 'requirements engineering', 'requirements gathering', and 'requirements specification'. The term 'requirements construction' emphasizes that requirements are socially constructed [14], influencing the co-construction of technologies and users [17] in practice, too.

This paper makes two contributions. At first it analyses boundaries between participants - different IT experts (IS experts from a vendor and software (SW) experts a client), and intended users representing different occupations and organizational positions - through an ethnographic study in an outsourced requirements construction project. Secondly, it makes visible the value of the concept of the boundary borrowed from the social sciences as analysing obstacles in knowledge sharing between participants, and barriers in user participation, both in the IS research and in practice.

The paper is organized as follows. The next section discusses studies of boundaries both in social sciences and in Information Systems (ISs). The third section describes an ethnographic field research setting and reports on empirical analysis of the project. The fourth section discusses results leading to the findings and outlines directions for future research. The final section summarizes the results.

2 Studies of Boundaries

Instead of doing a new literature review in the studies of boundaries in social sciences we mostly rely on Lamont and Molnar's [18] and Pachucki's et al [19] recent reviews. According to Lamont and Molnar the concept of boundary has been at the center of research in anthropology, history, political science, social psychology, and sociology [18]. They survey literatures in areas like social and collective identity; class, ethnic-racial, and gender inequality; professions, knowledge, and science; and communities, national identities, and spatial boundaries [18]. In social sciences, 'boundaries are part of the classical tool-kit of social scientists' [18] (p. 167).

Boundaries are situational and influenced by the cultural background and available resources and they emerge in the context of action by the particular set of people as selected co-operators [20] (p. 11). She distinguishes moral, socioeconomic and cultural boundaries. The cultural boundary is drawn on the basis education, for example, and therefore we see it as very interesting for the analysis aspects of this paper. Symbolic boundaries are conceptual distinctions made by social actors to categorize objects, people, practices, and even time and space, and they separate people into groups, and they are an essential medium through which people acquire status and monopolize resources [18] (p. 168). Social boundaries in turn are related to social differences, which appear in 'unequal access to and the unequal distribution of resources (material and non-material) and social opportunities' [18] (p. 168).

Boundaries are in most cases treated as markers of difference, however they can be conceptualized also as interfaces facilitating collaboration [18] (p. 180). Lamont and Molnar note that some research, boundary objects [21] as an example, focus not only on the exclusive aspects of boundaries, but also on their role in connecting social groups and making coordination possible [18] (p. 177, 187). In Information Systems, the application of the concept of the boundary object [21], [22] has been more common than the focus on boundaries as such [2], [23], [24].

Lamont and Molnar introduce the studies of professional boundaries in social sciences. In Information Systems Levina and Vaast [23] focus on spanning the boundaries of diverse professional and organizational settings, and boundary spanning competence in practice. They rely on the concepts of the boundary spanner, boundary object, and Bourdieu's theory of practice (referring to Bourdieu and Wacquant [25]). Even though they do not explicitly focus on the boundaries as such, they introduce the practice-based perspective on knowledge management in organizations, which, they claim, allows us to understand the nature of boundaries in practice [23], (p. 337).

Levina and Vaast prefer the concept of field rather than the concept of community of practice. They introduce the emergence of fields as a phenomenon, where agents develop continuity in their local practices allowing them to act knowledgeably in a given material, historical, and social context. By engaging in fields, agents pursue a joint interest (an inclination and ability to succeed in a given endeavor), and produce different kinds of resources (capital), which they can accumulate and use as the bases of power. Referring to Bourdieu [25] Levina and Vaast distinguish four key species of capital: economic capital (money, time, technology); cultural capital (professional expertise, education, the ownership of information); social capital (which social networks an agent can rely on); and symbolic capital (the ability to name any other resource as valuable, the power to name and classify things) [23], (p. 337). However, agents are also distinguished from others, and differentiate themselves from outsiders who do not do the same [23].

In this paper we approach boundaries as markers of differences and means of division, while Star and colleagues, and followers approach boundaries as a means of communication [18]. This does not mean that we are not interested in communication across boundaries. On the contrary, the first author and her colleague currently investigate boundary spanning (labeled as use-design mediation) across the divergent words of users and designers in two ISD contexts.

The concept of boundaries is useful for understanding 'how professions come to be distinguished from one another - experts from laymen, science from non-science, and disciplines between themselves' [18] (p. 177). We apply the notion professional boundary for making visible how IS and SW professions come to be distinguished from one another, and furthermore varying IT experts from professional office workers, for instance, in our case.

Whereas in the Scandinavian trade unionist and participatory design (PD) traditions [26], [27], [28], [29] knowledge sharing and mutual learning between participants is aspired, recent research on outsourcing [12], [13], which touches upon boundaries in a client-vendor relationship, views such knowledge overlaps expensive and unproductive. Related to clients' knowledge, Tiwana [13], for example, views the business process knowledge rather than work practices of intended users, which in turn are at the core of PD. Iivari and colleagues [14] view the business process knowledge and the knowledge on work practices as parts of organizational knowledge domain of professional IS developers. Yet, PD has proven to be difficult in practice [30], [31], and there is only a little evidence of how PD and ethnographic approach for bridging the gap between users and designers [5], [6], [7], [8] are applied in outsourced ISD practice and without academic intervention. Indeed, in an outsourced ISD project to be introduced in the next section, SW developers did apply neither PD nor ethnography. Dibbern's and colleagues' [12] and Tiwana's [13] research on outsourcing gives one possible explanation to it. This and other issues relating to boundaries in the project will be further discussed in the next and fourth section.

In spite of the recognition of the client-vendor boundary, Tiwana [13] does not focus on other boundaries, for example boundaries between different IT experts. Glass and colleagues [32] claim that in time when three of the major computing fields, Computer Science (CS), Information Systems (ISs), and Software Engineering (SE) began to formalize its curriculum, the differences were significant, and the overlaps were minimal, implying that three fields were doing a good job of distinguishing their content [32]. This form of professional boundary has been brought out more recently in [14] by comparing the body of knowledge of the fields of SE and ISs. IS application knowledge and ISD process knowledge is viewed as distinctive contrasted to related disciplines such as CS, SE, and Organizational Science [14].

The aim of this paper is not to go into details of the both professions and their distinctions [14], [32]. However, this distinctive nature of the fields has ramifications in practice too. Iivari and colleagues [14] identifies five knowledge areas as parts of an IS expert's body of knowledge (ISBoK): technical, application domain, organizational IS application, and ISD process knowledge. Tiwana [13] views application-problem-domain expertise and technical expertise as a knowledge base of the SW vendor. It is claimed that SE expertise is not enough in professional ISD [14]. Because the project to be studied concerns ISD in the client, we apply the concept of ISBoK for the analysis of the encountering of expertises in practice. We analyse how does participants' knowledge relate to the ISBoK.

3 An Ethnographic Field Study in the Collaborative Project

The ethnographic field study to be introduced below focuses on the requirements construction phase of an IS development project and provides rich insights into the boundary shaping, knowledge sharing and collaboration in practice. The project participants came from the client and the vendor organizations and represented different occupations and organizational positions. The six-month project was part of a two-year outsourced IS development project including specification, design, implementation, and varying testing phases. From the point of view the SW vendor it succeeded well. In this research it will not been investigated if it was economically reasonable to outsource ISD (cf. [12]), or how usable the client stakeholders viewed the new system after implementation.

As a part of her ethnographic involvement one author of this paper worked as a SW developer on the vendor side, participating in the collaborative requirements construction sessions conducted on the client's premises. Research data contain twelve full-day video-recorded collaborative requirements construction sessions, field notes [33], from participant observation [34], interviews and informal discussions, and numerous documentary sources. Interaction analysis [35] was used, and in video analysis with colleagues experienced in ethnographic 'working on the fringes' [36].

The client is a local funding department in a national-level operating charity organization. Every year over one thousand health and social welfare organizations receive funding through it so that applications are reviewed, prepared and proposals submitted to the Government, which makes the final decision. The department includes two offices. To develop its work process with information management, the old computer system became the target for development. One aim was to digitalize paper work in the offices. There had been two preceding development projects, which had yielded two subsystems for the preparing office. The third subsystem was developed for the supervision office that pays the granted funding, monitors, supervises and evaluates how it is used. An external software vendor developed the SW application; a qualified SW company located five hundred kilometres away from the client.

In the supervision office consisted of an office manager and ten employees. They were intended users, even though computer users do not consider themselves 'users' [37] (p. 112). Participants representing them were a secretary, a senior inspector, two inspectors and the office manager. In addition three of four IS developers from the client organization were involved in the project. They were experts with the current information system and involved in the development of communication between the client and its interest groups. They were: the system manager (familiar also with work analysis), the UI expert (familiar with user interfaces (UI), labeled 'UI expert' here), the HW expert (familiar with hardware (HW) issues, labeled 'HW expert'). Even though the office manager, the system manager and the HW expert were not nominated as participants, they participated in many requirements construction sessions (project documents, field notes, video recordings).

Three SW developers from the vendor worked in the project. Two fieldwork partners, ethnographers, participated in the project as SW developers and participant observers.

Participants' responsibilities and tasks were defined in the project plan. The senior inspector from the client was nominated to serve as a project manager. He was responsible for administrative tasks, overall coordination, inviting relevant participants and organizing collaborative sessions. In addition, 'producing the use environment description and evaluation of requirements specifications' (project plan) were his duties. The SW vendor, in turn, was 'responsible for conducting and steering specification sessions, documenting the outcomes of sessions and conducting tests of the specifications' (project plan). Unified Modelling Language (UML), Rational Rose, Flow Charter and Visual Basic were designated as description and documentation tools. Descriptions of the current system and some other documents of the previous projects were also mentioned in the project plan as sources of information for the project. (project documents)

However, the participants could not always follow the project plan, and actual management of the project was not clear to some participants. After five months the HW expert mentioned to the fieldworkers that he assumes that the vendor's senior SW developer is the project manager. The fieldworkers assumed in turn that the system manager might be a coordinator because on after couple of weeks from the beginning she explicitly listed the required outcomes and tasks of the project to the wall of the meeting room (field notes, video recordings).

However requirements were produced as a kind of co-operation but as these included very contradictory and diverse user needs, several iterations were needed to ascertain and formally specify them. In addition, the IT experts from two organizations had conflicting views of how to envision the context of use. The system manager intervened the project, did work on process modelling and took care of also some other responsibilities originally appointed to the SW developers on the vendor side.

4 Boundaries in the Outsourced Requirements Construction Project

Through an ethnographic data analysis two forms of professional boundaries were identified. Firstly, a clear professional boundary existed between external SW developers and client's office workers. Secondly, a professional boundary existed between in-house and external IT experts, reflecting practices of in-house ISD and software development. Thirdly, in addition to the two professional boundaries, an authority boundary between the client's managers and operatives was encountered.

4.1 Professional Boundary between Office Workers and SW Developers

There existed expertise differences between external SW developers and client's office workers, who were not IT experts. However, the latter were experts in their own occupations having the best organizational and application domain knowledge [14]. Application domain knowledge refers to knowledge about the application domain for which an information system is built. Organizational knowledge is knowledge about the social and economic processes in the organizational contexts, in which the IS is to be developed and used. An important part of organizational knowledge is the work processes in the organizational context to be supported by the IS [14]. In the beginning of the project it was implicitly expected that the users as participants bring along user requirements for new system. However, knowledge sharing between the client's office workers (users) and IT experts, in particular with the external SW developers, was not seamless. The gap between them was clearly evident. For instance, the secretary could not follow the discussion on requirements led by the SW developer and conducted with help of the old systems' documentation.

The gap was not as evident between the users and the in-house IS developers, since the latter ones worked in the same department (and in the same building) with the intended users and knew them and their work at some level. As a consequence the in-house IS developers had application domain and organizational knowledge to some extent. This made it possible for them to act as *mediators* between the users and the external SW developers (see earlier analyses in [38], [39]. We also found that the SW developers could gain organizational and application domain knowledge during the project, however that was not possible without these mediators.

The SW developers were not willing to get closer to the organizational work domain supported by the new system, i.e., the work of intended users. They viewed collaborative requirements construction sessions as places for gathering SW requirements - not for discussing the users' work. They did not mention in public that they do not want to understand users' and their work practices, but they told to the fieldworkers that instead of the communicating with the users they preferred collaboration with the system manager, the HW expert, and the office manager (field notes). They explained that it is presumable that the users do not understand requirements specifications and are not able to tell about systems requirements and decide which of the needed features should be implemented (field notes).

The only situation, when the secretary's actual work was near to be seen by the SW developers was at the beginning of the project, when copies of secretary's work documents, forms etc. were presented and discussed. Later during two requirements construction sessions the secretary herself tried to make her work visible to the participants. She fetched a big stack of her work documents put into office folders and explained in detail her ways of organizing and filing the documents, and how she used particular colours for coding them, etc. She repeatedly invited others to get to know her workspace and see how she did her job. Yet, nobody responded to the invitations. All her efforts were futile and essential aspects of her work remained unclear to the participants. In particular the SW developers could not grasp what knowledge she needed for her tasks, and how tasks related to her co-workers' tasks. These aspects and their relationship to the context of use were discussed again and again during the project (video recordings, field notes).

4.2 Professional Boundary between IS Developers and SW Developers

The vendor was a qualified SW company with an emphasis on software quality and process improvement (public information of the vendor). According to the first author's participant observations in this particular project, her access into the intranet of the vendor, and review on the preceding project documents of the client-vendor relationship, the vendor's approach to the SW development included typical knowledge areas of SW development (see SWEPOK, referred in [14] and [32]).

The senior SW developer's agenda for the first two sessions was to evaluate and discuss use cases derived from the old system's specifications and user interface models. However, the agenda was altered by the system manager, who had recently taken a course on work ergonomics and wanted to take the secretary's work into closer consideration. In her email to the participants she proposed using of a wall chart technique for modelling users' work process and information and work flow analyses to be conducted before returning to the definition of use cases. The SW developers were not able and willing to conduct such analysis or participate in such kind of requirements construction.

As a result, the system manager together with the secretary and the office manager conducted the modelling. Using the wall chart technique the current work process was described and the new work process constructed. The representations were recorded as research material by the fieldworkers, the wall charts in photographs and the work processes in ABC Flow Charter files. In this phase, the ethnographic field study turned into intervention as the principal SW developer had not recorded the work processes accurately. However, later the SW developers used that part of the research material in the subsequent requirements construction. Despite their insufficient knowledge of the users' actual work, with help of this material the SW developers could envision new use cases and user interface models.

The intervention initiated by the system manager was a manifestation of organization level IS modelling, which has been well known a long time in IS, in particular in Scandinavia (cf. change analysis in ISAC and pragmatic design in PIOCO, referred in [41]). See also more recent Contextual Design [42], for example.

On the other hand, though UML and the vendor's own 'Guide for object-oriented analysis' (OOA) were listed in the project plan, they were not applied as an actual ISD method or an ISD approach [43]. OOA was barely applied at a technique level [43] and UML notations were used for some SW specifications but neither became applied in the requirements construction or sharing of viewpoints between users and developers. To some extent they were used in collaboration between the in-house IS developers and the external SW developers. They were used mostly for transferring requirements as SW specifications to SW developers of subsequent phases of the ISD, but application in user-designer collaboration was lacking. In this paper we do not have space for an in-dept study of modelling methods-in-practice in the project, however it would be interesting in the future.

4.3 Authority Boundary

Users were supposed to be equal participants in the outsourced ISD project. The office manager mentioned that he and the system manager are not going to participate in the sessions so that the users and the SW developers could 'freely do envisioning'. However, he mentioned during the first session that the client had decided that it would 'need - in the beginning - an implemented system that fills up minimum requirements'. The explicitly mentioned reason was that the old computer system was expensive to maintain. The client needed the third part of the system quite fast, because the first and the second part of the whole system were already ready. The office manager made it clear during the first session that they are not going to change the current work practices. They assumed that they would get the implemented system earlier in that way. (video recordings and field notes)

At the beginning it was implicitly assumed that the participants self-evidently understand the work of each other. However, as the analysis has already revealed in many situations they could not do that. When the wall chart technique was applied and workflows became explained to others, the system manager tried to advocate the secretary, i.e. represent her in political sense [38], however the office manager advocated himself and the inspectors using managerial power in the situation (video recordings). As mentioned by the office manager in the first session and again in the wall chart session, one of the main purposes of the system to be developed was to provide information in a digital form to the inspectors and the office manager when making decisions on funding payments. It turned out that particularly the secretarial work was rather invisible to other client representatives, who conducted the workflow analysis. The SW developers, who were passive observers, did not understand it either. This became evident during the subsequent session when the secretary's tasks and the context of use were again and again discussed (video recordings and field notes).

The new system being developed had aspects of decision support system (DSS), management information system (MIS) and CSCW (Computer Supported Co-operative Work) system (e.g. the workflow aspects). However, it was not designed to support the secretary's work practice as a whole, but only the managers' decision making work. Ultimately, the secretary, although an operational-level worker, was in practice responsible for taking care of managerial level activities. It involved setting the stage for well-grounded and accurate decisions, providing factual and exact information on and for the interest groups and applicants, and organizing it based on several types of funding activity related needs and complex reason sets stored in paper and electronic documents. Furthermore, she was responsible for the entire calculating work, numerical checking, etc. and took care of paying based on the accepted funding decisions, informing the interest groups among other tasks. Although her tasks were listed in the work process model, they were represented as simplified tasks.

The authority and the professional boundaries intertwine. The boundary between the client's IS developers and the vendor's SW developers prevented sharing understanding of aims and responsibilities. Markus and Mao [9] implicitly assume that an external developer is a change agent. In our case the client's senior inspector was nominated to that position. However, he was not active at all in facilitating collaboration and managing the organizational change. Also the external SW developers were neither willing nor capable to do that. Instead the office manager and the system manager acted as change agents, the both did so in their different ways. The office manager advocated the inspectors' and his own work, and the system manager tried to advocate the secretary's work.

5 Discussion and Concluding Remarks

Based on our exploration on a requirements construction project, outsourced IS development applies knowledge areas from ISs and SE. The methodology difference between fields became visible in the project. Related to the boundary between the ISs and SE, the IS developers could focus on organizational alignment, which Iivari et al [14] argue to be distinctive in IS compared to SE. The SW developers in turn were experts in software development process. Because of the authority boundary, resources were not offered for more intensive analysis of the secretary's actual work practices as part of the organization level IS modelling. As a consequence, neither workplace studies [44] nor cooperative design [45] were done in the project.

Related to the boundary between SW developers and users, the project plan did not include any explicit methods for making users' work visible to design [46], [28]. This relates also to the professional boundaries within divergent computing fields and research communities. At first requirements construction is understood in different ways in various research communities [14]. The boundary between requirements engineering (RE) and workplace studies is known. Jirotka and Wallen [47], for example, have discussed the relationship between workplace studies and requirements engineering (RE) for computer systems, focusing primary on user requirements. They claim that those activities have much in common. An exact definition of the term 'requirements engineering' does not exist [47]. They note that 'various perspectives reveal that requirements engineers must understand a domain well enough to determine requirements for computer systems intended for use in that setting' (p. 242). Still they highlight their differences. The widely accepted view of goals and aims of traditional RE is to introduce the hypothetical and new system 'in terms of functionality of some technological innovation', but 'not to produce a carefully warranted analysis of the existing social organisation' (p. 244). Conventionally systems requirements are categorized based on the systems properties they specify, such as functional (e.g., behaviour of a system) and non-functional (e.g., constraints and responses to particular user needs) capabilities [48], [49]. 'Work place studies produce description of the rich interrelationships between work, technology and naturally occurring activities and epitomize the ISD approach of 'making work visible'' [47], (p. 245). In the project described above SW specification methods were applied in the too early phase, which prevented SW developers to gain application domain and organizational knowledge [14] effectively.

Secondly, again related to the boundaries within computing fields and research communities, the Scandinavian trade unionist and participatory design (PD) traditions have put forward the importance of active worker/user participation in systems development, and provided tools for understanding and envisioning the context of use [26], [27], [28], [29], [45]. Ethnographically informed analysis and design [5], [6], [7], [8] is viewed as a tool for systems developers for bridging users' work practice and systems design. Like we noted before, while knowledge sharing and mutual learning between participants is aspired in the PD tradition, recent research on outsourcing [12], [13] views knowledge overlaps in the client-vendor relationship expensive and unproductive. Related to clients' knowledge, Tiwana [13], for example, focuses on the business process knowledge rather than work practices of intended users, which in turn are at the core of PD.

However, PD has proven to be difficult in practice [30], [31]. In the outsourced ISD project, neither in-house IS developers nor external SW developers were equipped with knowledge about work place studies, PD or ethnography. Dibbern's and colleagues' [12] and Tiwana's [13] research on outsourcing gives only one possible explanation of it. The SW vendor's visits in the clients' site are expensive to the client. A second explanation might be that IT experts do not know methods for gaining organizational and application domain knowledge or collaborative methods in practice. Even though we have not conducted a careful analysis of education in the disciplines of computing, based our experiences in education work in one university, we claim that there is a lack of courses concerning PD, ethnography, and work place studies.

Related to the both authority and professional boundaries between 'experts and laymen' [18] (p. 177), in the context of computerization of workplaces it is important to focus on 'low-status' office work performed largely by millions of women [50]. The authority boundary was clear between the secretary and the office manager. The secretary's participation possibilities were weakened when the service type of work remained unrelated to the decision making process done by the higher-level status inspectors and the office manager, which in practice rested on her knowledge of the client's interest groups, for example. Clement [50] claims that conventional systems development approaches are inadequate for dealing with the interpersonal aspects and required skill of service work. However, skills are vital to work operation, but are very difficult to formalize [50]. These skills 'lack the authoritative status they would enjoy if associated with higher-ranked, more formally qualified personnel' [50] (p. 400). Participation possibilities were weakened even more as she was not expert in SW development techniques and tools, which were applied in too early phases of the ISD. She could not contribute to envisioning the context of use and the web of users [51]. Suchman [46] emphasizes that too often people's way of working is analysed based on the work performance rather than understanding the principles of work. She continues that in many forms of service type of work practices, we can recognize frequently the trivial fact: the better the work is done, the less invisible such expertise is for others not involved in the activity in practice.

Our study of boundaries in theory and practice makes visible barriers and obstacles of knowledge sharing between users, IS experts and SW experts in outsourced ISD. Knowledge about boundaries is useful for IS experts, PD practitioners and academic researchers in their attempts to develop both user-designer and client-vendor relationships. This paper challenges both IS and SW experts to complement their organizational and application domain knowledge with ethnography and PD tools. Ethnographic informed analysis and participatory design for outsourced ISD should be further researched. Paths for future work include for example to compare this study of boundaries and lessons learned with distributed PD research in [16], and to study mediation across the boundaries.

Acknowledgements

We thank Professor Juhani Iivari (Professor of Information Systems at the University of Oulu, Finland) for critical and constructive comments. In addition, Professor Michèle Lamont (Professor of European Studies and Professor of Sociology and African and African American Studies at Harvard University) helped our work by email discussions. Finally, our respectful thanks go to the three anonymous reviewers of this paper, whose critical and constructive comments and understanding about the topic helped us to improve the paper.

References

1. Bansler, J.P., Havn, E.: The Nature of Software Work: Systems Development as a Labor Process. In: Vaan den Besselaar, P., Clement, A., Järvinen, P. (eds.) Information System, Work and Organization Design, pp. 145–153. Elsevier Science Publisher B.V., North-Holland (1991)
2. Bergman, M., Lyytinen, K., Mark, G.: Boundary Objects in Design: An Ecological View of Design Artifacts. Journal of Association for Information Systems 8(11), 546–568 (2007)
3. Tellioglu, H., Wagner, I.: Cooperative work across cultural boundaries in systems design. Scandinavian Journal of Information Systems 11 (1999)
4. Grudin, J.: Interactive Systems: Bridging the Gaps between Developers and Users. IEEE Computer 24(5), 59–69 (1991)

5. Anderson, R.J.: Representations and requirements: The value of ethnography in system design. Human-Computer Interaction 9, 151–182 (1994)
6. Viller, S., Sommerville, I.: Ethnographically informed analysis for software engineers. International Journal of Human-Computer Studies 53(1), 169–196 (2000)
7. Hughes, J.A., King, V., Rodden, T., Anderson, H.: Moving out from the control room: Ethnography in system design. In: Conference on Computer-Supported Cooperative Work, pp. 429–439. ACM Press, Chapel Hill (1994)
8. Karasti, H.: Bridging Work Practice and System Design: Integrating Systemic Analysis, Appreciative Intervention and Practitioner Participation. Computer Supported Cooperative Work, The Journal of Collaborative Computing 10(2), 211–246 (2001)
9. Markus, M.L., Mao, Y.: User Participation in Development and Implementation: Updating an Old Tired Concept for Today's IS Contexts. Journal of the Association for Information Systems 5(11-12), 514–544 (2004)
10. Sabherwal, R.: The Evolution of Coordination in Outsourced Software Development Projects: a Comparison of Client and Vendor Perspectives. Information and Organization 13, 153–202 (2003)
11. Dibbern, J., Goles, T., Hirschheim, R., Jayatilaka, B.: Information Systems Outsourcing: A Survey and Analysis of the Literature. The DATA BASE for Advances in Information Systems 35(4), 6–102 (2004)
12. Dibbern, J., Winkler, J., Heinzl, A.: Explaining Variations in Client Extra Costs Between Software Projects Offshored to India. MIS Quarterly 32(2), 333–366 (2008)
13. Tiwana, A.: Beyond the black box: Knowledge overlaps in software outsourcing. IEEE Software 21(5), 3–10 (2004)
14. Iivari, J., Hirschheim, R., Klein, H.K.: Towards a distinctive body of knowledge for Information Systems experts: coding ISD process knowledge in two IS journals. Information Systems Journal 14(4), 313–342 (2004)
15. Orlikowski, W.J.: Knowing in practice: Enacting a collective capability in distributed organizing. Organization Science 13(3), 249–273 (2002)
16. Öberg, K.D., Gumm, D., Naghsh, A.M. (eds.): Special Issue on Distributed PD: Challeges and opportunities. Scandinavian Journal of Information Systems 21(1), 23–106 (2009)
17. Oudshoor, N., Pinch, T. (eds.): How users matter: The co-construction of users and technology. The MIT Press, Cambridge (2003)
18. Lamont, M., Molnar, V.: The Study of Boundaries in the Social Sciences. Annual Review of Sociology 28, 167–195 (2002)
19. Pachucki, M.A., Pendergrass, S., Lamont, M.: Boundary processes: Recent theoretical developments and new contributions. Poetics 35(6), 331–351 (2007)
20. Lamont, M.: Money, Morals, and Manners: The Culture of the French and the American Upper-Middle Class. University of Chicago Press, Chicago (1992)
21. Star, S.L., Griesemer, J.R.: Institutional ecology, "translations" and boundary objects: Amateurs and professionals in Berkeley's Museum of Vertebrate Zoology, 1907-39. Social Studies of Science 19, 387–420 (1989)
22. Star, S.L.: The Structure of Ill-Structured Solutions: Boundary Objects and Heterogeneous Distributed Problem Solving. In: Huhns, M., Gasser, L. (eds.) Readings in Distributed Artificial Intelligence, vol. 2, pp. 37–54. Morgan Kaufmann, Menlo Park (1989)
23. Levina, N., Vaast, E.: The Emergence of Boundary Spanning Competence in Practice: Implications for Implementation and Use of Information Systems. MIS Quarterly 29(2), 335–363 (2005)
24. Carlile, P.R.: A pragmatic view of knowledge and boundaries: boundary objects in new product development. Organization Science 13(4), 442–455 (2002)

25. Bourdieu, P., Wacquant, L.J.D.: An Invitation to Reflexive Sociology. University of Chicago Press, Chicago (1992)
26. Kensing, F.: Methods and practices in participatory design. ITU Press, Copenhagen (2003)
27. Schuler, D., Namioka, A. (eds.): Participatory Design: Principles and Practices. Lawrence Erlbaum Associates, New Jersey (1993)
28. Kyng, M.: Making Representations Work. Communications of the ACM 38(9), 46–55 (1995)
29. Saarinen, T., Sääksjärvi, M.: The missing concepts of user participation: An empirical assessment of user participation and information systems success. Scandinavian Journal of Information Systems 2, 25–42 (1990)
30. Bødger, S., Iversen, O.S.: Staging a Professional participatory Design Practice – Moving PD beyond the Initial Facination of User Involvment. In: NordiCHI 2002, pp. 11–18 (2002)
31. Nardi, B., O'Day, V.L.: Information ecologies: Using technology with heart, 2nd printing. The MIT Press, Cambridge (1999)
32. Glass, R.L., Vessey, I., Ramesh, V.: Research in software engineering: an analysis of the literature. Information and Software Technology 44, 491–506 (2002)
33. Emerson, R.M., Fretz, R.I., Shaw, L.: Participation Observation and Fieldnotes. In: Atkinson, P., Coffey, A., Delamont, S., Lofland, J., Lofland, L. (eds.) Handbook of Ethnography. Sage Publications, London (2001)
34. Atkinson, P., Hammersley, M.: Ethnography and Participant Observation. In: Denzin, N., Lincoln, Y. (eds.) Handbook of Qualitative Research, pp. 248–261. SAGE, Thousands Oaks (1994)
35. Jordan, B., Henderson, A.: Interaction Analysis: Foundations and Practice. Institute for Research on Learning, Palo Alto, Ca (1994)
36. Star, S.L.: Infrastructure and ethnographic practice: Working on the fringes. Scandinavian Journal of Information Systems 14(2), 107–122 (2002)
37. Grudin, J.: Interface. Communications of the ACM 36(4), 112–119 (1993)
38. Tuovila, S., Iivari, N.: Bridge Builders in IT Artifact Development. In: Österle, H., Schelp, J., Winter, R. (eds.) 15th European Conference on Information Systems, pp. 819–830 (2007)
39. Iivari, N., Karasti, H., Molin-Juustila, T., Salmela, S., Syrjänen, A.-L., Halkola, E.: Mediation between Design and Use – Revisiting Five Empirical Studies. Human IT 10(2) (2009)
40. Blum, B.I.: Beyond programming. To a new era of design. Oxford University Press, New York (1996)
41. Iivari, J., Lyytinen, K.: Research on Information Systems Research in Scandinavia–Unity in Plurarity. Scandinavian Journal of Information Systems 10(1&2), 135–186 (1998)
42. Beyer, H., Holtzblatt, K.: Contextual Design: Defining Customer-Centered Systems. Morgan Kaufmann, San Francisco (1998)
43. Iivari, J., Hirschheim, R., Klein, H.K.: A dynamic framework for classifying information systems development methodologies and approaches. Journal of Management Information Systems 17(3), 179–218 (2000/2001)
44. Luff, P., Hindmarch, J., Heath, C. (eds.): Workplace Studies: Recovering Work Practice and Informing System Design. Cambridge University Press, Cambridge (2000)
45. Greenbaum, J., Kyng, M. (eds.): Design at Work. Cooperative Design of Computer Systems. Lawrence Erlbaum Associates, New Jersey (1991)
46. Suchman, L.: Making Work Visible. Communications of the ACM 38(9), 56–64 (1995)

47. Jirotka, M., Wallen, L.: Analysing the workplace and user requirements: challenges for the development of methods for requirements engineering. In: Luff, P., Hindmarch, J., Heath, C. (eds.) Workplace Studies: Recovering Work Practice and Informing System Design, pp. 242–251. Cambridge university press, Cambridge (2000)
48. Davis, A.M.: Software Requirements: Objects, Functions, and States. Prentice Hall, Englewood Cliffs (1993)
49. Flynn, D.J.: Information Systems Requirements: Determination and Analysis, 2nd edn. McGraw-Hill, London (1997)
50. Clement, A.: Computing at Work: Empowering Action by Low-Level Users. In: Kling, R. (ed.) Computerization and Controversy. Value Conflicts and Social Choices, 2nd edn., pp. 383–406. Academic Press, London (2000)
51. Millerand, F., Baker, K.S.: Who are the users? Who are the developers? Webs of users and developers in development process of a technical standard. Information Systems Journal (forthcoming)

Is Standard Software Wiping Out Socio-Technical Design? - Engaging in the Practice of Implementing Standard ERP Systems

Lene Pries-Heje

Department of Informatics, Copenhagen Business School,
DK-2000 Frederiksberg, Denmark

Abstract. Many organizations have experienced severe business disruptions and socio-technical misfits that persist for years after going live with ERP systems,. Deciding on the right mix of configuration, customization and process change seems to be very challenging. Understanding how design teams (ERP consultants and organizational representatives) actually decide on the mix has received very little attention within ERP research, however. This paper presents a focus group study on how ERP professionals perceive ERP implementations, and how their perception influences the approach used to implement the ERP system. As a result, four different perceptions of the nature of the design process have been identified. The perceptions manifest themselves as four distinct metaphors used by ERP experts to explain what implementations are about and the nature of the cooperation with the user organization. The research findings imply that the practice preferred by ERP consultants is very likely to result in a narrow focus on the design of the IT-artifact, and that joint optimization of the social and the technical sub-system will very seldom be realized.

Keywords: ERP implementation, socio-technical design, focus groups.

1 Introduction

In the introduction to the book *Second-wave Enterprise Resource Planning Systems* [1] the challenge of implementing ERP package software is formulated thus: *Apart from all the normal problems of information system project management, the novel difficulty for teams implementing Enterprise Software Systems is to decide which mix of configuration, customization, and process change is best for the organization.*

Empirical studies reveal that many companies have difficulties realizing a useful design and therefore experience moderate to severe business disruptions when going live with ERP package software, resulting in recovery difficulties. Sometimes, the only way to stabilize the situation is to increase staffing permanently and reduce efficiency expectations. Furthermore, it appears to be a turbulent ride when 'go-live' results in a long lasting disinclination toward the ERP system [2, 3]. A hostile attitude toward the new ERP system makes it very difficult to improve the situation without conceding the user organization changes to the IT artifact. These difficulties imply that the socio-technical design plays an important role in the difficulties that organizations experience.

As a whole, the ERP literature provides very few insights into how the design teams, as well as the organizations as a whole, actually engage in ERP. Thus, the need for research providing insights into how ERP implementations are engaged, and how implementation teams actually make decisions regarding configuration, customization and organizational change. A case study conducted earlier by the author of this paper [4]is an example of research actually seeking to provide such insights. It found that the approach used to implement ERP in a Danish company with 1,200 employees was intended, and set up, to provide broad participation and focus on the socio-technical design, but in practice, the design team ended up focusing on the technical design. The approach used in the case organization was found to have been heavily influenced by the implementation method suggested by the vendor, and it allowed the external ERP consultants to dominate the design process. As a result, more priority was given to technical design issues.

Thus, the aim of this current research is to provide a deeper understanding of how ERP professionals perceive ERP implementations, and how this perception influences the approach used when deciding on the mix of configuration, customization and process change. Hence, the overall research question formulated is: How do ERP professionals perceive ERP implementation, and how does it influence the implementation approach used?

2 Theoretical Background

It is often argued that ERP implementations are different from traditional systems development. This is especially so because it is perceived to be desirable or necessary to adapt the organizational processes to the ERP package software [5-9]. However, ERP projects are, in general, expected to involve a mix of organizational change, configuration of the ERP software and customization of the ERP software.

Deciding on alternative ways to realize the mix of organizational change, the configuration of the ERP software and the customization of the software should, at least in this writer's mind, qualify as ***design***. And design is here understood as a cooperative enterprise "where different people with different professional backgrounds and different motives are engaged in creating something new, the object of design" [10 p. 18]. Following this idea of design as a cooperative enterprise, design can be understood as an activity mediated by design artifacts, where the design artifacts can serve both as explicit means of cooperation and as means for the sharing of experiences, insights and visions about the design object. Implementing ERP systems, both the organizational processes and the ERP software, seems to be the object of design, and, to some extent, the two design objects have to inform each other. Which of the two design objects has priority remains unclear.

The scope of the ERP system is often the organization as a whole, and thus it can be seen as a common system serving many heterogeneous user groups at the same time. When considering design politics and user participation, the totality of the system could be addressed using a management perspective, or that there are differing perspectives, depending on various stakeholders' organizational positions and roles [11]. Using the latter perspective, the realization of the system would be a compromise between the interests and needs of many different user groups, and the goal would then be to balance these interests. This perspective is similar to the socio-technical approach which takes as its premise that employers and employees have a common interest in developing useful computer systems [12-14]. The socio-technical approach also addresses the organization as a whole, and within socio-technical research, the techniques for stakeholder participation in the organizational arena have been discussed and developed.

According to socio-technical theory, both the social and the technical sub-system should be given priority when designing information systems, and joint optimization of the two sub-systems is the goal. To apply this basic understanding of socio-technical design on ERP implementations, it is necessary to have knowledge about, and concern for, the social as well as the technical sub-system present when deciding on the mix of configuration, customization and process change (making design decisions).

Having knowledge about the social sub-system, especially in the sense of business knowledge or organizational knowledge, seems to be recognized within research on ERP implementations. Participation of organizational staff in ERP implementations is considered to be essential for success [7, 15, 16], and is expected to provide a better fit of user requirements, thus achieving better system quality, use, and acceptance [17]. The design team should be balanced or cross-functional, and comprise a mix of external consultants and internal staff, and the internal staff should develop the necessary skills for design and implementations [18-20]. Both business and technical knowledge are important [19, 20]. Not only is sharing of information among the various parties involved vital and requires partnership trust [21], but the team also needs to be empowered to make rapid decisions [20].

Thus, user participation and knowledge issues are widely recognized to be important success factors, but very few insights into how this have actually been engaged in organizations have been provided by ERP research. Within the ERP literature, the problems of ERP implementation have not been addressed as problems of design processes, but rather as problems of involvement, change management and commitment.

This research is framed by an understanding of ERP implementations as a cooperative socio-technical design process, that is, a design process aiming for joint optimization of the social and technical sub-systems, and requiring external ERP experts and heterogeneous user groups to cooperate balancing different interests when deciding on the design.

3 Research Method

In order to answer the research question - How do ERP professionals perceive ERP implementation, and how does it influence the implementation approach used? - this research used focus groups. The main arguments for using focus groups were the following: First, there was the ability to bring consultants and internal ERP experts together *outside a specific project* to discuss and share insights about ERP implementations. Second, it provided an opportunity to observe a large amount of interaction on a topic *chosen by the researcher* in a limited period of time. Third, it provided data about attitudes and decision making related to the implementation process (deciding on the mix of configuration, customization and process change) and the techniques and tools used. Fourth, agreements and disagreements discussed among peers provided direct access to similarities and differences in the participants' opinions and experiences. Thus, focus groups could provide insights into the common (socially constructed) understanding of ERP implementations as a practice seen from the perspective of the ERP professionals.

Assembling the focus groups, I, the researcher, had to balance many different requirements and practical obstacles. For example, the participants needed to have solid practical experience implementing ERP package software, and preferably they should come from different organizations. I decided to use my network's network (as recommended by Bente Halkier [22]). Since I had graduated from Copenhagen Business School in 1991, I knew that many of my "class mates" worked as ERP consultants or they would know someone who did. I therefore wrote to them and asked if they would pass on an invitation in their network. I received 15 positive responses and aimed for three groups with five participants each. Due to an influenza epidemic at the time, I ended up with two successful focus groups, each with five participants. All the participants had extensive experience implementing ERP systems. Having between 5 and 20 years of experience as ERP professionals, they had experience in implementing many different ERP standard systems (e.g. SAP, Oracle, Baan, Navision, Axapta, Multi+).

Despite recommendations not to spend more than two hours in a focus group session [22, 23], I decided on four hours with a generous break half way through. I had more questions and exercises than could be conducted in two hours, and I knew that it would be very difficult to arrange for the participants to come twice. Based on my personal experience with consultants, I found it reasonable to expect them to be able to concentrate and participate in longer sessions. When working at customer sites they often had to be very alert for a whole day. In addition to a break half way through, I decided to use different aids and exercises to avoid monotony, and I also focused the discussions in different ways.

3.1 Data Collection

Planning the focus groups the amount of structure and moderation for the focus group session had to be considered. The literature suggests three different models: a loosely structured model, a very structured model and a combined funnel model [24]. I decided on the combined model which encouraged a more general discussion in the beginning, but which also could apply more structure later to ensure that the group discussed specific issues.

The data collection was, to some extent guided by a very general understanding of socio-technical theory. The focus group study had three main parts given equal priority: *part one* focused on whether knowledge and consideration of the social sub-system (as existing practice) was present when making design decisions; *part two* concerned on knowledge and consideration of the technical sub-system when making design decisions; and *part three* related to if/how the concern for the social subsystem (as future practice/work processes), as well as for the technical sub-system were balanced in order to consider joint optimization. Following the funnel model, each of the three parts started with a more general question, allowing the participants an open and unstructured discussion, which was then followed by a few more specific questions. Finally, each part concluded by asking the participants to evaluate the ability of specific techniques and tools' (design artifacts) to support generating and sharing knowledge.

I documented the focus group sessions by sound recording and video filming. I took photographs of notes on the whiteboard and kept all papers used for exercises. The sound recording was then transcribed (more than 100 pages) and the photographs were incorporated into the text. The focus group discussion and data analysis were conducted in Danish; all citations in this paper have thus been translated into English, with great effort made to be as faithful to the original Danish language as possible.

3.2 Data Analysis

The analysis of the focus group data was conducted in three steps. First, the opening question to the focus groups (*"What is ERP implementation about and why is it difficult?"*) was analyzed using mind maps to "code" the conversation/discussion, where coding means a systematic way of understanding and keeping track of the research data. For each theme introduced in the discussion a mind map was made, sub-themes were noted as branches, and different contributions to the sub-themes were noted as offshoots. For each contribution a unique identifier (focus group #, participants' initials, and a line reference to the transcript) was noted. This made it possible for me to follow who introduced and who contributed to a specific theme or sub-theme, who agreed or disagreed with whom, and who backed up others' claims. As I was reflecting on the themes discussed, I noticed that different metaphors were used by the participants to explain the nature of ERP implementations and share insights about ERP implementations. Upon careful scrutiny, four different metaphors could be identified (*a standardization war, a game, an ERP driven change project, a business expert driven change project*). The metaphors were not necessarily mutually exclusive, as some participants contributed to more than one metaphor, but it was clear that each participant had a dominant metaphor. The metaphors are described in greater detail in section 4.

The next step in the analysis was to go back to the transcripts and look for different dimensions of the metaphors. Here, the roles that different stakeholders (management, ERP experts, organizational representatives in design team, end user, and the software) were expected to play were significant. The results of the analysis are described in greater detail in section 5. The final step of the analysis was the reflection on the implications that the metaphors had on the perceived nature of the design process and how it influenced the approach used/preferred by the ERP professionals.

4 Metaphors as the Main Finding

In this section, the four metaphors found in the first step of the analysis are presented. For each metaphor, selected important citations are provided to allow the reader insights into how the metaphors were derived from the empirical material.

4.1 The Standardization War Metaphor

The quotation below is the one that gave rise to the "standardization war" metaphor: *"It is much about standardization and integration... You get into trouble if you do not win the **standardization war**...Having everybody use the same system is both the challenge and the goal."* (# 1/18).

Other participants in focus group 1 also build on this metaphor, e.g., explaining how the previous IT system may influence the war. *"If the customer wants a tailor made system, you* (the implementation team) *are sure to be **defeated**."* (# 1/28).

The war metaphor is used to describe the relation between the external consultants and the user organization, for example, the external ERP experts talk about taking users hostage and fighting with the user organization. *"Here we took three countries hostage you could say, in a nice way, but three countries were **taken hostage**."* (# 1/56). *"In each country we had **a fight** over customizations needed because of local legislation."* (# 1/60).

The war metaphor is also used in the second focus group, but here it is taken up by an internal ERP expert to explain the hostile attitude the user representative experiences when interacting with the ERP consultants *"I have seen consultants **take my user representatives as hostages**. I know it can sound harsh but this I how I see it. Some of them (the user representatives) are not used to or tough enough to go up against consultants."* (# 2/241).

In the external ERP expert's mind, the "war" is legitimate because standard systems are cost effective and serve a greater purpose – integration and standardization: *"You want one integrated system sharing master data, using the same processes and input screens... it is all about standardization and integration. No one thinks that is fun."* (# 1/18), or it is alright because the system works to serve management: *"I was once part of a company's group management, the situation was that we had some subsidiaries that needed to have the system **enforced on them**"* (# 1/10).

The ERP experts perceive themselves as being on *a mission* working for management (and standard systems) against the user organization. *"With vendor XX the **mission** was to define the business case and follow it through; **force it through** the organization... The perception was that we* (the consultants) *acted as an auxiliary arm to management."* (# 1/20). The ERP experts' believe in the good of standards/ERP software, that it is very strong, and therefore they consider it important to be forceful in their contact with the user representatives *"Use standards don't develop different obscure corners to the system because the user organization claims their life depends on it."* (# 2/13).

Another way to legitimate the "war" is the perception of end users as being unable to see what is best for them. *"Customer XX used 11 segments in their chart of accounts, one of them the VAT code ... Basically this destroys the idea of a standard system. "* (# 1/24). They are unable to see what they do critically and therefore need someone from the outside to open their eyes: *"I also experience a wish to map the old world to the new. Often because you had no other way to handle the complexity in your old world than e.g. to build it into the chart of accounts. Now you have a large application portfolio providing functionality but...."* (# 1/27). Thus, if the user organization is given the power, they will not be able to see the idiosyncrasy in their processes, and it will be impossible to implement a standard system: *"They (user representatives) try to customize the system as much as possible to the organization's way of working instead of living with the more limited possibilities the standard system provides. Suddenly it is no longer a standard system."* (# 1/23).

4.2 The Game Metaphor

The game metaphor can be recognized in the following citation: *"I think this is a problem of great importance in this **game**."* (# 1/17). Here the "game" is characterized by many different players (stakeholders) having different goals and different rules to play by, both on the vendor side and the customer side: *"For the vendor, it is about selling licenses... at the end it is all about earning some money. For the customer, it is getting a solution to some basic problems."* (# 1/16).

The number of participants in the ERP game is huge, and the different and goals sometimes questioned. *"Many different goals also on the vendor side; sales person, PR-sales consultant, implementation consultant, programmer, support department and after sales"*, and at the customer side: *"It can be one person who wants to thumbprint something. Obviously, the person believes it is for the good of the company, but it is important for him that he made it happen. In the organization there may be others with completely different goals, and maybe somebody that actually will suffer from the decision."* Participants in the game cannot predict the next move of stakeholders or the outcome: *"For me, one of the main issues is that those involved in preparing and signing the contract are too distant from fulfilling the contract and actually taking part in the work... It gets more and more impossible to oversee the consequences of such a project."* (# 1/17).

Related to this metaphor, the participants emphasize that an ERP system is not just a standard system, it has several possible solutions that need to be evaluated and negotiated. *"One of the more important things about the large systems is the enormous customer base. Over the years experience is collected,... thus not just one way to do things, but a number of variants."* Also, when using this metaphor the external ERP expert believes in the completeness of the software *"... there should always be a solution which any company can live with, or at least use and find right for them."* (# 1/41).

Thus, the focus group participants who initiated and developed the "game" metaphor emphasize the unpredictable nature of ERP implementations, and the fact that success is not a given, that it depends on the stakeholder's point of view. ERP experts have to adjust their behavior and strategy to maneuver in this unpredictable and changing environment. *"Business consultants representing smaller areas cannot oversee the consequences of implementing a standard system covering the entire organization. All they do is think about their own area and require what will make them stand well with their own group. But it is an integrated standard system that we are implementing, they don't understand that data entered in one module is made available elsewhere. This kind of relations IT people have to help explain, plus cut down business requirements that come out of the blue. The way you* (as an external ERP expert) *have to act is questioning everything all the time. Should this really be included? Are you sure this is necessary? What do you need this for? Can't it be done in a different way? I have seen many business people requiring what is easy for them to get acceptance for in their hinterland."* (# 2/25).

4.3 The Business Expert Driven Change Project Metaphor

Contributions to the "change project" metaphor can be found in both focus groups, but it was this statement that identified it for this researcher: *"It is important to approach it (ERP implementation) as a **change project**, which is the major challenge. If you approach it as a business change project, then very different mechanisms come into play from the very beginning. It creates a very different communication with the organization. The expectation you create in the organization is different compared with perceiving it simply as an implementation of an IT system. It is very, very different."* (# 2/21).

Using this metaphor, business cases (suggestions for re-engineering) are developed internally in the client organization before the ERP experts are asked to help configure the ERP software; the ERP consultants' task is to help find software solutions that accommodate the business cases in the best possible way. Thus, the organization is responsible for the re-engineering: *"Regarding responsibilities and challenges, I don't think the organization can expect 'a brilliant consultant' to take over the responsibility or require them to give the right advice. It is the organization's own responsibility* (develop business cases and manage the change process). *If you are not aware of your own responsibilities, then you make a big mistake, and excuse me, but then you bring it on yourself... You should rather get the right employees in key roles; have them ask the right questions, someone that knows the market and understands both IT and the structure: both advantages and disadvantages - someone that has all-round knowledge and is able to make the connection to the business."* (# 2 S 57).

Some objections were made that it was too time consuming, and if the project had a deadline, that it might be impossible. The same person replied: *"It is my experience, that if you are the kind of organization that needs a tender process, then it takes time, maturing time - attitude time, I might say. Top management is involved and you are turning many stones. You get into all corners and hopefully you have time to consider it thoroughly. You also have time to make a risk profile for your project, so that you start the project with your eyes open and know how to do it."* Thus, it is emphasized that rushing into the configuration process might not be a good idea and that an organization needs to prepare for meeting the external consultants. *"... instead of starting the project too quickly, because you want to finish soon and then shooting yourself in one foot. Becoming a project manager in that situation is not goo, because you get into discussions that actually should have been taken upfront while making a thorough analysis including a business case. That is very important to have it done that way."* (# 2/59).

4.4 The ERP Expert Driven Change Project Metaphor

Participants contributing to the *ERP expert driven change project* metaphor also contribute to the *war metaphor,* thus the two metaphors are, to some extent, overlapping. The main difference lies in the anticipated role of the software and the ERP experts. Using the pure war metaphor, the software is expected to have best practice business processes built into the software, in the belief that any organization will be able to adapt its practice to the built-in processes. Using the ERP expert driven change project metaphor, however, it is emphasized that ERP consultants are working for management; thus, they are expected to have suggestions for re-engineering the business processes and then be able to justify them with business cases. This is done prior to the configuration and customization, or during configuration and customization. *"When I was working for XX* (consultant company implementing ERP) *then you had the idea that what was driving the project was business cases. Thus your mission* (as an ERP consultant) *was to develop the business case and follow it through the organization. On as large a scale as possible... you worked for management."* (# 1/20).

The ERP expert driven metaphor also has a little overlap with the *business driven change project* in that the assumption is shared that change can be planned and executed. *"If it* (the ERP project) *is supposed to change and develop the business, then it is very process oriented. You have to be open to what kind of project.... It is here the business case comes in; what do we gain and what will it cost? .... You have to know it and plan accordingly!"* (# 2/24).

5 The Metaphors and the Perceived Role of Different Stakeholders

As mentioned earlier, after identifying the four metaphors, the next step was to go back into the empirical material looking for the dimensions that made the metaphors distinct. Analyzing the discussions in more details, looking at who developed/contributed to each metaphor, and how they described and discussed the metaphors, it became clear that the role of different stakeholders was to dominate the discussion. Five distinct roles were discussed, namely: the role of the ERP experts, organizational representatives participating in the design team, management, the role of end users, and the role of the standard software. Space in this paper does not permit the details of how the perception of each role was derived from the empirical material.

But after having identified the five roles, it was verified that each of the five roles was discussed for each metaphor, and that the key characteristics were noted. The results are given in Table 1.

Table 1. The perceived roles of stakeholders for the four metaphors

	A standardization war	A game	ERP expert driven change project	Business expert driven change project
Perception of the ERP consultant's role	• Defending the (IT-) Standard software • Working for standards/management	• Serving a specific stakeholder in the organization (typically the IT department) • Recognizing stakeholders on both sides (change over time → the game changes over time) • Guarding the standard system	• Working for management • Developing business cases and re-design processes • Deploying the standard software as much as possible • Defending the standard	• Working for the design team as IT (ERP) experts • Developing IT design suggestions based on the business case/requirements specification, and deploying the standard software as much as possible
Perception of the organizational representatives' role (as part of the design team)	• Informants only → provide low level knowledge (details) about existing business processes • Testing the configured software • Contributing to end user training	• Provide knowledge about organizational practice • Negotiating design suggestions in the organization • Focusing on the IT artifact • Approving and testing the configured software	• Informants only → provide low level knowledge (details) about existing business processes • Testing the configured software • Contributing to end user training	• Strategic focus (IT artifact secondary) • Serving as design experts who is able to optimize the business and work processes • Guiding the design team's work with the business cases
Perception of management's role	• Deciding on the ERP system • Defending (dictating) the standard	• An important stakeholder • Sponsor • Court of appeal regarding design decisions and conflicts between stakeholders • Support standard IT for cost reasons	• Deciding on the ERP system • Approving business cases (ensure strategic fit) • Defending (dictating) the new processes	• Developing or approving business cases (ensure strategic fit) • Communicating why change is important • Ensuring resources for the project
Perception of the end users' role	• Adapting to the standard • Passive – receiving training in the new IT-system	• A stakeholder • Influencing the design team and the final design, directly or indirectly • Influencing other stakeholders • Receiving training in the new IT system	• Adapting to the standard • Passive – receiving training in the new IT-system	• Needing to be included for psychological reasons and, to some extent, for knowledge diffusion • Receiving training in new socio-technical processes
Perception of the system's role	• Best Practice • Standard software • Common infrastructure	• Supportive infrastructure (hosted by IT department) • Cost-effective IT solution • Offering built in processes that work for most organizations	• Providing common (standard) processes in the whole organization • Standard software used to inspire the re-design of business processes	• Designing the IT artifact is secondary to designing new business processes • As much reuse (standard) as possible

6 Discussion of the Findings

As described in the methods section, the third step of the analysis was the reflection on what implications the metaphors had on the perceived nature of the design process, and how they influenced the approach used/preferred by the ERP professionals.

The ware metaphor – the nature of the design process: This metaphor implies that the primary focus is on the design of the IT artifact, and that the business processes built into the software are considered to be useful for any organization. Standardization is in itself considered to be a goal. The cooperative aspect of design is limited, and organizational representatives are expected to provide details regarding the existing work processes that allow the consultants to configure the software. Only on very rare occasions does design actually take place, and thus, in practice, the responsibility for design (both the IT artifact and the prescribed business processes) is placed with the predefined standard software. The ERP professionals subscribing to this metaphor favor an approach where management is expected to defend/dictate using a standard system; user representatives serve only as informants, and take on the responsibility of testing the configured standard system. The user organization provides the requirements, and alternative design suggestions are limited to configuration. The ERP experts are not interested in detailed knowledge about the social-sub system, but are concerned only with abstract business process descriptions.

The game metaphor – the nature of the design process: This metaphor implies that the design process is perceived as a negotiation involving all stakeholders. The standard software and the ERP experts are also stakeholders, with the potential of being very influential stakeholders. The power balance between different stakeholders differs from one project to another, and depends on local conditions. The ERP professionals subscribing to this metaphor favor an approach similar to the war metaphor (implementing a standard system with support from management); the main argument here is not so much best practice, but rather the cost and risk related to customizing the software. There seems to be more concern for understanding the current organizational practice, that is, not to sympathize with the user organization, but to be able to argue why/how the standard software can be used.

The ERP expert driven change project metaphor – the nature of the design process: This metaphor implies that the design of both the software and organizational processes is the responsibility of the ERP experts. The ERP experts are working for management developing (re-engineering) business processes, using the standard system as inspiration whenever possible. The new business processes are supported by business cases that quantify the benefit of the new process. User representatives are, in some cases, not involved at all; instead, existing documents and observations serve to provide knowledge about the existing practice, and thus the focus is on the product that the process is expected to produce. The approach preferred by the ERP professionals subscribing to this metaphor is somewhat similar to the war metaphor. Here, the responsibility for design is not placed with the standard software, but with the ERP experts. The user organization is only involved in providing detailed knowledge about business processes needed for configuration and data definitions in order to test the software and to receive training in the new system.

The business expert driven change project – the nature of the design process: This metaphor implies that the design process is driven and dominated by internal business experts (business process designers) cooperating with management. The design takes the business strategy as an outset. The participants subscribing to this metaphor perceive deep knowledge about the current organizational practice to be important. First, there is the need to understand the social and physical context that the processes are supposed to accommodate. The preferred approach is to design business process (supported by business cases) and let them serve as high level requirements for the design of the IT artifact. The ERP experts are then given the responsibility to utilize the standard system as much as possible. The end users are not expected to be directly involved in the design process, but the business process designers are expected to watch over their interests.

Summing up, how does the research result relate to the notion of ERP implementations as cooperative socio-technical design? Three of the four metaphors indicate that an ERP implementation is not perceived as a cooperative socio-technical design process. *The war metaphor* places the responsibility for design with the standard system, and social aspects are given no or very little priority. *The ERP expert driven change project* places the design responsibility with the ERP expert, and social aspects are given no or very limited priority. *The business driven change project* places the responsibility for the process design with the business experts, and the design of an IT artifact (that support the specified to-be processes) with the ERP experts. It is somewhat unclear as to how much and how the end users are allowed to influence the design of the to-be processes, but the internal business experts participating in the focus groups seem to be very aware of the need for a satisfying socio-technical design in order to ensure effective and efficient work processes. For *the game metaphor,* the design process may actually be approached as a cooperative design process, giving priority to social as well as technical aspects, depending on how the stakeholder negotiation is allowed to play out. Several constraints for the ERP implementation project may pull the ERP implementation approach in the direction of the war metaphor, although it is perceived as a game, e.g., budget and time constraints, or allowing the ERP software or the ERP consultants a dominating position in the stakeholder negotiations.

When considering technology development projects in general, the arguments vary as to why and how users should participate. At one end of the spectrum, users participate solely to provide (professional) designers with an understanding of the local work situation. The design work is initiated by management or design professionals, and is carried out by designers. Users have no, or very limited, influence on the design, and they are only invited to participate when their input is considered valuable to the designer. At the other end of the spectrum, users participate not only because their knowledge is considered to be valuable, but also because their interests in the design outcome are acknowledged. Thus, users participate in negotiating and deciding on how projects are negotiated and supported, and they participate in all phases of a project.

When considering the four metaphors, three of them (the war metaphor and the two variants of the change project metaphor) seem to result in an approach where the users are participating only to provide the designers with the information needed to configure the software. The game metaphor may allow socio-technical design issues to be negotiated and reconciled in the organization, but it may also result in a stakeholder fight where some stakeholders (and here the ERP experts and the ERP software also qualify as stakeholders) are given more priority than others. The war metaphor and the change project metaphor with an ERP expert perspective seems very likely to result in a lack of user involvement, but also the two other metaphors could make it difficult for the users to see the importance and personal relevance of the (design of the) system.

7 Conclusion

The overall research question for this study was: How do ERP professionals perceive ERP implementation, and how does it influence the implementation approach used?

The answer to this question is four-fold, namely, four different perceptions of ERP implementations; four different metaphors, where each metaphor has implications for how the role of not only ERP experts, but also user representatives, management, end users and the ERP standard software, are perceived. The metaphors are found to influence the perceived level of detailed knowledge that the ERP consultants need about the organizational practice, as well as the nature of the design process. The research findings imply that the practice preferred by ERP consultants is very likely to result in a narrow focus on the design of the IT-artifact, and that joint optimization of the social and the technical sub-system will very seldom be realized

References

1. Shanks, G., Seddon, P.B., Willcocks, L.P. (eds.): Second-Wave Enterprise Resource Planning Systems - implementing for effectiveness, p. 449. Cambridge University Press, Cambridge (2003)
2. Markus, L., et al.: Learning from Adopters' Experiences with ERP: Problem Encountered and Success Achieved. In: Shanks, G., Seddon, P.B., Willcocks, L.P. (eds.) Second-Wave Enterprise Resource Planning Systems, pp. 23–55. Cambridge University Press, Cambridge (2003)
3. Pries-Heje, L.: Time, Attitude, and User Participation: How Prior Events Determine User Attitudes in ERP Implementation. International Journal of Enterprise Information Systems 4(3), 48–65 (2008)
4. Pries-Heje, L.: Coexistance or no existence: ERP systems as process protocols. 2009: The IT University of Copenhagen (2009)
5. Bancroft, N.H., Seip, H., Sprengel, A.: Implementing SAP R/3 - How to introduce a large system into a large organization, 2nd edn. Manning Publication Co., Greenwich (1998)
6. Markus, M.L., Tanis, C.: The Enterprise System Experience – From Adoption to Success. In: Zmud, R.W., Price, M.F. (eds.) Framing the domains of IT management: Projecting the future through the past. Pinnaflex Educational Resources, Cincinatti (2000)
7. Kawalek, P., Wood-Harper, T.: Finding of Thorns: User Participation in Enterprise System Implementation. Advances in Information Systems 33(1), 13–22 (2002)
8. Parr, A., Shanks, G.: Critical Success Factors Revisited: A Model for ERP Project Implementation. In: Shanks, G., Seddon, P.B., Willcocks, L.P. (eds.) Second-Wave Enterprise Resource Planning Systems. Cambridge University Press, Cambridge (2003)

9. Fenema, P.C.v., Koppius, O.R., Baalen, P.J.v.: Implementing packaged enterprise software in multi-site firms: intensificaton of organizing and learning. European Journal of Information Systems 16, 484–598 (2007)
10. Bertelsen, O.W.: Design Artefacts: Towards a design-oriented epistemology. Scandinavian Journal of Information Systems 12(1-2), 15–27 (2001)
11. Bjerkness, G., Bratteteig, T.: User Participation and Democracy: A Discussion of Scandinavian Research on System Development. Scandinavian Journal of Information Systems 7(1), 73–98 (1995)
12. Bjørn-Andersen, N., Hedberg, B.: Designing Information Systems in an Organizational Perspective. Studies in the Management Sciences Perscriptive Models of Organizations, vol. 5 (1977)
13. Markus, L.: Power, Politics and MIS Implementation. Communication of the ACM 26(6), 430–444 (1983)
14. Mumford, E.: Redesigning Human Systems, p. 303. Information Science Publishing, Hershey (2003)
15. Nah, F.F.-H., Zuckweiler, K.M., Lau, J.L.-S.: ERP Implementation: Chief Information Officers' Perceptions of Critical Success Factors. International Journal of Human-Computer Interaction 16(1), 5–22 (2003)
16. Robey, D., Ross, J., Boudreau, M.: Learning to Implement Enterprise Systems: An Exploratory Study of the Dialectics of Change. Journal of Management Information Systems 19(1), 17–46 (2002)
17. Esteves-Sousa, J., Pastor-Collado, J.: Towards the unification off critical success factors for ERP implementations. In: 10th Annual Business Information Technology conference, Manchester, UK (2000)
18. Gibson, N., Holland, C., Light, B.: Enterprise Resource Planning: A business Approach to Systems Development. In: 32nd Hawaii International Conference on Science Systems HICSS, Msui, Hawaii (1999)
19. Sumner, M.: Critical Success Factors in Enterprise Wide Information Management Systems Projects. In: Americas Conference on Information Systems, Milwaukee, WI (1999)
20. Parr, A., Shanks, G.: A Model of ERP Project Implementation. Journal of Information Technology 15(4), 289–304 (2000)
21. Stefanou, C.J.: Supply Chain Management (SCM) and Organizational Key Factors for Successful Implementation of Enterprise Resource Planning (ERP) Systems. In: Americas Conference on Information Systems, Milwaukee, WI (1999)
22. Halkier, B.: Fokusgrupper. Samfundslitteratur, Roskilde (2002)
23. Morgan, D.L.: Focus Groups as Qualitative Research, 2nd edn. Qualitative Research Methods Series. Sage publications, Newbury Park (1997)
24. Morgan, D.L.: Focus Groups as Qualitative Research. Sage publications, Newbury Park (1988)

Facing the Lernaean Hydra: The Nature of Large-Scale Integration Projects in Healthcare

Eli Larsen[1] and Gunnar Ellingsen[2]

[1] Norwegian Centre for Telemedicine,
[2] University of Tromsø
[1,2] Sykehusvn 23, 9019 Tromsø, Norway
eli.larsen@telemed.no, gunnar.ellingsen@hn-ikt.no

Abstract. Despite initiatives and actions, only minor steps towards better communication systems have been achieved in healthcare. We examine this phenomenon empirically through three Norwegian healthcare projects, all of which started in 2005. The projects were initiated and funded by the Norwegian government and were aimed at establishing inter-organizational integration in healthcare. We examine the nature of these projects, and elaborate on how they tended to escalate and increasingly become enmeshed with each other. The top-down approach, with a high degree of requirement specification up front, creates a large gap between the different stakeholders involved. As an alternative, we propose a more restrained strategy in line with the information infrastructure concept: development in an inter-organizational setting must be carried out in small steps and with substantial influence by users and vendors.

Keywords: National projects, healthcare, coordination, interdependency strategy, integration, information infrastructures, ANT.

1 Introduction

A Western health care infrastructure is distributed across several institutional boundaries that typically involve general practitioners, hospitals, nursing homes, and home care services. This presents challenges for healthcare personnel who need a complete picture of the patient's condition. An example is when a patient is transferred from a hospital to the home care service; information about medication and care is essential to provide a quality service. As a result, improved electronic cooperation and integration in the healthcare sector have become an essential part of governmental strategies in Western countries [1-4]. In some instances, the government has even become directly involved in running several large-scale projects, such as the National Programme for IT in England [5] and the ePrescription project in Norway [1].

Despite these initiatives, only minor steps towards the improvement of electronic inter-organizational collaboration have been achieved [1, 6]. In the Netherlands, a number of national projects met pitfalls and challenges [7]. Conclusions from evaluation and status reports in Norway are similar [8]. As a result, there is a call for even more governmental control and coordination [1, 8, 9].

However, large integration projects run by the Health Directorate seem to present a paradox: while many healthcare stakeholders call for more governance [10], the same stakeholders complain about how these top-down interventions are misplaced or fail to provide working solutions. We examine this phenomenon empirically through three national healthcare projects, which all started in 2005. The projects were initiated and funded by the Norwegian government and were aimed at establishing inter-organizational integration in healthcare.

The study contributes empirical insight into complex large-scale projects with top-down organizing. We elaborate on how these projects tend to escalate and increasingly become enmeshed with each other, thus complicating any governmental action. As an alternative, we propose a more modest strategy in line with the information infrastructure concept. Based on this, we address the following research question: What is the nature of government-initiated inter-organizational integration projects in health care?

Our analysis proceeds along the following three dimensions: Firstly, we elaborate on how the size and scope of national IT projects escalate and how they increasingly become interdependent on each other. Secondly, we explore how the government's top-down pre-specification needs substantial translations among the vendors to make requirement specifications work. And thirdly, given the many stakeholders and the different associated interests, we critically examine how integrations tend to redistribute the costs and the benefits unevenly among participants.

As a theoretical basis, we employ the concept of information infrastructure and supplement it with Actor Network Theory (ANT) to emphasize how infrastructural integration projects are complex, interdependent and unpredictable.

The rest of the paper is organized as follows: The next section describes the theoretical framework and concepts used in this paper. The methods section describes and explains the methods for the research. Next, we present in-depth information about three nationally initiated inter-organizational projects, followed by the discussion and conclusion.

2 Theory

Many of today's healthcare organizations have a large installed base [11] of information systems. General practitioners (GPs) use electronic patient record systems (EPRs) in their practice; hospitals run composite systems containing hospital-based EPRs, laboratory systems, radiology systems, and patient administrative systems. Many nursing homes have also introduced EPRs, and special-purpose systems are used by many emergency care units. While these different systems function effectively within the institution they are supposed to support, integration between them is often lacking or problematic [6, 7].

The lack of integration may have serious consequences. An example is information about medication held in EPRs in GP practices, hospitals and home care services. In most countries, this information is not integrated and must be cut and pasted into ordinary letters for transmission between the different health care providers. This may cause adverse drug events [12] because physicians may prescribe new medication without being aware of existing medicine regimes. A study from a hospital in Norway found that 20% of the hospitalizations of elderly people were caused by adverse drug events [13].

Accordingly, in many Western countries, national strategy on IT in the healthcare sector emphasizes the importance of achieving a smooth information flow between the systems in the different organizations [1-4]. In many instances, the health authorities even undertake a direct role in coordinating and running IT projects [14]. In this regard, it is assumed that the authorities have the resources and the power to run the projects in a structured and controlled manner, and that they are able to coordinate activities between the different and often autonomous stakeholders in a top-down manner [8, 9, 14].

Unfortunately, experience from many studies of large-scale projects indicates that a top-down approach is risky and often fails. The size and inter-organizational scope of these infrastructures make integration efforts very complex. Typically, many stakeholders, infrastructures and vendors are involved, and a recurrent characteristic is that the projects tend to suffer from insurmountable delays, overrun budgets, as well as escalation of ambitions and scope [15, 16].

In contrast, considering coordination from the perspective of information infrastructure invites a more careful approach. Such an approach recognizes that overall control of systems in the healthcare sector is almost impossible, for the reasons provided above. The question then becomes how we can scale (cf. integrate) information infrastructures in healthcare without at the same time scaling the associated projects. Some clues to an answer may be found in the way that Star and Ruhleder [17] describe how infrastructures are *emergent*. They grow slowly over time, building on the installed base.

What also increases complexity in this domain is that there is not just one project, but several. As a result of their inter-organizational scope, many of the projects have interrelated and partly overlapping aims. Consequently, the government faces challenges related to coordinating and prioritizing *between* them. One complex project may escalate into a bundled collection of complex and mutually interdependent projects. In a sense, integration projects *are* about creating interdependencies between different systems. Data exchange formats have to be agreed on and work processes shaped, etc. However, the danger is that several overlapping projects may be too tightly coupled. From a system perspective, Perrow [18] uses the notion of loose and tight coupling to describe the degree of dependencies between the various components. He warns that tightly coupled systems have very little slack with only limited ways to accomplish a task. In a more process-oriented perspective, these dependencies may be conceptualized through the lenses of Actor Network Theory (ANT), where people and artefacts as actors are linked together in networks [19, 20]. The basis for the actors' participation in the network is that they pursue specific interests and will negotiate with and possibly ally themselves with other actors to try to achieve their goals. The flexibility of ANT enables us to zoom in on several of the characteristics of the projects while at the same time examining their increasing scale, their different strategies and their interdependency.

However, due to the high degree of complexity of national projects, it is not surprising that many demand for even more governmental intervention and top-down control, in accordance with the management literature [21]. This typically includes agreeing on a clear-cut requirement specification up front, followed by a well-defined bid-for-tender, and finalized by acquisition of the new system. However, considering the (coordination) challenge through the lenses of ANT, we are invited to see that it is extremely difficult to have everything settled up front. Firstly, this is not just a relatively standalone design task involving one customer and one vendor. Instead, there is a heterogeneous ensemble of existing systems and organizations that must coordinate their activities. ANT emphasizes how achievements are a result of negotiation of the actors' interests. In such a process, an agreement between two actors may result in a displacement of their original goals, or as Latour notes: "We can portray the relation between two agents as a translation of their goals which results in a composite goal that is different from the two original goals". It follows that top-down requirements from the authorities cannot just be imposed on vendors and user organizations. Rather, there is a great deal of work on the vendors' part in order to translate high-level requirement specifications on integration into the designer's specific needs in the development phase, which revolves around screen layout, specific exchange formats and data structures. In turn, the developed systems and the associated functionality need to be translated to the end-users' practice. Hence, there is a chain of translations and adaptations between the different actors in the network.

One might believe that integration is positive for everybody. However, the distributed, negotiated and partly unpredictable character of networks [19, 20] indicates that the envisioned effect of integration is not given per se. Several studies have also pointed out how integration delimits action [22]. Hence, integration brings not only benefits, but also costs [23]. As many of these projects are run at a national level, these issues have direct implications for the health authorities' strategy on integration: the assumed benefits and costs have to be carefully balanced. To take the argument further, given the many different institutions involved, one may experience that the costs and benefits may be unevenly distributed among the participants [24]. Naturally, this will also be reflected in each stakeholder's willingness to allocate resources as well as to pay for integration projects. From an ANT perspective, the actors involved (vendors, institutions, authorities, etc.) may pursue completely different interests, thus prohibiting potential compromises and making it hard to keep the actors in line.

3 Method

An interpretative approach [25] is used to develop a better understanding of the mechanisms influencing the development of tools for electronic cooperation in the healthcare sector. The empirical material has been gathered through a longitudinal process that started in 2004 and is still ongoing. In this period, the first author has collected empirical data from the following information sources:

- Strategic documents and evaluation reports for ICT in Norwegian health care for the period 1997 onwards.
- Project documentations for each of the three projects
- 25 semi-structured interviews with vendors, policy makers and public authorities. The interviews were conducted by the first author and lasted between approximately 60 and 160 minutes

The first author was formerly a project member in the core EPR project, one of the analysed projects, and has thus worked as an insider [25]. This has given her valuable insight into how these projects have been run and has enabled easier access to key actors in all of these projects, who would otherwise be difficult to make appointments with. Nonetheless, throughout the data collection and analyses process, she had to re-examine her own perceptions of what was going on in these projects. After initially ascribing the problems and delays primarily to the vendors, she increasingly considered the challenges to be much more complex, involving interests, relationships and interdependencies between many actors.

4 Background: Problems Due to Inadequate Cooperation

Norway has a publicly managed healthcare sector divided into the primary health service and the hospitals. An important part of the primary health care is the self-employed GPs, who number almost 3000. Today, almost 100% of the GPs and the hospitals use EPRs. In 1990, the authorities established KITH, a dedicated centre, which prepares national standards for secure electronic cooperation within healthcare. Norway was one of the first countries in Europe to establish an infrastructural network for interaction in the healthcare sector [9]. Currently, more than 80% of the GPs and 100 % of the hospitals are connected to the Norwegian Health Net [1]. During more than 30 years, a vast number of standards for exchanging medical certificates, discharge letters, referrals, laboratory orders and laboratory results have been developed. In spite of this, establishing substantial volume services between different health institutions has taken more time than anyone would have expected when taking into account the first national plan for ICT in Norwegian healthcare from 1997. In 2006, only 8% of referrals to Norwegian hospitals and about 50% of discharge letters were sent electronically [8]. A high number of versions of the messages are making the communication even more challenging. In 2009, only 8% of the messages flowing between the health institutions were approved by the authorities [26]. Electronic medical certificates were required by law from January 2010. At this date, 33% were sent electronically [26]. Thus, a key concern in the current national strategy plan is to revitalize the efforts related to improved workflow and seamlessness [26].

4.1 Three Nationally Initiated Inter-organizational Projects

During a few months in 2005, the public administration started several linked projects: ePrescription, Core EPR and ELIN-k. The projects were to be finished within a period of three to four years.

The three projects had a common goal of increasing the degree of regional cooperation, and were thus perfectly aligned with the Norwegian strategy [1].

Table 1. Key information concerning the three projects

Project	Design strategy	Funding	Period
ePrescription	Database with prescriptions	30 million Euro	2005 ->
Core EPR	Database with medication records	3 million Euro	2005 - 2009
ELIN-k	Messages directly between institutions	2 million Euro	2005 ->

4.2 ePrescription – "A Living Hell"

In 2004, the Ministry of Health initiated a project called ePrescription, which stood for electronic prescriptions. The most important argument for this was a regulation that instructed the National Insurance Administration to document all prescriptions handled by the pharmacies. However, implementing electronic prescriptions was also expected to provide benefits for pharmacies, which could handle prescriptions faster and with fewer errors. The doctors saw the potential for decision support, improved quality, and less time spent on writing prescriptions. The patients could have their prescription distributed to any pharmacy, and the authorities could distribute changes to regulations more efficiently. The project was to be completed in 2009.

The following actors were included in the project: Norwegian Pharmacist's Union, National Insurance Administration (NIA), Norwegian Medical Association (representing physicians) and Norwegian Medicines Agency (NMA), which concerns all information concerning medicine in Norway. The project was managed by the Directorate of Health.

The ePrescription project was established with funding from the parliament of about 30 million euros. The EPR vendors received funding for parts of their development costs.

First of all, the authorities wanted an electronic prescription system to document the use of medicine and control the public financing aspect of medicine distribution. In the beginning of the project, the management targeted its efforts toward this end. However, the physicians' representative was dissatisfied with the system that had been outlined, as the physicians' perspective was lacking. The system did not allow for some kind of support during the prescription phase, such as interaction control and product information. Neither was it possible to send orders to the pharmacy for those patients who got their medicine packed in separate single-use doses. The physicians are vital in the prescription process. Without their goodwill, prescriptions would probably still be in a paper-based format, and this would have undermined the concept of substantial electronic cooperation concerning prescriptions. In 2007, a new version of ePrescription was designed, but pilot testing was based on the first version.

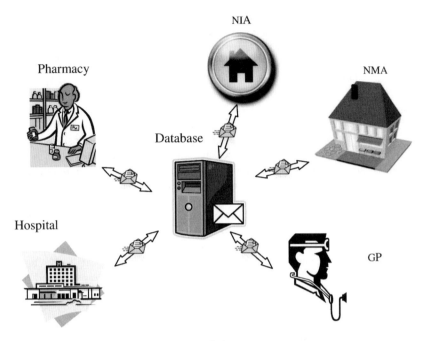

Fig. 1. ePrescription concept

The first version of ePrescription did not provide the functionality that the doctor wanted. We had to tear it apart and build it up completely from the ground. The first version did not have any future perspective and was not possible to develop further into an adequate service. [Project member]

Another problem was that the three vendors of the hospital-based EPRs demanded more specific requirement specifications before they were willing to develop anything. As a result, the project initiated working groups in the hospitals to work out user requirements for hospitals. It was difficult to launch an initiative and recruit volunteers in large institutions like hospitals, and therefore about two years passed before the working group was able to deliver. Only one EPR vendor for GPs developed functionality for the first version of ePrescription. The remaining two were not able to participate because they had recently introduced new EPR systems that needed a great deal of attention.

Much involvement from doctors was in the form of interviews, meetings, and workshops. The EPR vendor participated in much of this work. During this process, the specification changed extensively:

The technical specification of the message we were supposed to get from the Norwegian Medicine Agency was only ten percent OK when we started developing. [..] They had defined classes and stuff that they wanted to use in the message but the message itself was not defined. And there were a lot of changes in the class structure afterwards. [EPR vendor]

The Norwegian standardization organization, KITH, was included in the project when the testing phase started:

It [the message] was supposed to be finished before we started developing because we needed something to test against. The result was that we had to go several rounds with the Norwegian Medicine Agency to say that the message that had been constructed was in fact not a message, but rather a text string. So we had to go some rounds with KITH where they standardized the message. [..] In the end of the summer [2007] we had a fairly good data model on the message, but still we received a lot of errors in the messages, wrong data type, etc.[..] Several kinds of things like this influence the time of development. [EPR vendor]

Even after KITH had established the structure of these messages, a great deal of testing and error detection was necessary in order to communicate seamlessly between the actors. In the ePrescription project, only one of six vendors participated actively during the first three years. The workload necessary for establishing communication between the EPR and the rest of the actors, for instance the prescription database, was very time-consuming and several times greater than initially expected. This project, with a budget of 30 million euros, offered the vendor 175 000 euros – which is about 0.6% of the total budget.

A pilot test was launched by the Minister of Health in a small municipality in Norway in May 2008. The EPR vendor insisted that it should be postponed for a few months, but this was refused.

Those who manage the [ePrescription] project have obviously decided to keep it on schedule, and this is said in such a way that you understand that there is a lot of prestige in the project – as if there is somebody who will rap them over the knuckles if they don't. [Profiled health actor]

The EPR system that was integrated with ePrescription was a completely new system, but unfortunately the vendor had not had time to test it sufficiently in-house. The ePrescription was installed just a few days after the installation of the new EPR. This caused even more trouble for the pilot users, who received too much experimental software to test in a busy working day. The EPR vendor was mainly delayed because the development tool they had used, Microsoft's FoxPro, was not supported any more. The vendor then had to start its development from scratch, only two years back in time. As a result, the combined functionality offered to users was not good enough and was characterized as a "living hell" in the Norwegian media. The pilot was aborted after only three months. The next pilot test is now scheduled for the beginning of 2010.

4.3 ELIN-k: Communication with the Municipal Sector – "The Best Public Project in Which I Have Ever Participated"

In 2005, the Norwegian Nursing Council initiated the ELIN-k project, which focused on electronic information exchange of health information in the municipalities. More specifically, this concerned the nursing homes, home care service, emergency wards, hospitals and medical offices (GPs).

The goal of ELIN-k was to develop 13 standardized message formats that enabled the different institutions to communicate. ELIN-k was the first project that used standardized electronic messages in the municipal healthcare sector – both internally and to other parts of the health care sector. The messages were logistics, applications, medication and diverse information messages. In a revised project plan from February 2006, the project was scheduled for completion in February 2008.

The Norwegian Nursing Council and the Norwegian Association of Local and Regional Authorities were in charge of the project. The latter was considered to be an important actor because it represented the users and the owners of the ICT solutions in the municipalities. The Nursing Council represented the users on an occupational level. The inclusion of the Norwegian standardization centre, KITH, was considered essential.

The communication flow had to be tightly integrated in the ICT tools that already existed in the health care sector. Therefore, a total of seven vendors, covering all sectors within the healthcare, signed contracts with the project. Six municipalities wanted to run pilots.

The funding of the project was a package deal between the Ministry of Health, Innovation Norway (the Norwegian Association of Local and Regional Authorities) and the Norwegian Nursing Council. The EPR vendors would get about 50% of the stipulated development cost of the project. The package totalled about 1.5 million euros.

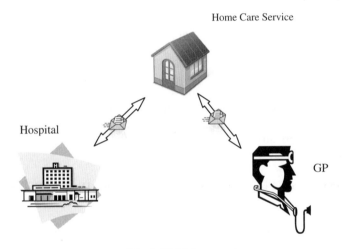

Fig. 2. ELIN-k concept

One of the most essential messages included in the project contained medication information. The prescription is the first step in creating this information. Hence the prescription should also be the basis for information that the home care service or the hospital needed. This caused some trouble for ELIN-k, because medication was the essential part of the ePrescription project, and here a standard was in the process of being developed. A common data model was necessary in the medication module.

The main activities in the project were development, laboratory testing, approval, pilot testing, evaluation, and adjustment of requirements. In the beginning of the project, the specifications had to be worked out more in detail in order to create a description that developers could take further. The project used a working method that involved users in cooperation with vendors to specify the requirements and to adjust them. Several meetings and workshops were arranged and included users from the pilot municipalities and sometimes also EPR vendors. These gatherings were considered useful from the vendors' point of view. The vendors were involved from the very beginning, but were not very active during the first two years. The amount of work with regards to user requirements was more time-consuming than initially expected. Several rounds of description and justification were necessary in order to fit the workflow and standards.

But the function descriptions are very difficult to follow and they have also changed a lot without a good specification. [..] The function descriptions do not always agree with the standardized messages. [EPR vendor]

Considerable delay was also caused by a lack of resources on the vendor's part. The specifications for the first phase in the project, communication between nursing homes and medical centres, were finished in 2006 and the vendors were supposed to deliver in spring 2007. An informant among the vendors explained:

The vendors are heavily tied up in other things too. They have to upgrade their own system and requests from their customers. Then IPLOS [a demand from the authority] has been going on at the same time, we have been forced to prioritize IPLOS over the messages. All these projects that are going on at the same time steal from the same resources and there is very little coordination between them. [..] The Directorate pushes on and does not respect that we are tied up with other things. [EPR vendor]

During the spring of 2009, one of the EPR vendors within medical centres and one within the municipal sector delivered the functionality in the EPR and the first message was sent from one of the pilot sites. This was two years later than first planned. Unfortunately, the project run out of money in 2009 and will not be able to include all the planned messages. In sum, the EPR vendors were positive to the way the project had been organized and several stated that it was the best public project in which they had participated.

4.4 A National Core EPR – "I Can't Imagine That Our Doctors Will Pay for This"

In 2004 Trondheim Municipality applied for project money announced by the Directorate of Health. It received support in December 2005 and named the project: Core EPR. The goal of the project was to develop, implement and test the functionality of a core patient record. This was a database consisting of all the medication information of the patients. The database should be easy to access for those treating the patients. Patients who had their medicine administered by the home care service were the ones who were planned to be included in the pilot. The first pilot installation was planned to take place in late 2006, and the service was to be evaluated and completed by the end of 2008.

The project was run by Trondheim Municipality and included eight EPR vendors (three GP EPRs, three municipal EPRs and two hospital EPRs). KITH was also included because new standards for the cooperating EPR systems had to be developed.

The funding of the project was a package deal between the Ministry of Health, Innovation Norway and Northern Norway Regional Health Authority. The EPR vendors would get about 50% of the stipulated development cost of the project. The package included about 3 million euros.

Some sort of coordination with the ePrescription project was expected, as the electronic prescription was considered the most significant input to the database. The Core EPR was to be used in several different health care institutions: hospitals, home care services, nursing homes, emergency wards and GP practices. This implied that the medication information had to be presented in a proper and adapted way in each institution.

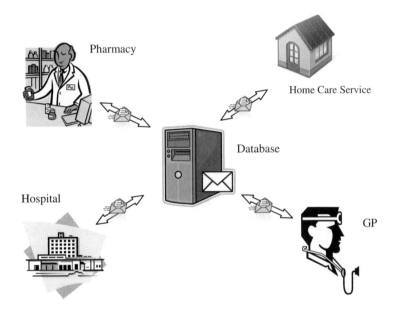

Fig. 3. Core EPR concept

However, the first version of ePrescription did not split up the information elements in such a way that the information could be presented differently to the hospital and to the home care service. As a result, the progress in the Core ERP was slowed down until the ePrescription team drew up new specifications in version two.

The core EPR consisted of two main parts: (1) a database and (2) integrated EPRs that read and write information into the database. A high-level requirement specification was made in the beginning of the project. This was based on user participation and was mainly written by the Norwegian standardization company, KITH. While interested in the project, the vendors had concerns about whether they would be fully funded and whether they had the development resources available within the specified time limit. As they saw it, there was little potential for making money from the new functionality:

This might be a good service, but I can't imagine that our doctors are willing to pay for this. [EPR vendor]

Due to feedback, the project had to find a source of finance so that the EPR vendors could get payed for their effort. This process lasted for more than a year.

Basically, the project team wanted to include as few EPR vendors as possible, but felt forced to include all the vendors and to produce a national solution because funding from Innovation Norway was not available otherwise.

The development of the Core EPR database was assigned to ProfDoc – the largest EPR vendor in the GP market. The contract was signed based on the preliminary specification. By the end of 2006, the project had raised funding for 50% of the development that the EPR vendors needed to do in order to adapt the EPRs to the database. Most of the other vendors also signed a contract. User workshops and technical workshops were arranged and the specifications were further developed. This process was difficult for the EPR vendors.

We give input to the specification all the time, but we don't receive any feedback. We just hear from the project that "yes, we have included it in the specification", but we don't know which part of our input has been taken into account. We have to wait until the next meeting and read the documents that are sent to us in connection with it, and see if our input is taken into account. [EPR vendor1]

It seems like those who work with the specification and the EPR vendors live in two separate worlds [...] when we get an answer to a question, it is often on a level that is useless to us. [EPR vendor2]

None of the EPR vendors started to make adaptations in their systems for the Core EPR. The vendor that developed the database delivered it and installed it in the local area network at the municipality and claimed that it was according to specifications. The municipality claimed that they had not received sufficient documentation together with the database.

If they don't understand it, then it is because they don't understand their own project – and that is a bit curious! [EPR vendor]

The project made no progress and was terminated in 2009 without achieving any kind of testing.

5 Discussion

5.1 Escalation and Interdependencies

In this section, we analyse how national projects coordinated by the authorities tend to escalate, overlap with each other, and increasingly become mutually interdependent [18], which curbs progress and may ultimately cause failure. From an ANT perspective, we consider each of the projects as a growing network due to an increasing number of actors with regard to participants, details on requirement specifications, funding and the like [19, 20].

In its simplest form, the authorities wanted electronic prescription to document use of medicine and to control the public financing aspects of medication distribution. In the first round, this implied giving preference to the requirement specification from the National Insurance Administration and the pharmacies. However, this was not in line with the interests of the physicians' representatives. They argued that the doctors were an essential part of the service and if the functionality for physicians was not included now, it would probably take many years to achieve anything that worked, if this was possible at all. Since the requirement specification was more or less pre-specified, they argued very strongly in favour of having the physicians' functionality added. Otherwise, the risk existed that by the time the project period was complete, nothing would be developed for them and the funding would be spent.

As a result, during the project period the requirements from the hospitals and the GP practices were also included. When the project management re-designed the specifications, all actors had their say, and the project agreed on a solution that worked for everybody. However, keeping everybody satisfied resulted in an enormous escalation of the requirement specification.

In the Core EPR, lack of funding caused the escalation. Initially, the project team wanted to test a simple medication database and integrate a few EPR systems, but the project was forced to include all the EPR vendors to obtain sufficient funding. The authorities had funded only the part of the project that included project costs for the public staff of the project. In turn, much of this funding was used to find funding sources for the EPR vendors. Finally, after nearly a year, funding was granted from Innovation Norway – a governmental funding institute that stimulates nationwide industrial development. In this process, the project grew from a small local project into a project with national dimensions.

Basically we wanted to develop a small Core EPR between only three systems, but due to the pressure we were forced to have a national focus – and then everybody had to be included. [Project manager, Core EPR]

In ELIN-k, they experienced that the specifications needed substantial work in order to fit into the workflow in the three different institutions.

Since the projects concerned medication, there were overlapping functionalities between them. Therefore, the vendors wanted to use the same data model for medication information in all the three projects. While this was an obvious strategy for the vendors, it tightened the dependencies between the projects. Since the ePrescription was to contain all active prescriptions for a limited time span and the Core EPR was to contain the complete medication regime for a limited patient group, this implied that the Core EPR project had to wait until the ePrescription definitions were ready. Unfortunately, the first draft of the electronic prescription was not in a data format that the Core EPR could use, causing a new delay in the Core EPR project. Even in the relatively simple ELIN-k project, the lack of a defined medication message hampered the progress. The participants argued that the project was dependent on the specifications defined in both ePrescription and the Core EPR. The ELIN-k project considered it was best to wait for the definition from the ePrescription rather than defining anything themselves, in turn potentially adding some constraints to the ePrescription project. This situation was enforced because ePrescription was recognized as having more influence and status than the other two projects and was run directly by the Directorate.

Furthermore, since all the projects had signed an agreement with the same EPR vendor, a serious resource dependency emerged. The vendor had signed up with all the projects because it felt the pressure of being the largest vendor in the GP practice market (70–80% of the market), and knowing that progress was dependent on them. However, as the amount of development work was underestimated, the vendor became a bottleneck in the process. Even worse, the ePrescription solution could not be integrated with the vendor's EPR version because of the new data structure. As the vendor was in the middle of redesigning its EPR, it was not willing to adapt the old EPR version to the ePrescription format. Instead, most of the vendor's resources were allocated to the task of redesigning its EPR software, causing even more delays.

5.2 Translating Top-Down Requirements into Practical Work

Large-scale integration projects in healthcare need coordination between the different stakeholders and their associated information systems. As this is recognized as a complex task, often subject to delays, it is a common perception that the authorities should impose more governance to ensure that the projects are run more predictably [1]. This was also a key theme at the Norwegian national HelsIT conference 2008 [27]. Many representatives from the healthcare institutions called for more interventions from the authorities regarding stricter project plans, well-defined requirement specifications, fixed completion dates and complete standardization formats up front.

In contrast, we believe that more governance and having everything settled up front may be the wrong strategy. Lessons learned from many studies on information infrastructures indicate how these systems emerge gradually and never top-down [17]. Many translations, adaptations, and negotiations need to be done at a practical level where many heterogeneous stakeholders are involved [20 p 36]. Predefined specifications fit poorly with this:

It is not possible to start some kind of development based on the specification [in one of the three projects] - we must rewrite the whole damn thing. It is on such a theoretical level that all of it needs to be explained in a practical frame. [EPR vendor]

We get these projects that are kind of agile processes where we receive a requirement specification that is not finished – then we work with it continuously, but then also the time schedule is shifted all the time because when the requirement specifications are not frozen – you accept modifications and then you must modify the final date. [...] And that is the problem with public projects. They have specified a final date and at the same time put up an agile process that will change on the way. [EPR vendor]

Accordingly, a major problem is that the authorities expect the vendors to sign up on development contracts that have a fixed closing date and a limited budget, but still expect an agile and dynamic development process.

The paradoxical consequence is that the vendors also end up demanding more pre-specifications from the authorities to avoid losing money on emerging demands from the users and unforeseen circumstances. Consider how the vendors did not want to start developing anything in the ePrescription project until a detailed requirement specification was on the table. Consequently, the stakeholders take part in and contribute to a self-reinforcing process where everybody is demanding more detailed requirement specifications up front, which in turn causes more delays, keeping the spiral going. Ultimately, in the ePrescription project the vendor maintained that it received funding for only 20–25 % of its work.

This unfortunate process is bound to continue when the new system is put into real use. While the vendors deliver in accordance with high-level requirement specifications, the software has not really been tested. So instead of having a stepwise negotiation process [20] for requirements between vendors and users, the system – in accordance with high-level requirements – is pushed onto the users. The probability of failure then increases dramatically, which was eventually the case in the ePrescription project.

5.3 Uneven Distribution of Costs and Benefits

An essential part of ANT is how actors are associated with and manoeuvre in accordance with their interests [19, 20]. In this light, each actor will pay attention to the consequences of the integration effort, and may easily ask: "What is the benefit, and what is the cost for me?" Along these lines, an uneven distribution of the costs and benefits for different user groups may explain failure.

In the ePrescription project, the most obvious benefits were associated with the authorities' need for control over the financial aspects of the medication distribution. In the Core EPR project, the benefits were found in nursing homes and the home care service. Accordingly, the benefits were not found directly among those who generated medication information, namely the physicians. They tended to see the new integrations as a cost. At least, this was not something the GPs would pay for or prioritize compared to other pressing tasks. In comparison, the success in the ELIN-k project may partly be ascribed to the municipality sector's willingness to put some money on the table to achieve integration with EPRs in the GP practice and hospitals.

What is surprising, then, is that many of the large integration projects are promoted as a joint effort among stakeholders who are only moderately interested in the project. Even if the government provides some limited start-up funding, this seems to be asking for trouble:

There is very little willingness in the Norwegian administration [...] to finance public joint initiatives via the state budget. We are supposed to follow the line principle, which means that it is those with needs who should take the responsibility. This has been a central principle in Norwegian administration and I believe that this principle has been like a nightmare for the governmental administration – when I look at what other countries have been willing to finance in governmental projects. [Member of the Directorate of Health]

The principle of matching costs to needs entailed identifying those actors who had most to gain from this project. Interestingly, in this case it is basically the Norwegian administration itself that has most to gain. Hence, in accordance with its own principle of weighing the benefits against the costs [23, 24], it should take on more of the economic burden of the project. If not, the burden of taking on the costs of developing the integrations easily becomes a joint effort that very few actors are interested in. Specifically, in the ePrescription and Core EPR project, the costs spilled over to the EPR vendors in the latter project, the vendor received only 0.6 % of a budget of 30 million euros.

Consequently, since the income is low and the new integrations do not do much for the vendors' market share, they do not see much benefit in the process. Accordingly, when vendors need to prioritize between different development tasks, it should not come as a surprise that they give preference to assignments from their primary customers, which ensure a steady cash flow. This is beneficial for both the customers and the vendors who appear as allies in these matters [20]. However, at the same time this puts the vendors in the unfortunate position of being regarded as the core reason for the major delays in these projects. A member of the Health Directorate expressed deep concern:

All the projects that I am concerned with in any way report delays due to (EPR) vendors, all of them - all of them! [Member of the Directorate of Health]

However, as we have emphasized, the problem is more complicated; the modest interest among end-users and the vendors combined with the government's funding policy may cause the project to drift off course.

6 Conclusions

In this study, we found that it is extremely difficult to manage large-scale projects top-down on a relatively detailed level, exercising a high degree of control. Information and workflow are so enmeshed in each other that it requires much effort and detailed insight to deal with the challenges as they emerge during the project phases. Organizing development within traditional project management - with a high degree of requirement specifications up front with pre-specified completion dates - creates the danger that every stakeholder will demand to have their interests inscribed in the requirement specification from the outset. Based on the study, we draw the following conclusions:

Firstly, we believe that development in inter-organizational settings requires a stepwise approach with substantial influence by (real) users. Early cooperation between developers and users will result in detailed specifications and will make the users able to understand the service that is being developed. A service that is developed in close cooperation with users will encourage the users to adopt the solution if it adds value to their work and is thus a service that the users will be willing to pay for.

Secondly, if the users are not willing to commit in early development phases, a model that is almost fully funded might be necessary to enable significant progress. Basically, this will also reflect the fact that the authorities are the driving force behind the required new functionalities. Alternatively, the authorities could channel funding via the users in order to convince the vendors prior to the authorities' request. The reason for this is that the vendors are more loyal to their customers than to the authorities because their users give them a stable income.

Thirdly, scientific studies on national inter-organizational services seem to be lacking. The importance of such studies will increase as demands for inter-organizational collaboration increase, in healthcare as well as in other areas. We suggest that new projects focusing on new inter-organizational ICT services should be financed with earmarked research money - focusing on project processes. It is important that these funds are given to research groups that study several projects in order to build up a substantial body of knowledge. The research funding must be grounded among the participants in the projects, in order to achieve access to the various actors.

References

1. Norwegian Ministries of Health Social Affairs: Te@mwork 2007 - Implementation Plan (2006),
   http://www.helsedirektoratet.no/vp/multimedia/archive/00017/IS-1433E_17193a.pdf
2. Swedish Social Departement. National ICT strategy (2009),
   http://www.regeringen.se/content/1/c6/12/47/97/9af34a6e.pdf
3. Danish National Strategy, Digitalisation of the Danish Healthcare Service (2007),
   http://www.sdsd.dk/~/media/Files/Strategi/Strategy_english.ashx
4. UK Department of Health. Delivering 21st Century IT Support for the NHS (2001),
   http://www.connectingforhealth.nhs.uk/resources/policyandguidance/delivery_21_century_IT.pdf
5. Parliamentary Office of Science and Technology. New NHS IT (2004),
   http://www.parliament.uk/documents/upload/POSTpn214.pdf
6. Ham, C.: Integrating NHS Care: Lessons from the Frontline (2008),
   http://www.nuffieldtrust.org.uk/ecomm/files/Integrating_NHS_Care.pdf
7. Roos, A.d.: Implementing an electronic health record in the Netherlands: pitfalls and challenges (2007),
   http://albertderoos.nl/pdf/Implementing%20an%20electronic%20health%20record%20in%20NL.pdf
8. Auditor General Norway. Evaluation on ICT in hospitals and electronic interaction in the health service (2008),
   http://www.riksrevisjonen.no/SiteCollectionDocuments/Dokumentbasen/Dokument3/2007-2008/Dok_3_7_2007_2008.pdf
9. Norwegian Health Directhorate. Teamwork 2.0 (2008),
   http://www.helsedirektoratet.no/vp/multimedia/archive/00047/Samspill_2_0_-strate_47719a.pdf
10. Gaventa, J.: Triumph, deficit or contestation?: deepening the "deepening democracy" debate., Brighton, UK, IDS (2006)
11. Bowker, G., Star, S.L.: Sorting things out: classification and its consequenses. Inside technology. MIT Press, Cambridge (2000)
12. Nebeker, J., Barach, P., Samore, M.: Clarifying adverse drug events: a clinician's guide to terminology, documentation, and reporting. Annals of internal medicine 140(10), 795 (2004)
13. Buajordet, I., Ebbesen, J., Erikssen, J., Brors, O., Hilberg, T.: Fatal adverse drug events: the paradox of drug treatment. Journal of internal medicine 250(4), 327–341 (2001)
14. Hyppönen, H., Salmivalli, L., Suomi, R.: Organizing for a national infrastructure project: the case of the Finnish electronic prescription (2005)
15. Fleming, N.: Bill for hi-tech NHS soars to £20 billion (2004),
    http://www.telegraph.co.uk/news/uknews/1473927/Bill-for-hi-tech-NHS-soars-to-20-billion.html
16. Ellingsen, G., Monteiro, E.: Big is beautiful:electronic patient records in Norwegian hospitals 1980-2001. Methods Inf. Med. 42, 366–370 (2003)
17. Star, S.L., Ruhleder, K.: Steps Toward an Ecology of Infrastructure: Design and Access for Large Information Spaces. Information Systems Research 7, 111–133 (1996)

18. Perrow, C.: Complexity, coupling and catastrophe, in Normal accidents, pp. 62–100. P.U. Press (ed.) (1984)
19. Latour, B.: Science in Action. Harvard University Press, Cambridge (1987)
20. Latour, B.: Pandora's Hope. Essays on the Reality of Science Studies. Harvard University press, Cambridge (1999)
21. Davenport, T.: Process innovation: reengineering work through information technology. Harvard Business School Pr., USA (1993)
22. Boudreau, M., Robey, D.: Enacting integrated information technology: A human agency perspective. Organization Science 16(1), 3–18 (2005)
23. Rolland, K., Monteiro, E.: Balancing the Local and the Global in Infrastructural Information Systems. The Information Society 18, 87–100 (2002)
24. Berg, M., Goorman, E.: The contextual nature of medical information. International Journal of Medical Informatics 56, 51–60 (1999)
25. Walsham, G.: Interpreting information systems in organizations. John Wiley & Sons, Inc., New York (1993)
26. Health Directorate Norway. Messages Status pr 1 (January 2010), http://www.helsedirektoratet.no/vp/multimedia/archive/00282/Rapportering_pr__1__282759a.pdf
27. KITH NTNU. HelsIT 2008 (2008), http://www.kith.no/templates/kith_WebPage____2164.aspx

Bootstrapping Revisited: Opening the Black Box of Organizational Implementation

Espen Skorve and Margunn Aanestad

University of Oslo, Dep. of Informatics. P.O. Box 1080 Blindern, N-0316 Oslo, Norway
{espen.skorve,margunn}@ifi.uio.no

Abstract. This paper contributes to the literature on implementation strategies for enterprise information systems. Based on a study of the implementation of a hospital wide clinical information system in a major Norwegian hospital, we discuss various dimensions along which implementation strategies can be adapted. We utilize the concept of *bootstrapping* which was introduced to the IS field in the context of design and implementation of information infrastructures. Applied to the context of enterprise information system implementation, it addresses the challenges in dealing with organizational diversity.

1 Introduction

Challenges related to organizational implementation of information systems has been a core research topic in the IS field since its inception. Researchers discovered early on that reality deviated from simplistic models of deployment, and involved a mixture of organizational and technical change. Keen [1] claimed that IS development and implementation was a strongly political affair, often overshadowing the technical issues. He described strategies of counter implementation where different actors tried to prevent disruption of existing status quo. Users' resistance as explanation for implementation failure was also a focus in Markus' seminal paper [2]. However, she found simplistic explanations, such as inadequate designs or users' subjective reasons for resistance insufficient, and advocated the interplay between specific system features and aspects of the organizational context as the major mechanism behind implementation challenges. Such multi-factor interaction models have also been proposed by others. Leonard-Barton described implementation as a process of mutual adaption of technology and organization [3]. Through iterative 'cycles of adaptation', the initial misalignment of technology and user environment could be reduced. Understanding change as gradual and iterative alignment has resonated in other studies [4][5], and improvisational models have been introduced [6][7][8]. With improvisation comes the need to flexibly adapt implementation strategies to the context and to the emerging results from implementation activities.

Improvising implies the ability to change and adapt. This requires the ability to acknowledge *differences*; both with respect to the organizational context and the technology, as well as the availability of differentiated strategies. Based on a qualitative longitudinal study of the implementation of a hospital wide patient information system, we investigate available repertoires of implementation strategies as well as selection criteria as resources for improvisational implementation. We focus on the need for differentiated implementation strategies and seek to formulate insights into the diversity of organizational IS implementations. That this represents particular challenges in healthcare is well known [9][10][11], especially when conventional waterfall or big bang implementation approaches are applied in the context of strategic projects [12]. As professional bureaucracies, hospitals offer a considerable autonomy to its employees. Keen thus argued that "the change process must be explicitly managed" [1] in the context of organizational pluralism, which he regarded a major cause of inertia and subsequent implementation failure. While the hospital in our case already had an electronic patient record (and multiple other ISs) implemented, the new system was supposed to replace the paper based medical charts as the last part of a complete digital patient information infrastructure. Thus the system would reach into core clinical practices more profoundly than the EPR, which is primarily used for documentation purposes. As a hospital wide infrastructure, the implementation was considered of great strategic significance.

After a selective review of relevant research, including contributions addressing implementation of enterprise information systems, groupware and networked technologies in healthcare, we introduce bootstrapping as an analytical lens on differentiated implementation strategies. Next we account for our approach and present the case. The analysis unpacks the details of differentiated implementation strategies, while the discussion addresses our application and expansion of bootstrapping as an analytical tool. We conclude with some remarks on what it takes to design and deploy an effective 'organizational bootstrapper'.

2 Related Research

Enterprise-wide systems pose specific challenges in addition to general implementation challenges: These are on one hand related to the need to balance overall standardization with local needs, and on the other hand the expected and wished-for, but difficult reengineering of the organization. This tends to 'mess up' linear strategies of deployment. In the following section we present studies that describe adjustments and variations in strategy as a result of these challenges.

Three decades ago Keen, Bronsema and Zuboff [13] studied the development and implementation of enterprise-wide systems in a multinational corporation. They described several changes in strategy, in pace and in focus. The project managers changed their strategy from 'parachuting (i.e. merely 'dropping' the code in the local branches), to 'acculturation', which was geared towards creating local competency and ownership. "Parachuting is a naïve strategy; it is gradually abandoned under the pressure of experience" [13]. Similarly the project's pace was adjusted. Initially the management pursued a 'crash' pace (rolling out as quickly as possible), but were forced to switch to a 'filter' pace, where the progress followed the organization's capacity to assimilate changes. In parallel, the project focus shifted from techno-centric to organizational.

Choice of implementation strategy was also a core issue in Markus et al.' [14] discussion of challenges that face implementation of multi-site enterprise systems. They reviewed and discussed five different strategy constellations where balancing central control and local autonomy was the central issue, and where risks and benefits differed. Similar concerns were also central to Hertzum [15], who described three generic types of implementation strategies and their benefits and risks. With the *big bang* strategy, a system is released to all customers simultaneously. This is often technically simpler, as it does not require a transition period, but it is risky. With the *case-based* release strategy, a few, straightforward cases will be initially handled by the new system. The proportion of work handled by the new system gradually increases until the switch is complete. This approach requires parallel facilities, and as such it can be costly and confusing for users. The third approach Hertzum called the *region-wide* release. Here a subset of the users (e.g. geographically bounded) start using the new system. This limits potential problems to fewer users and allows easier training. However, it may be difficult to find regionally confined cases, so transition mechanisms between the two systems may be needed.

Some researchers have advocated that such phased, partial and incremental strategies are useful because they allow learning along the implementation trajectory. This argument was proposed by Robey et al. [16], who claimed that learning is a core challenge in ERP implementation. Partial and piecemeal adoption facilitates learning processes in the organization, as it helps companies spread the learning process over time. This allows project participants and users the time to assimilate the new work situation and recover from the stress and strain of implementation. Robey et al. described how firms that used such an incremental strategy deployed different tactics. Some implemented the system in one site at a time, others limited the number of modules to implement, or used parallel systems, while other chose to upgrade the package in small increments. These alternative strategies for implementation were seen as results of the learning process; stimulated by the tension between old and new knowledge.

Nordheim and Päivärinta [17] studied enterprise-wide knowledge management systems, and found that learning in the KM context happened in more areas and for more reasons than identified by Robey et al in their case study on ERP systems [16]. However, they also argued that "adoption and adaptation of immature technology may require more learning and flexibility for emergent project coordination than adaptation of mature technology with available benchmarks, predictable benefits, and experiences from other enterprises."[17]. This argument hints to the openness of the system, an issue which has been addressed e.g. by Scheepers [18]. Customizable systems that are highly malleable and can be configured for many purposes need to tackle divergent and unique needs of different user communities. Scheepers argued that this calls for a richer conceptual framework for understanding challenges of implementation. With customizable systems one cannot assume a homogeneous internal 'user market'. Consequently a useful implementation strategy would be to subdivide the market into more homogeneous segments. This strategy would allow a focus on various users' unique attributes (their needs and potential profitability) and as such help prioritization during implementation.

Such considerations of the users, their interests and needs, were also addressed by researchers studying groupware adoption. As largely voluntary and novel tools, groupware applications were vulnerable to non-adoption. The debate between Grudin [19], Markus and Conolly [20] and Grudin and Palen [21] provided explanations for this phenomenon. The researchers identified several social mechanisms that encouraged or mitigated users' adoption of groupware. These technologies were prone to 'collective action dilemmas', as benefits were not produced by the system alone, but hinged on the proper usage and commitment of other users. The concept of 'critical mass' represented the number of users necessary for these shared applications to be perceived as valuable.

From this brief review of selected literature from the vast area of implementation studies, we can indicate some core aspects: Different implementation strategies have different benefits, costs and risks. Learning is crucial, both about the application and its 'fit' with the organization, where organizational pluralism and user heterogeneity is a core factor. While the literature indicates the importance of these factors, they do not provide us with specific selection criteria for how to approach implementation, where and how to start, which users to begin with etc. Thus we introduce the concept of bootstrapping.

2.1 Bootstrapping Infrastructural Technologies

The concept of bootstrapping [22][23] was proposed to address start-up challenges related to introduction of new networked communication technologies in healthcare contexts. The argument was that these technologies, similar to groupware applications, require a rather large user base for the effects to be realized. Initially there are no benefits to be found for the prospective users, and the network must be 'bootstrapped' in order to achieve critical mass. The bootstrapping algorithm offers a way to create that critical mass when use cannot be formally mandated or economically subsidized. At the core of the algorithm lies the recognition that users are different, as are use areas, organizations, situations and technologies. A mindful sorting of users, applications and technologies can help implementers to identify a few users that may gain benefits even without a large network. The sequence of introducing new users, applications and technologies need to be carefully scrutinized, so that each step is sustainable in its own right in terms of costs and benefits. This way, pragmatic choices of starting point and sequence of expansion may allow a network to reach the point where self-reinforcing mechanisms kicks in to drive further growth. In its initial form [22] the algorithm was presented like this:

"1. Start by design the first, simplest, cheapest solution we can imagine and which satisfy the needs of the most motivated users in their least critical and simplest practices and which may be beneficial by supporting communication and collaboration between just a few users.
2. use the technology and repeat as long as possible: enrol more users
3. if possible: explore, identify and adopt more innovative (and beneficial) ways of using the solution, go to 2
4. use the solution in more critical tasks, go to 2
5. use the solution in more complex tasks, go to 2.
6. improve the solution so new tasks can be supported, go to 2"

While this formulation of bootstrapping primarily addresses the problem of *diffusion* – how to reach critical mass when use is optional – use of the system in our case was intended to become mandatory. Thus the focus here is on a different problem; more precisely that of designing an implementation strategy where a novel and undefined technology meets a complex organization. However, the algorithm's basic principles of sorting between different users and different applications are still relevant to the selection of starting point for the implementation. So is the way the algorithm encourages strategic thinking around further sequence of expansion. These are the issues we will explore in relation to our case study.

3 Background and Methods

The medical charts project is perceived as being of great strategic importance to the hospital: "Rikshospitalet is considering the digitizing of information as a core issue of its overall strategies [24]. When we say Digital Hospital, we mean that "all relevant information in the hospital is produced, distributed and used electronically"" [25]. The medical charts are considered the last third of a complete patient information infrastructure, and digitizing the charts is thus imperative to the overall hospital strategy. But the medical charts are equally important at operational level; tightly entangled as they are in everyday (and often critical) clinical practices: "We can't manage for five minutes without the medical charts. Then the patient would be dead – many would die if we didn't have this information. So this is essential – that it works" (nurse). The charts provide (in a blink for a trained eye) an instant overview of the patient's current condition as well as the direction in which it is evolving.

The fieldwork from which the data presented here is derived started ultimo 2007, and is still ongoing. Primary sources of information include interviews with members of the project group, clinicians directly involved in or influenced by the project as well as other (more or less peripheral) stakeholders. Eleven semi structured interviews have been conducted; all recorded and transcribed. A second source of information has been field notes from participant observation in project group meetings as well as in the clinic. Ten such sessions have been conducted, most of them in relation to project group activities. Our third source of information has been relevant documents and correspondence. Including the project's requirements specification, the internal evaluation of the pilot as well as strategic documents from different levels, this amounts to several hundred pages of written material.

As our study initially was of a very exploratory nature, most 'focal points' were tentative and many of them were rejected as patterns of more interesting topics started to emerge from our material. One such topic was what we perceived as the contours of fundamentally different approaches to initial phases of the implementation, based on the participants own reflections on the process. The analysis is based on an interpretive approach [26]. Our focus has thus been on understanding the participants' own perceptions of issues relevant to how the implementation could and should have been initiated, much in line with the hermeneutic principles suggested by Klein and Myers [27]. Special attention has been paid to statements and observations that highlight the consequences of selected approaches, as well as what could and should have been done differently. This has enabled us to distinguish and differentiate three different approaches and their tradeoffs, as shown in our analysis.

While the concept of 'bootstrapping' initially played the role of a 'sensitizing devise' [26], shaping the direction in how we approached our empirical material, it also came to be a tool applied in our analysis.

4 Implementing the Medical Charts System: Visions Face Reality

The pilot is the first real encounter between visions and clinical reality. During the pilot in the thorax surgical department (ultimo 2006), the discrepancy between visions and reality became a problem that eventually led to a premature termination of the pilot. In the following account we describe the challenges that were encountered, how they were handled, and the subsequent adaptations of implementation strategies.

4.1 Visions of Efficiency Meet Complexity

The system should automatically harvest data from medical equipment, relieving the nurses from manually filling the paper chart. It turned out, however, that this involved more than simply transferring data from the equipment to the medical chart; it required professional discretion and knowledge of contextual factors. For instance, blood pressure is measured in catheters also used to draw blood samples or give intravenous fluids. As fluids must be infused with a pressure exceeding the patient's blood pressure, this has a direct effect on blood pressure measurements at the catheter. When manually registering pressures, the nurse would therefore first stop the infusion, then read the value, before starting the infusion again. MetaVision, however, harvested these values continuously, regardless of any external influences. Thus most values recorded in MetaVision were erroneous. The nurse could choose to leave the chart with a majority of faulty entries, or to manually delete all but the samples where the infusion was turned off. Doing this, however, was a lot more time consuming than manually recording the information:

"The rule was that I should zero out these pressures in MetaVision. Then I had to frame the interval with erroneous pressures, and then delete it, or mark it as invalid. Then it would disappear from the screen. That was fair enough, I guess. But I had to do it *three* times – for systolic blood pressure, mid blood pressure and diastolic blood pressure. So it is three processes every time, adding up to far more manual work in recording blood pressures than we ever had to do with pen and paper" (nurse).

The doctor's prescription of medication, an activity that is performed in seconds or minutes on the paper charts, was also subject to radical changes:

"Before we started using MetaVision, it took me 10-12 minutes to prescribe all medications and remove the thorax drain for the two post-operative patients. Then I had also evaluated the patients; can they be moved to the in-patient ward, or must they stay one more day. After we started to use MetaVision I spend 50 minutes on the same procedure" (surgeon).

Bootstrapping Revisited: Opening the Black Box of Organizational Implementation 117

The increased time consumption was attributed to the transition from free text to structured data: "When you prescribe in the paper chart, you do so in free text. If you say to [those that make electronic charts] that I want to prescribe in free text, they respond that; no, no, no – that is not possible. A prescription must consist of data elements" (surgeon). The result was that for every entry in the list of medication, the doctor had to traverse multiple levels in MetaVision's menus, first to find the correct medication – then to find the right dosage for every time the medication was to be administered. "And that places me in a dilemma. I already come to work half an hour before I am supposed to. Am I now supposed to come *an hour* earlier, just because my employer has decided that we must have a computer system that currently doesn't work well enough?" (surgeon).

4.2 Quality of Documentation and Patient Care

MetaVision's lack of ability to distinguish correct from erroneous measurements had consequences for the quality of information crucial to clinical decisions. And when the basis for making such decisions is degraded, the decision making processes and ultimately, the quality of patient care is at risk. As a reduction in 'production' was not acceptable to the management, and a reduction in care for each individual patient was unacceptable to the clinicians, they decided to maintain the old paper charts in parallel with MetaVision, and base all decisions on them instead.

The changes in medication procedures imposed by the new system and a subsequent workaround for anesthesia also surfaced a discrepancy in the view on this between surgeons and anesthetists that had not previously been an issue:

"What is done in MetaVision when the patient comes from the OR is that the anesthesia doctors prescribe standard packages, already entered in the system. Then you get a list of fluids and medications that can be administered to the patient whenever needed. They just load a post op package, and ta-da, you have a 100 medications that the nurses can administer whenever needed. Then I ask myself; what are then the quality gains of switching to an electronic charts system?" (surgeon).

The significant increase in time consumption required for prescriptions also had consequences for the quality of information, patient care and working conditions, especially in relation to the doctors' morning-round:

"Some of the younger doctors spent an hour extra every morning because it took so much longer to do the prescriptions. That put us in a time squeeze. Some of the doctors doing the morning-round were due for surgery later. They had two choices; they could leave the sedated patient waiting in the OR for half an hour, or they could skip the prescription of medication. They chose the latter. When they left before doing the prescriptions, we nurses didn't have the written prescriptions needed for us to effectuate them. So we only administered what we were *certain* the patients should get. The rest was put on hold. The result was that patients who needed important medications at 9-10 didn't get them until 12-1-2. And the timing is critical, so the doctors became mad that we hadn't given the medication at the correct time" (nurse).

4.3 Visions of Integration Meet Local Terminology

The visions of cross context integration through increased information sharing were not realized in the pilot, much due to insufficient information quality. However, the pilot uncovered another challenge related to this integration – standardization of terminology. Naming the parameters for which data was to be harvested in MetaVision was a huge (and initially underestimated) challenge:

"We knew what parameters we needed. We needed heart rate, we needed blood pressure – systolic and all that. We just made a bunch of them. Then we reached a point where we realized that this was not the way we could do it. We had to be more systematic. A parameter could not be used more than once – for instance bleeding on the drain; if we named that *drain*, we also had a *process* called drain" (nurse).

This problem was partly related to variations in the clinical terminology being used in different contexts: "In regular hospital language we are pretty sloppy. One and the same word can mean different things, depending on context. That works fine, as long as all parties understand what it is about. But when this is on a PC, it has to be clear and unambiguous terms that can be understood by everyone" (nurse). This led to the establishing of a project-within-the-project, aiming at standardizing terminology across the hospital.

4.4 Adaptations, Learning and Continuation

It was commonly acknowledged that the project was entering territory unknown to the vendor as well. Thus the software was (and still is) continuously being revised and released in new versions to accommodate Norwegian legislation, fix bugs and adjust and add functionality. A new graphical interface layer has been developed for the medication module to 'imitate' free-text entries by hiding the structured data elements behind an auto-text search engine. Similarly, data automatically harvested from the medical equipment is no longer considered valid until manually approved; thus eliminating the need for deleting erroneous entries.

Though not primarily intended as such, the pilot thus served as a learning opportunity for the whole project organization. A considerable self reflection in the project group after the pilot resulted in a thorough evaluation report. This, combined with other learning experiences from the pilot, led to a radical change in strategy for the continuation of the project – a change that appears to have had significant impact on the transition from a pilot few were happy with to an implementation that currently seems to have wide support in the clinic.

So what did they learn, and what impact did this have on the continuation of the project? We discovered that the answer depended on who we asked. Users from the thorax pilot advocated different approaches than those suggested by users in anesthesia, who were involved in the next phase. In the following sections we discuss how both of these contemplations offer interesting insights on learning and improvising in implementation strategies.

4.5 Experience before Dependency (The Thorax Approach)

Though the project as such was decided to proceed in a stepwise manner, the pilot in the thorax department was intended as a big bang implementation, covering all patients in all units from day one. Some of the participants were skeptical to this approach from the start, and in hindsight most involved parties seem to agree on this: "And the way this was implemented; everything was suddenly supposed to be completed in *one* morning, and we were supposed to start with a lot of patients simultaneously. I believe it would have been better to start off more carefully – for instance with a single patient" (nurse).

"I think the idea of starting with a narrow, but long chain was good. I don't think I would have rejected that again. I believe that would have been smart – to follow one or two patients all the way through; these are the *MetaVision patients*" (head of department). The *long, narrow chain* refers to two different but related aspects of the implementation. *Long* is about the fact that the pilot was supposed to cover all units of the department. This was perceived as necessary in order to gain experience with how the system would support the transfer of patients and information between different units and practices. *Narrow* concerns the number of patients for whom the new system was used, thus reducing the degree of dependency on the system.

4.6 Simplicity before Complexity (The Anesthesia Approach)

The choice of thorax as venue for the pilot was based on the department's status as technology-intensive and the assumption that if it could be done there, it would be easy to include the rest of the hospital. In hindsight this decision was challenged, both by the clinicians and in the project group: "We were not the right place to start. They should have gone for a simple inpatient ward if that was what they wanted to develop an application for. It became too much with our postoperative children, intermediary, reception, department patient in for evaluation or control – it was too many different groups of patients" (nurse).

Though the pilot was limited to the thorax department, it included actors from other departments, like for instance anesthesia, who operates across *all* surgical units of the hospital. Thus, participants from this department made their own experiences with and reflections on the project and the system:

"Had I known then what I know *now*, I would have put my foot down *thoroughly* when we started, and said that – we will do this, but we will start with *anesthesia*. We will start with an anesthesia record, and replace the current anesthesia charts. It's a limited area – it is a solvable task. Then we use all resources on making *that* good and correctly implemented. With thorough education and such, I am convinced we would have avoided a lot of problems. […] Start with a limited area – and intensive care is a lot more complex activity than anesthesia" (head of anesthesia).

After prematurely ending the pilot at thorax, focus was shifted towards creating a working solution for anesthesia before proceeding to other departments. The initial assumption about thorax that *if we can make it there, we can make it anywhere* might have been correct. The problem was that they *couldn't make it there* – at least not based on the current software and approach.

"So we decided to postpone intensive care – and that was smart. That is what we should have done from the start. To focus on *one* thing... [...] We chose to start with anesthesia. That was smart. It is a lot easier to make an anesthesia application than an intensive care application" (head of anesthesia). The technical functionality is not really that different, but the intensity and complexity of its use and use situation *is*. Thus the functional requirements are harder to meet in intensive care than in anesthesia, even though most of the underlying functionality is overlapping. This shift in strategy – from *complexity first* to *simplicity first* – has resulted in an implementation of MetaVision that today is working well for anesthesia; the paper charts have been replaced in all operating rooms and in the post operative rooms. Focus is currently on including the intensive care units as well.

4.7 Current Status

Initially, the project had rather extreme expectations to its progress. The first project manager withdrew partly due to what he considered unrealistic time frames. In hindsight his worries were well founded; deadlines have continuously been adjusted according to a growing awareness of the project's complexity, and strategies have been forced to prioritize *learning* over *immediate change*.

From doing the most *difficult* first, focus changed to doing the *simplest* first. The plan was to then build on what could be achieved through this. After what has to be characterized as a successful implementation in anesthesia, MetaVision was introduced in the children's intensive care unit. Here challenges related to intensive care reentered the picture, and it is interesting to note that issues initially perceived as problematic in this unit no longer seem to represent a problem. One example of this is the visual presentation where MetaVision requires them to traverse multiple tabs in order to assemble the same picture as the paper charts gave in a glance. When I ask whether it is MetaVision or the practitioners that have changed, the answer pointes to the users: "We have simply gotten used to it" (nurse).

Though the introduction of the new system did not proceed painlessly, the project seems to have induced a series of learning experiences that eventually *could* lead to a successful outcome. It is to this aspect of the process we now turn.

5 Bootstrapping Organizational Implementation

With an understanding of organizational implementation as "the activities that prepare organisations and users for a new system as well as the activities that prepare the system for the transition period during which it enters into operation and takes over from previous systems and artefacts" [15], we apply bootstrapping as our analytical lens when we compare the initial approach to the pilot with what we have called the thorax approach and the anesthesia approach. Our focus is on how these approaches differed, and in particular which learning potentials they offered, which issues each of them addressed as well as issues *not* addressed.

5.1 The Pilot Approach

While the overall project strategy was based on an incremental approach with the thorax surgical department as first step, the pilot was planned as a big bang [15] implementation. From day one (set according to plan rather than readiness) the new system should encompass *all* medical charts information for *all* patients in *all* units of the department. Combined with the ambitious timeframes this linear strategy [28] – based on the vendor's previous experiences from single unit implementations – generated a considerable complexity. The diversity in practices and functions the system would have to support increased both 'longitudinal' and 'latitudinal'. By 'longitudinal' diversity we point to the heterogeneity of practices in and functions of operating rooms, intensive care, post operative, intermediary and inpatient rooms. By 'latitudinal' diversity we point to the heterogeneity of the patients, their diagnoses and the current stage of their (often lifelong) patient trajectories. Within a tight timeframe the system would thus have to prove useful to a wide range of functions, of which most were critical to daily operations and existing practices in the department. Making all patients dependent on this also generated a considerable risk; if something went wrong or didn't work as intended (which often proved to be the case) this would be likely to affect *all* patients, increasing the consequences and scope of any 'rescue operation' or workaround. The 'cost' of the implementation for the clinicians was also multiplied in another dimension, as the extra workload associated with the implementation was on a per patient basis. Covering ten patients would thus generate five times as much extra work during the pilot than just covering two.

The sources of learning experiences were considerable, including issues such as bugs, logical flaws, use of terminology, support of multiple practices in multiple contexts, reuse of information and integration. However, the linear strategy was more focused on changing than on learning, as tends to be the case for strategies were most is planned ahead. Rather than building on the installed base, the pilot's primary aim was to change it. However, much due to its size and strength, it proved difficult to change. Rather than being a resource to the implementation, the installed base thus came to represent an obstacle. This conflict – between the new system and existing practices – finally led to a premature termination of the pilot.

5.2 The Thorax Approach

The alternative approach outlined in hindsight by clinicians in the thorax surgical department is based on changing *one* major dimension. The 'long, narrow chain' points explicitly to the number – and subsequent diversity – of patients initially covered by the new system. This is consistent with a case based approach [15] and also a more adaptive strategy [28], especially if the nurses' request for time to learn the system-in-use were accommodated. The new system would still encompass all units of the thorax surgical department, but not necessarily from day one, and not for all medical charts information for all patients. This would represent a reduction of *latitudinal* diversity and subsequent complexity, as well as a reduction of the risk and extra workload associated with the implementation.

The potential for learning would still have been considerable, as issues of bugs, logical flaws, use of terminology, support of multiple practices in multiple contexts, reuse of information and integration would remain. And with a stronger focus on learning rather than changing, the harvest of such learning experiences could have been supported more effectively. By not planning too much ahead, the installed based could have been mobilized into improving the system and the implementation process before generating too many dependencies and too much risk. The installed based would also have been smaller, and maybe less powerful, as an important aspect of the context's multiplicity no longer would have to be taken into consideration. Adapting to rather than opposing the installed base, as well as reducing the extra workload on the clinicians in this phase is likely to have improved the chances for learning and a more desirable outcome of the pilot. However, this approach was never implemented, as a third strategy gained precedence when the thorax surgical department chose to reject continued use of the system.

5.3 The Anesthesia Approach

When anesthesia was decided as venue for the next phase of the project, many of the following principles were implemented. As such this is based on the clinicians' reflections both on the pilot and the continuation of the project.

Even though the anesthesia section provides services to the entire hospital, it consists of *one* unit, and its functions are fairly homogenous. Starting there would thus be more in accordance with a regional approach [15] and also a more adaptive strategy [28]. While the new system would have to encompass all medical charts information for all patients, the scope would be limited to one single unit, and a less complex set of functions. With this approach, the *longitudinal* diversity, and subsequent complexity, would thus be considerably reduced.

The potential for learning would still be considerable, even though some dimensions would be lost. While issues of bugs, logical flaws, and to some extent use of terminology, would remain, issues related to the support of multiple practices in multiple contexts, reuse of information and integration would be less likely to surface. However, this decrease in the range of learning potentials could increase the impact of remaining learning experiences, as learning becomes more focused. As for the thorax approach, the installed based would have been smaller, easier to build upon and maybe less powerful, as its complexity would have been radically reduced. Thus adaptation rather than conflict would be more within reach here as well, with improved chances for learning and a more desirable outcome as final result.

5.4 The Multiple Facets of Bootstrapping

Table 1 summarizes tradeoffs associated with different approaches, and illustrates how bootstrapping is not about finding the one-right-way, but rather about identifying and selecting between different tradeoffs, considering both operational and strategic costs and gains.

Table 1. Approaches and tradeoffs

	Pilot	Thorax	Anesthesia
Strategic approach	Linear/Big bang	Adaptive/Case	Adaptive/Regional
Focus on	ICT	Risk	Complexity
Short term goal	Changing	Learning	Learning
Diversity	Longitudinal *and* latitudinal	Longitudinal	Latitudinal
Progress	Project driven	'Business' driven	'Business' driven
Installed base	Large	Medium	Small
Usability for	Everyone	All clinicians	All patients
Learning potential	A lot about a lot	A little about a lot	A lot about a little
Learning efficacy	Low	Medium	High
Learning issues	Everything and nothing (unfocused)	Bugs, logical flaws, use of terminology, support of multiple practices in multiple contexts, reuse of information and integration	Bugs, logical flaws, (to some extent) use of terminology, support of single practice in single context
Issues not covered		*Latitudinal* diversity and volume; suitability for multiple patient groups Dependability; *one* tool for *all* patients	*Longitudinal* diversity; support of multiple practices in multiple contexts, reuse of information and integration

The initial approach to the pilot held little resemblance with the bootstrapping algorithm, where fundamental principles include *building* on the installed base, starting 'small' and avoid applications where 'user investments' are not immediately rewarded with benefits for the users who invest their time and effort to make it work. *Some* of the fundamental principles of the bootstrapping algorithm would have been implemented through the thorax approach, as it could have reduced dependencies to a not-so-risky size, and used the experience gained to expand and enroll more users. *Other* fundamental principles would have been (and to a large extent were) implemented through the anesthesia approach, primarily through reduced complexity and subsequent functional ambitions.

6 Discussion

While bootstrapping in the original contribution was applied to the diffusion of new information infrastructures where the enrollment of users was primary focus, we have shown the concept's applicability to other contexts as well.

Recruiting users was not a central issue in the medical charts project. Rather the main purpose of initial exercises was to pave the way for a complete rollout by developing a working solution through customizing the system and 'adjusting' the clinical practices. The initial strategy did, for several reasons, not adequately support this. Applying the bootstrapping concept to our analysis helped us to contrast this and the alternative strategic approaches that emerged in the course of the project; what the distinguishing features were and what differences these (could have) made to the bootstrapping of a hospital wide implementation. Thus we have focused on the possibility of making the perceived benefits of enterprise systems exceed the pain of their implementation, and to reduce the amount – and undesirable consequences – of surprises they inevitably will produce. To achieve this we believe it is necessary to understand the design and implementation of 'organizational bootstrappers'.

A bootstrapper is 'the little' program that gets 'the big' program going. To most of us (software programmers included) the bootstrapper is a black box; we might know *what* it does, but have no idea of *how* it does it. This is partly due to the bootstrapper's close relationship to the hardware, of which most of us don't care as long as it works. However, for those that design and implement bootstrappers, there are certain requirements that must be met and certain things that must be known; either in advance or learned during the design and execution of this little program. Analogue issues face those designing and implementing the first steps of an enterprise system implementation in order to enhance the chances for a 'successful' outcome. Where and how to start are thus important decisions to make. To do so it is imperative to reflect on available alternatives; what are the different 'mechanisms' at work; what are their effects and implications; what are their 'costs' and benefits; what do they *do* and what is postponed; what can be learned from them and what can *not*? This requires an intimate knowledge of the analogue to the hardware in this context; *the organization and its practices*. Bootstrapping enterprise information systems is as dependant on this as bootstrapping an operating system is on the computer hardware. Next, in order to base any decisions on this, it is also necessary to question what 'the big' program needs to 'know' *before* it can get going; what must be in place already and what can be added later? *Bootstrapping*, both as a metaphor and as an algorithm, encourages and enables us to take a closer look at these questions, thus *opening the black box of organizational implementation*.

As we have illustrated, there can be several ways to design and deploy bootstrappers, and there is not likely to be a one-best-way; different approaches will represent different tradeoffs. In the medical charts project we identified three different configurations of tradeoffs, as summarized in table 1. Which configuration to select depends on a complex set of factors, ranging all the way from enterprise strategies, through the project group composition and all the way down to operational realities. In the medical charts project, the first configuration didn't yield the desired results. Thus a different configuration was tried, with an outcome much closer to what they were striving for; an organizational bootstrapper.

7 Conclusions

So what does it take to design and deploy an effective organizational bootstrapper? We have already pointed to the significance of an intimate knowledge of the organization and its existing practices, but equally important is knowledge about and ability to prioritize the project's strategic and short term goals. Finally – and maybe most important of all – is *learning*. Synthesizing the tradeoffs associated with different approaches in hindsight (like we have done in this paper) is fairly easy; doing so by pre-analysis is a lot harder. The willingness and ability to learn – often through trial and error – is therefore essential. Awareness of these issues is prerequisite to this, and the concept of bootstrapping stimulates such awareness.

As for the theorizing of organizational implementation, the concept offers an analytical tool for making sense of the first – often fumbling – steps of such processes. We have illustrated how it draws attention to the variety in possible approaches, and how each approach represents a tradeoff where something is gained, something is lost, and always at a price someone has to pay. We regard bootstrapping as an *adaptive* strategy, with a focus on the complexity and dynamics of developing "a viable match between the opportunities and risks present in the external environment and the organization's capabilities and resources" [28]. In relation to organizational implementation, bootstrapping also takes into account opportunities and risks in the 'internal environment' as crucial to the understanding of organizational change initiatives and their outcomes.

References

[1] Keen, P.G.W.: Information Systems and Organizational Change. Communications of the ACM 24(1), 24–33 (1981)
[2] Markus, M.L.: Power, Politics, and MIS Implementation. Communications of the ACM 26(6) (1983)
[3] Leonard-Barton, D.: Implementation as mutual adaptation of technology and organization. Research Policy 17, 251–267 (1988)
[4] Tyre, M.J., Orlokowski, W.J.: Windows of Opportunity: Temporal Patterns of Technological Adaptation in Organizations. Org. Science 5(1), 98–118 (1994)
[5] Majchrzak, A., Rice, R.E., Malhotra, A., King, N., Ba, S.: Technology Adaptation: The Case of a Computer-Supported Inter-Organizational Team. MISQ 24(4), 569–600 (2000)
[6] Orlikowki, W.J., Hofman, J.D.: An Improvisational Model for Change Management: The Case of Groupware Technologies. Sloan Management Review, 11–21 (1997)
[7] Orlikowski, W.J.: Using technology and constituting structures: A practice lens for studying technology in organizations. Organization Science 11(4), 404–428 (2000)
[8] Ciborra, C.U.: De profundis? Deconstructing the concept of strategic alignment. Scandinavian J. of IS 9(1), 67–82 (1997)
[9] Elingsen, G., Monteiro, E.: Big is beautiful: electronic patient records in large Norwegian hospitals 1980–2001. Methods Inf. Med. 42, 366–370 (2003)
[10] Ellingsen, G.: Coordinating work in hospitals through a global tool. Scandinavian J. of IS 15, 39–54 (2003)
[11] Vikkelsø, S.: Subtle Redistribution of Work, Attention and Risks: Electronic Patient Records and Organisational Consequences. Scandinavian J. of IS 17(1), 3–30 (2005)
[12] Jones, M.: Learning the lessons of history? Electronic records in the United Kingdom acute hospitals. 1988–2002. Health Inf. J. 10(4), 253–263 (2004)
[13] Keen, P.G.W., Bronsema, G.S., Zuboff, S.: Implementing Common Systems: One Organization's Experience. Sloan Working Papers, pp. 1265–1281 (1981)

[14] Markus, M.L., Tanis, C., van Fenema, P.C.: Multisite ERP implementations. Communications of the ACM 43(4) (2000)
[15] Hertzum, M.: Organisational Implementation: A Complex but Underrecognised Aspect of Information-System Design. In: Proc. of the second Nordic conf. on HCI. ACM Int. Conf. Proc. Series, vol. 31, pp. 201–204 (2002)
[16] Robey, D., Ross, J.W., Boudreau, M.C.: Learning to Implement Enterprise Systems: An Exploratory Study of the Dialectics of Change. J. of MIS 19(1), 17–46 (2002)
[17] Nordheim, S., Päivärinta, T.: Implementing enterprise content management: from evolution through strategy to contradictions out-of-the-box. European J. of IS 15(6), 648–662 (2008)
[18] Scheepers, R.: A conceptual framework for the implementation of enterprise information portals in large organizations. European J. of IS 15(6), 635–647 (2006)
[19] Grudin, J.: Why CSCW Applications Fail: Problems in the Design and Evaluation of Organizational Interfaces. In: Proc. of the Conf. on CSCW, Portland, Oregon, pp. 85–93 (1988)
[20] Markus, M.L., Connolly, T.: Why CSCW Applications Fail: Problems in the Adoption of Independent Work Tools. In: Proc. of the Conf. on CSCW, ACM CSCW'90, pp. 371–380 (1990)
[21] Grudin, J., Palen, L.: Why Groupware Succeeds: Discretion or Mandate? In: Marmolin, Sundblad, Schmidt (eds.) Proc. from the Fourth European Conf. on CSCW, pp. 263–378. Kluwer Academic Publishers, Dordrecht (1995)
[22] Hanseth, O., Aanestad, M.: Bootstrapping networks, communities and infrastructures. On the evolution of ICT solutions in health care. Presented at ITHC: Erasmus University, Rotterdam, The Netherlands (September 6-7, 2001)
[23] Hanseth, O., Aanestad, M.: Design as bootstrapping. On the evolution of ICT networks in Health Care. Methods Inf. Med. 4 (2003)
[24] The Digital Hospital,
http://www.rikshospitalet.no/ikbViewer/page/no/pages/
hygiene/om/menypunkt?p_dim_id=44068
[25] Vision,
http://www.rikshospitalet.no/ikbViewer/page/no/pages/hygiene
/om/menypunkt?p_dim_id=44381
[26] Walsham, G.: Interpreting Information Systems in Organizations. John Wiley, Chichester (1993)
[27] Klein, H., Myers, M.: A Set of Principles for Conducting and Evaluating Interpretive Field Studies in Information Systems. MISQ 23(1), 67–94 (1999)
[28] Chaffee, E.E.: Three models of strategy. Academy of management review 10(1), 89–98 (1985)

Configuration Analysis of Inter-Organizational Information Systems Adoption

Kalle Lyytinen[1] and Jan Damsgaard[2]

[1] Department of Information Systems, Case Western Reserve University
Cleveland, Ohio, USA
[2] Center for Applied ICT, Copenhagen Business School, Denmark & School of Information Systems, Curtin University of Technology, Australia
kjl13@po.cwru.edu, jd.caict@cbs.dk

Abstract. Investigations of the adoption of Information Systems (IS) have successfully sought to predict a singular organization's or user's propensity to adopt an IS. Encouraged by the success researchers have approached the diffusion of Inter-Organizational Information Systems (IOIS) as a special instance of IS adoption and extended existing diffusion models with extra-organizational factors. Unfortunately, the validity and usefulness of these models have been inadequate in explaining IOIS diffusion. In this paper we dismiss the organization as the unit of analysis and we propose an alternative unit for IOIS adoption studies that we call an adoption configuration. Each such configuration has a diffusion scope determined by its topology, a way of relating adopters defined by its underlying mode of interaction, and a style of using the service determined by the mode of appropriation. Configuration based analysis calls for a redirection of IOIS diffusion studies both at the theoretical and the methodological level. Diffusion theories need to synthesize across multiple adoption levels. Methodologically scholars need to work with sparse and incomplete multi-level process data as to explain the emergence and dynamics of viable (and failed) configurations.

Keywords: Inter-organizational information systems, IS diffusion and adoption, and configuration analysis.

1 Introduction

The Information System research community has been quite successful in explaining the adoption of single Information Systems (IS) in organizations [1-5]. Analogously researchers have approached the diffusion of Inter-Organizational Information Systems (IOIS) as a special instance of IS adoption and extended the IS diffusion models with additional extra-organizational factors. The underlying goal remains from IS adoption; namely to explain a single organization's propensity to adopt an IOIS [6-12]. Regrettably, scholars following this reasoning have not gone far enough in recognizing the essentially different attributes that affect the IOIS adoption as compared to IS adoption. One simple difference for example is that a single organization cannot adopt an IOIS on its own – it takes at least two adopters to do the

IOIS tango! Hence, the use of a single organization as the unit of analysis limits the investigation to 'one end' of the IOIS, it truncates the networked nature of the system, it hides specific technological features of the embedded IOIS, and it ignores institutional influences upon the adoption process. Hence explaining IOIS diffusion by refining and expanding the number of salient antecedents for IS adoption and organizing them in increasingly elaborate ways is not the right approach. Such approach just complicates the models, yields diminishing returns in terms of explained variance, and fails to address the process or emergent nature of IOIS diffusion. If the "true" nature of IOIS is recognized the adoption needs to be examined more holistically as occurring concurrently among a number of interrelated organizations in an environment.

A fresh approach is to rethink the basic premises and start by reconsidering the unit of analysis and its ontology. For example in the past literature a major gap in research is that the organizing vision underlying the adoption of the IOIS has not been linked to the structure and functionality of the system. Adoptions of IOIS happen only, when a match is found between these factors i.e. the organizing vision and structure and functionality are interrelated – in other words when a viable IOIS design has emerged. This together with the networked nature of IOIS suggests that we must shift from examining singular adopters to analyzing organized constellations of organizations and technologies that are *adopted as a whole*. We call these emergent units *adopter configurations*. The notion of adopter configurations shifts attention from singular IOIS adopters to clusters of organizations with heterogeneous technological capabilities and their strategic and structural arrangements in explaining adoption outcomes.

The idea of configurations, as such, is neither new nor revolutionary. Organization scholars and economists have for a long time recognized structural and dynamic features of ensembles of people (i.e. organizations or teams) or organizations (i.e. markets). Configuration analysis also underlies Mintzberg's theory of *structures in fives* where for example a stable environment favors the *machine bureaucracy* [13]. Our contribution in this paper is to articulate the value of the idea of configurations for the study of the IOIS and its implications for IOIS diffusion theory and research methodology.

The remainder of the paper is organized as follows. In section 2 we introduce the main tenets of past IOIS adoption studies and summarize their main challenges. In section 3 we formulate key concepts – adopter configuration and adopter ensemble – that underlie IOIS configuration analysis and describe some typical configurations. In section four we outline theoretical and methodological guidelines for carrying out configuration based analysis and identify issues that need to be accounted for in the future study of the adoption of IOIS. The last section reiterates our main findings and notes some constrains in configuration studies.

2 IOIS and Its Diffusion and Adoption

An IOIS can be defined as: "automated information systems shared by at least two separate companies". An IOIS is built around information technology... "that facilitates the creation, storage, transformation, and transmission of information" [14].

The challenge scholars face in the study of IOIS adoption is that IOIS systems exhibit high levels of complexity and uncertainty, have contested and ambiguous organizing visions, are networked in nature, and involve heterogeneous technologies and functionality. Fundamental in the deployment is that the resulting IOIS service must be defined and propagated *in chorus* among several involved companies by adopting a shared organizing vision [8, 15]. This we can call the 'strategic positioning' of the IOIS service and it defines critical elements of how the IOIS will work held by key actors.

2.1 Diffusion and Adoption of IOIS

Since Diffusion Of Innovations (DOI) [4, 16] constitutes the original theory applied in most IOIS adoption studies (see e.g. [6-8, 10, 12, 17] we review next its basic premises and then evaluate some of its limitations.

Rogers [4] defines the diffusion of innovation as the process "by which an innovation is communicated through certain channels over time among the members of the social system". DOI assumes that the following characteristics apply to *all* adopters: 1) adopters are *independent*, and 2) they make *voluntary* decisions to *accept* or *reject* an *innovation* based on the 3) perceived *benefits* they expect to accrue from their 4) *independent use* of the innovation [18]. Accordingly, the DOI models explain IOIS adoption using the singular organization as the unit of analysis. It is further assumed that, the organization operates in a homogenous diffusion space i.e. the organization is similar in most ways with other organizations. It is further assumed that the adoption decision is a voluntary *go* or *no go* event. As a result a DOI models can be used to make bets on how likely it is for an organization to adopt an innovation in the next "round". The original DOI also did not recognize process or institutional factors that affect diffusion processes. Therefore DOI based IOIS diffusion models has been expanded with inter-organizational, institutional and environmental factors [7, 19, 20] generating a growing gallery of factors organized into increasingly complex structural models [6, 7, 9-12]. Currently, these models and their analyses are growing beyond tractability to the extent that they often obscure as much as they illuminate [21].

To summarize due to their theoretical assumptions DOI models cannot generate accurate accounts for reasons to adopt or reject *a specific IOIS system with certain properties in a context*. In this regard DOI models are not the best way to analyze the adoption and evolution of *IOIS as systems* but rather as *tools*. To overcome these limitations we next propose *configuration analysis* as an alternative theoretical approach to elucidate facets that provide understanding of IOIS adoption.

3 Configuration Analysis

The concept of adopter configuration suggests that IOIS adoption studies have to be sensitive to the whole *network* of interrelated actors and technology elements being meshed together during any individual decision to join an IOIS. The studies must also be open to inherent dynamism of configurations (this is in fact the diffusion analysis) and sensitive to the differences in configurations. In fact, IOIS become adopted over time through a series of *different* and *alternative* adopter configurations. The configuration concept thus forms a critical *observation and analysis unit* in IOIS diffusion research.

We define an *adopter configuration* as a set of interrelated adopters who share a specific organizing vision and appropriate a selected set of key functionalities for their common IOIS service. Each configuration can be specified by its organizing vision, structure, mode of interaction, typology, mode of appropriation and key functionality. In configuration analysis it is further assumed that these features *cannot* vary independently; i.e. a particular organizing vision obliges a certain interorganizational structure to be viable [22, 23]. Therefore there are only a finite number of viable configurations possible in any given adopter population at any given time. Each configuration entails a specific way of relating would-be adopters (mode of interaction and topology), and using the IOIS service (mode of appropriation and selected key functionality). These conditions vary between adopter configurations. The topology, for example, can vary from simple dyadic relationships, into complex industry-wide hubs, or distributed networks, and the mode of interaction can vary from voluntary and equal relationships (*match mode*) to obligatory and hierarchical interactions (*conflict mode*) [22]. Likewise the mode of appropriation can vary in terms of intensity, strategic emphasis and level of process integration, and the key functionality in terms of message exchange and coverage of order-fulfillment cycles.

We emphasize the criticality of the adopter configuration as the primary unit of analysis in the sense that no organization's adoption of an IOIS takes place outside a configuration. In turn, an individual organization may participate in multiple configurations, whilst each configuration always includes at least two organizations. Actors can participate in several adoption configurations, and thereby, their behaviors may involve adopting different or similar IOIS technologies multiple times. An adopter population can be defined by all actors which have participated (or could have participated) in at least one adopter configuration during the IOIS diffusion process. Some organizations may shift between configurations, or may drop out altogether (voluntarily or involuntarily) as they maneuver strategically to maximize their IOIS utility.

3.1 Properties of Adopter Configurations

The set of all configurations we call the *configuration ensemble*. Dynamics of configuration ensembles are critical in understanding the diffusion of IOIS. Hence, at any point of time we can observe several adoption configurations at any given industry or adoption context. Each configuration in the ensemble is dynamic in the sense that it can cease to exist, be transformed into an alternative configuration, or become stabilized. This is similar to Mintzberg's [13] description of how an organization transforms from one effective organizational form to another as the organization matures or changes in the environment or technology oblige it to do so.

These concepts also affect how one determines an adequate scope – the population – for the IOIS adoption study. Here, it is necessary to give up the concept of a constant and homogeneous population. Instead, the scope and size of the adoption population depends on the technological, temporal and institutional elements of adopter configurations, the shaping of the technology by the actors and promoters, and properties of the network (like modalities of interactions, trust, history, culture, or globalization). Accordingly, both the adopted technology and set of potential actors can and will change over time. Innovation in configurations is inherently complex and difficult to arrange or manage by single actors. Therefore diffusion processes behave often in chaotic or seemingly random manner. For example, the decision to adopt a new standard or create a new organizing version is not a unilateral decision, but it has wide ripple effects in the network. To orchestrate a coordinated simultaneous switch among heterogeneous and autonomous actors necessary to keep the IOIS operational is often an insurmountable barrier, and therefore many configurations never evolve beyond the original vision and structure. Often a number of "false starts" are needed in the diffusion arena before the right composition of services and solutions emerges victorious. For example, in Hong Kong it took almost a decade to establish a viable communitywide IOIS service after several initiatives stranded, because of the "wrong composition" of organizing visions, structure, actors and incentives [24, 25].

A configuration's characteristics are in addition *time* dependent in that its organizing vision, key functionality and topology can evolve at different stages of adoption into new types of functionality and organization. Hence, each specific configuration can be distinguished through its start and end time. Diffusion studies using configuration analysis need to describe and analyze the evolution of configurations (and associated adopter populations) and their interactions with potential partners, as well as other configurations. As there are only a limited number of viable configurations feasible in any population [22, 26] the convergence to such configurations happens relatively quickly during the diffusion trajectory. Once reached a fairly stable set of configurations typically prevails over an extended period of time [22]. Only when the environment experiences an abrupt change a new set of configurations becomes inevitable and organizations aligned with one configuration will attempt to move in concert to a different configuration [13, 22].

3.2 Typical IOIS Configurations

Adopter configurations can be identified by using their distinguishing features: key functionality, mode of appropriation, production and use lattices (topology), organizing visions, and structure. Archetypical configurations within IOIS diffusion are: dyadic relationships configurations, hub and spoke configurations, industry configurations and community configurations.

Dyadic relationship configurations occur where two organizations adopt the IOIS at the same time and they depend on each other's actions in exploiting it [27]. The organizing vision involves both companies. It can aim at virtual business integration (match mode) or it can operate in conflict mode where one company reaps most direct benefits. Existing power structures are replicated in the way the IOIS is organized

[27-29]. Characteristics to consider include: the complexity of key functionality, the communication structures [10, 30], user differences, characteristics of the innovation (like trialability, observability) [4], and types of innovation decision [31]. To understand dyadic relationships and their evolution organizational analysis is applicable as it highlights characteristics of organizations that might appropriate IOIS [4, 13, 32, 33].

Hub and spoke configurations spans industry wide and involve at least three actors. In this configuration the organizations' decisions are coordinated and depend on some "central" hub with strong technological capabilities and power. Similar to dyadic relationships a *Hub and spoke configuration* can evolve either in *conflict* mode or in *matching* mode. The organizing vision is normally that of a "middleman" or a "clearing house" [28, 34, 35]. In the matching mode a hub offers IOIS services to business partners as an additional benefit when doing business [36] or to obtain virtual business integration [37]. In the power based hub and spoke setup the hub initiates the IOIS and controls the business relations [35, 38, 39]. The hub often provides the spokes little choice in rejecting the IOIS [28, 34]. Appropriate theoretical lenses to study hub and spoke configurations are supply chain management [40] and power dependency analysis [41, 42].

Industry configurations span part of an industry and business relationships are shorter and less idiosyncratic than in the previous configurations. Industry configurations often depend on institutional involvement where the organizing vision is related to the concept of a "common good" for the industry. It is often an association [29, 43, 44] that promotes the organizing vision and convenes the mode of interaction. However, where no central association can or wants to get involved more strategic industry configurations might emerge. Often strategic IOIS networks operate exclusively and only invite organizations with complementary interests to participate. Industrial analysis expands the adoption investigation by identifying relevant industrial actors, their roles and types of relationships [22]. It caters for the networked nature of IOIS adoptions, adopter dependencies, and resource and power relationships among actors as to narrate emerging interactions between technologies, organizations and external institutions [37, 43, 45-47]. Industrial analysis thus locates the organizing vision within a broader industrial field by using strategy analysis [42], power and resource dependency analysis [41], and supply chain management [40].

Community wide configurations capture national IOIS initiatives that often include public institutions or governments [48]. National IOIS plans are often implemented to spur the national adoption of IOIS especially where it is envisioned to lead to a competitive advantage over other nations or regions [49]. *Institutional analysis* draws boundaries within the potential diffusion population by recognizing those regulatory regimes that act as focal points in constraining, or enabling IOIS diffusion. Institutional regimes can be identified using concepts from institutional theory, and political theory [48-50]. Though there are some comparisons of IOIS use at the national level [25, 49, 51-53], the influence of regulatory regimes during the diffusion of IOIS is not well understood [18, 54]. These include incentives, symbolic value given to technologies, or mobilization of bias etc. [49].

4 Conducting a Configuration Analysis

The benefits of configuration analysis are: 1) it addresses multitude of adoption contexts and dynamics inherent in IOIS adoption, 2) it recognizes shifting boundary conditions for IOIS diffusion; and 3) it integrates multiple theoretical views to account for the IOIS diffusion. Next we shortly address the pressing issues in conducting configuration analysis:

- When to use configuration based analysis?
- How does configuration analysis affect the organization's point of view?
- How do configurations evolve?
- What type of research methods and designs are needed for configuration analysis?

4.1 When to Use Configuration Based Analysis?

When the technology is networked, complex, flexible, and depends on coordinated action of would-be-adopters, technology providers, standards and institutional actors it signals that configuration analysis is appropriate. Also when the investigator interprets adoptions as a series of interrelated events in contrast to unrelated solo adoptions, it is appropriate to use the concept of configuration analysis as a basis for data collection and subsequent configuration based investigation.

In order to explain complex and layered behaviors associated with configuration analysis the investigator needs to mobilize several theoretical frames: technological, organizational, industrial and institutional. The necessity to use several frames emerges from the layered structure of the adoption dynamics though the breadth and depth of deployed frames may vary depending on the configuration and its scope. Technological analysis focuses on traits of the examined technology. 1) The nature of its application, i.e. is it a stand alone or networked technology. 2) The skills required to exploit the technology. 3) Its dependence on standards. 4) How open to interpretation the technology. E.g. enterprise portals and ERP systems are very different in this respect.

4.2 How Does Configuration Analysis Affect the Organization's Point of View?

Organizations often participate in multiple adopter configurations. The end product of a configuration analysis can be labeled a "dominant design," a set of configurations readily available to align an organization's technology, strategy, and structure in an effective manner. A dominant design of configurations is 'favorable' because it encapsulates a set of proven and effective ways to exploit IOIS. A firm that implements a configuration therefore secures a competitive edge over companies that don't. Although the understanding of these processes is central to the concerns of many practitioners in the field, the IS literature contains very few examples of analyses of this type.

4.3 How Do Configurations Evolve?

Configuration analyses by definition imply a process oriented analysis due to their imminent path dependency [54]. An investigator must investigate in motion interactions between adopters and configurations, and between configurations and thereby observe simultaneous changes at different levels: inside singular organizations, within adopter configurations, across adopter configurations, and within adoption ensembles. Critical in these analyses is also to observe quantitative and qualitative changes at each level: how individual organizations differ in their rationale, how adopter configurations evolve and change in character and size, and how adopter ensembles mature and become stable. Furthermore configurations transform over time due to maturity, to changes in other configurations or to changes in the technology.

4.4 What Type of Research Methods and Designs Are Needed for Configuration Analysis?

One normally starts by using generic adopter configurations as seeding categories. Then proceeds on identifying concrete instantiations of configurations from these categories based on the types of relationships implicated by the empirical data including demands for coordinating the infrastructure, standardization of technology, coordination in processes; or the impact of the industrial and the institutional regimes. The number of enacted adopter configurations is not decided a priori in configuration analysis.

There are two restrictions in engaging in configuration analysis: 1) complexity of theoretical models, and 2) diversity and inherent incompleteness of data. Configuration analysis calls for a theoretical attitude where one must orchestrate multi-theoretical inquiries of the evolution of each configuration. We have learned that this is not an easy task, as it requires careful and often painful ongoing disciplined conceptual refinement during the study [55, 56]. Moreover, for each configuration the scope and the nature of theoretical frames can vary. This can easily lead to escalating theoretical commitments and advanced models where investigators deploy multiple frameworks simultaneously located at different levels of analysis. This is challenging because moving between levels of analysis sets tantamount challenges for social scientists.

Configuration analysis also calls for longitudinal investigations where data sets are complex, unstructured, sparse and not bounded. Yet, without longitudinal data that are organized through the lens of configurations and ensembles our understanding of the variety and diversity of ongoing adoption processes becomes (too) limited. Unfortunately, this methodological stance is a tall order. It requires intensive fieldwork, long time spans to collect data, and working your access to multiple organizations. All this adds to the investigator's effort and makes it risky, and yet collected data sets remain incomplete and sparse. In this sense the approach to data and its analysis equals the use of historical research methods [57]. We feel that such risks need to be tolerated, if we as a discipline want to develop insightful theoretical accounts.

5 Conclusions

In this paper we have suggested a new approach – called configuration analysis – to study the adoption of IOIS. We note, however, that we are not against conducting individual adopter based (DOI) based analysis per se. We just call attention to its assumptions and limitations. We propose configuration analysis as a complementary approach, which can bring order and clarification to the multi-level and dynamic investigation of IOIS. Configuration analysis is an open, yet a systematic way of illuminating the IOIS adoption as a transformative and dynamic process. In configuration analysis the invariant is not a set of factors and a model that explain some variance, but a set of configurations around which viable IOIS adoption processes occur effectively.

We have formulated the key concepts of configuration analysis – adopter configuration and adopter ensemble – that help narrate theoretically the diffusion of IOIS systems. The concept of an *adopter configuration* carries the idea of a difference in the topology, mode of interaction, organizing vision, key functionality and mode of appropriation in adopted IOIS service. The social elements of the configuration include actor relationships – power, resource dependency, trust, capability-, the significance attributed to the technology by each actor (organizing vision); and the technical elements include specific capabilities of IOIS as defined by its key functionality. Each configuration weaves together both technical and social elements in a holistic fashion into a configuration that can lead to deeper and broader embedding of IOIS into organizations and adopter populations.

References

1. Davis, F.D.: Perceived Usefulness, Perceived Ease of Use, and User Acceptance of Information Technology. MIS Quarterly 13, 319–329 (1989)
2. Fichman, R.G.: Information Technology Diffusion: A Review of Empirical Research. In: DeGross, J.I., Becker, J.D., Elam, J.J. (eds.) Proceedings of the Thirteenth International Conference on Information Systems, Dallas, Texas, pp. 195–206 (1992)
3. Prescott, M.B., Conger, S.A.: Information Technology Innovations: A Classification by IT Locus of Impact and Research Approach. Data Base Advances 26(2&3), 20–41 (1995)
4. Rogers, E.M.: Diffusion of Innovations, 5th edn. The Free Press, New York (2003)
5. Venkatesh, V., et al.: User Acceptance of Information Technology: Toward a Unified View. MIS Quarterly 27, 425–478 (2003)
6. Chwelos, P., Benbasat, I., Dexter, A.S.: Empirical Test of an EDI Adoption Model. Information Systems Research 12(3), 304–321 (2001)
7. Huang, Z., Janz, B.D., Frolick, M.N.: A Comprehensive Examination of Internet-EDI Adoption. Inf. Sys. Manag. 25(3), 273–286 (2008)
8. Iacovou, C.L., Benbasat, I., Dexter, A.S.: Electronic Data Interchange and Small Organizations: Adoption and Impact of Technology. Management Information Systems Quarterly 19(4), 465–485 (1995)
9. Lee, S., Lim, G.G.: The impact of partnership attributes on EDI implementation success. Information & Management 42, 503–516 (2005)

10. Premkumar, G., Ramamurthy, K.: The Role of Inter-organizational and Organizational Factors on the Decision Mode for Adoption of Inter-organizational Systems. Decision Sciences 26(3), 303–336 (1996)
11. Premkumar, G., Ramamurthy, K., Crum, M.R.: Determinants of EDI adoption in the transportation industry. European Journal of Information Systems 6, 107–121 (1997)
12. Premkumar, G., Ramamurthy, K., Nilakanta, S.: Implementation of Electronic Data Interchange: An Innovation Diffusion Perspective. Journal of Management Information Systems 11(2), 157–186 (1994)
13. Minztberg, H.: Structure in Fives: Designing Effective Organizations, International Edition. Prentice-Hall, London (1983)
14. Johnston, H.R., Vitale, M.: Creating competitive advantage with Inter-organizational systems. Management Information Systems Quarterly 12(2), 153–165 (1988)
15. Swanson, E., Ramiller, N.: The organizing vision in information systems innovation. Organization Science 8, 458–474 (1997)
16. Rogers, E.M.: Diffusion of Innovations, 4th edn. The Free Press, New York (1995)
17. Jones, M.C., Beatty, R.C.: Towards the development of measures of perceived benefits and compatibility of EDI: a comparative assessment of competing first order factor models. European Journal of Information Systems 7, 210–220 (1998)
18. Lyytinen, K., Damsgaard, J.: What's wrong with the diffusion of innovation theory? The case of a complex and networked technology. In: Proceedings of the IFIP TC8 Working Group 8.6 conference, Diffusing Software Product and Process Innovations, Banff, Canada, pp. 173–190 (2001)
19. Fearon, C., Phillip, G.: An Empirical Study of the use of EDI in supermarket chains using a new conceptual framework. Journal of Information Technology 14, 3–21 (1999)
20. Teo, H.H., Tan, B.C.Y., Wei, K.K.: Organizational transformation using Electronic Data Interchange: The case of TradeNet in Singapore. Journal of Management Information Systems 13(4), 139–166 (1997)
21. Reimers, K., Johnston, R.B.: The use of an Explicitly theory-driven data coding method for high-level theory testing in IOIS. In: International Conference on Information Systems, Paris (2008)
22. Miller, D.: Configurations of Strategy and Structure: Towards a Synthesis. Strategic Management Journal 7, 233–249 (1986)
23. Miller, D.: Configurations revisted. Strategic Management Journal 17, 505–512 (1996)
24. Damsgaard, J.: The Diffusion of Electronic Data Interchange: An Institutional and Organizational Analysis of Alternative Diffusion Patterns, Aalborg: Ph.D. Thesis, R-96-2041, Department of Computer Science, Aalborg University (1996)
25. Surmon, L., Huff, S.: Hong Kong's Tradelink: An EDI vision, The University of Western Ontario, Western Business School: London, Canada (1995)
26. Lyytinen, K.J., Newman, M.: Explaining Information System Change: a Punctuated Socio-Technical Change Model. European Journal of Information Systems 17(6), 589–613 (2008)
27. Ali, M., Kurnia, S., Johnston, R.B.: A Dyadic Model of Inter-organizational Systems (IOS) Adoption Maturity. In: Proceedings of the 41st Annual Hawaii International Conference on Systems Sciences (2008)
28. Nagy, A.: Collaboration and conflict in the electronic integration of supply networks. In: Proceedings of the 39th Hawaii International Conference on System Sciences, Hawaii (2006)
29. Oliver, C.: Determinants of Inter-organizational Relationships: Integration and Future Directions. Academy of Management Review 15(2), 241–265 (1990)

30. Bouchard, L.: Decision Criteria in the Adoption of EDI. In: Proceedings of the 14th International Conference on Information Systems, Orlando, Florida, pp. 365–376 (1993)
31. Tornatzky, L.G., Klein, K.J.: Innovation Characteristics And Adoption-Implementation. IEEE Transactions on Engineering Management EM-29(1), 28–45 (1982)
32. Perrow, C.: Complex Organizations - A Critical Essay, 3rd edn. McGraw-Hill, Inc., New York (1986)
33. Williamson, O.: Transaction-Cost Economics: The Governance of Contractual Relations. The Journal of Law and Economics 22(2), 233–261 (1979)
34. Kumar, K., van Dissel, H.G.: Sustainable Collaboration: Managing Conflict and Cooperation in Inter-organizational Systems. Management Information Systems Quarterly 20(3), 279–300 (1996)
35. Webster, J.: Networks of Collaboration or Conflict? Electronic Data Interchange and Power in the Supply Chain. Journal of Strategic Information Systems 4(1), 31–42 (1995)
36. MacKay, D.: The Impact of EDI on the components sector of the Australian automotive industry. Journal of Strategic Information Systems 2(3), 243–263 (1993)
37. Kambil, A., Short, J.E.: Electronic integration and business network redesign: A roles-linkage perspective. Journal of Management Information Systems 10(4), 59–83 (1994)
38. Hart, P., Saunders, C.: Power and Trust: Critical Factors in the Adoption and Use of Electronic Data Interchange. Organization Science 8(1), 23–42 (1997)
39. Manabe, S., Fujisue, K., Kurokawa, S.: A comparative analysis of EDI integration in US and Japanese automobile suppliers. International Journal of Technology Management 30(3-4), 389–414 (2005)
40. Christopher, M.: Logistics and supply chain management: Strategies for Reducing Cost and Improving Service, 2nd edn. Prentice Hall, Upper Saddle River (1998)
41. Emerson, R.M.: Power-dependence Relations. American Sociological Review 27, 31–41 (1962)
42. Porter, M.E.: Competitive Advantage: Creating and Sustaining Superior Performance. The Free Press, New York (1985)
43. Damsgaard, J., Lyytinen, K.: The role of intermediating institutions in diffusion of Electronic Data Interchange (EDI): How Industry associations in the grocery sector intervened in Hong Kong, Finland, and Denmark. The Information Society 17(3), 195–210 (2001)
44. O'Callaghan, R., Eistert, T.: An Association's Leadership for Industry-wide EDI - The Case of AECOC in Spain. In: Krcmar, H., Bjørn-Andersen, N., O'Callaghan, R. (eds.) EDI in Europe: How It Works in Practice, pp. 277–297. John Wiley & Sons Ltd., Chichester (1995)
45. Bakos, Y., Katsamakas, E.: Design and ownership of two-sided networks: implications for Internet platforms. Journal of Management Information Systems 25(2), 172–202 (2008)
46. Cox, B., Ghoneim, S.: Drivers and Barriers to adopting EDI: A sector analysis of UK industry. European Journal of Information Systems 5, 24–33 (1996)
47. Delhaye, R., Lobet-Maris, C.: EDI Adoption and Standard Choice: A Conceptual Model. In: Doukidis, G., et al. (eds.) Proceedings of the 3rd European Conference on Information Systems, pp. 165–182. Print Xpress, Athens (1995)
48. Damsgaard, J., Lyytinen, K.: Building Electronic Trading Infrastructure: A private or public responsibility? Journal of Organizational Computing and Electronic Commerce 11(2), 131–151 (2001)
49. King, J.L., et al.: Institutional Factors in Information Technology Innovation. Information Systems Research 5(2), 139–169 (1994)

50. Damsgaard, J., Lyytinen, K.: Contours of Electronic Data Interchange in Finland: Overcoming technological barriers and collaborating to make it happen. The Journal of Strategic Information Systems 7, 275–297 (1998)
51. Damsgaard, J., Lyytinen, K.: Hong Kong's EDI Bandwagon. Derailed or on the right track? In: McMaster, T., et al. (eds.) Facilitating Technology Transfer Through Partnership: Learning from Practice and Research, pp. 39–63. Chapman and Hall, London (1997)
52. King, J.L., Konsynski, B.: Singapore TradeNet: A Tale of One City. Harvard Business School, Boston (1990)
53. Wrigley, C.D., Wagenaar, R.W., Clarke, R.A.: Electronic Data Interchange in International trade: frameworks for the strategic analysis of ocean port communities. Journal of Strategic Information Systems 3(3), 211–234 (1994)
54. Kurnia, S., Johnston, R.B.: The Need for a Processual View of Inter-Organizational Systems Adoption. Journal of Strategic Information Systems 9(4), 295–319 (2000)
55. Klein, K., Kozlowski, S. (eds.): Multilevel theory, research and methods in organizations - foundations, extensions and new directions. Jossey-Bass, San Francisco (2000)
56. Ragin, C.: The comparative method; moving beyond qualitative and quantitative strategies. University of California Press, Berkeley (1987)
57. Mason, R.O., McKenney, J.L., Copeland, D.G.: Developing an Historical Tradition in MIS Research. MIS Quarterly 21(3), 257–278 (1997)

An Analysis of Literature Reviews on IS Business Value: How Deficiencies in Methodology and Theory Use Resulted in Limited Effectiveness

Guido Schryen

Business Information Systems, RWTH Aachen University
52062 Aachen, Germany
schryen@winfor.rwth-aachen.de

Abstract. Enduring doubts about the value of IS investments reveal that IS researchers have not fully managed to identify and to explain the economic benefits of IS. This paper assumes that literature reviews, which represent a powerful instrument for the identification and synthesis of knowledge, have not tapped their full potential to address this issue due to deficiencies in methodology. The analysis of 18 literature reviews published in pertinent academic outlets during the past 20 years shows such deficiencies. Two of the most critical weaknesses identified are (1) the lack of theory use in most reviews and (2) a weak linkage of reviews, resulting in little progress in theory and framework development. The systematic identification of these weaknesses and the extraction of promising methodological examples from past literature are the main contributions of this work, which supports the composition of more effective literature reviews in future research.

Keywords: Literature review, Business value, Information systems, Methodology, Theory.

1 Introduction

Information systems (IS) started to be embedded in economic environments many decades ago and are even considered commodity inputs nowadays [1]. The reliance on IS has meanwhile occurred to an extent that, for some firms, such as Internet sellers, online banks, and telecommunication providers the failure of IS impedes or even renders business activities impossible. Beyond this firm-level impact, IS have also gained macroeconomic importance: according to the World Information Technology Services Alliance, the global marketplace for information and communication technology is likely to have topped $3.7 trillion in 2008 [2]. The economic relevance of IS has made research on "IS business value" highly attractive to researchers, who have shaped the academic discussion by publishing more than 1,000 research papers [3].

Some researchers provide sobering arguments on the economic relevance of IS. For example, [4;5] doubt the strategic power of IS and argue that IS are commodities and that any IS-based advantages will be soon eroded. Carr [1] sums up doubts by even entitling his paper "IT doesn't matter". Another discourse is rooted in empirical studies that do not find evidence that IS positively affected specific performance measures, such as productivity [8], stock market reactions [7], or "Return on Assets" [8]. Apparently, IS researchers have (at least not fully) managed to identify and to explain the economic relevance of IS so that business executives and researchers continue to question the value of IS investments, as Kohli and Grover [9] note in their recent review. However, answering this question is regarded fundamental to the contribution of the IS discipline [10].

This leads to the question of why IS researchers have not (yet) succeeded to demonstrate the economic value of IS. Possible explanations are that (1) the value of IS is actually limited and has been overrated by IS researchers [1;4;5], or (2) IS are economically valuable, but the specific types of value have not been identified or/and not clearly demonstrated [9]. Being an IS researcher, I believe in assumption (2) as I doubt that the wide use of IS in practice to support core business processes in many service and manufacturing industries is based on the error of practitioners, who would then have made suboptimal investment decisions. The consequence of believing in assumption (2) is to further assume that the main instruments for identifying and synthesizing (IS business value) knowledge, literature reviews, have not been used effectively. In this paper, the notion "literature review" refers to a paper that conducts the review of research papers as a task on its own; I do not investigate literature reviews that are conducted as a start of a research project. The particular appropriateness of literature reviews to preserve domain knowledge in general is stressed in an MISQ guest editorial [11].

Several authors published literature reviews on IS business value during the past 20 years in pertinent academic outlets. But what did go wrong? Haven't reviews managed to preserve findings, to build theories, and to prevent researchers from getting lost in the "jungle of literature", which is accompanied by a variety of methodologies, research objects, research models, and findings? Addressing these questions requires to analyze how literature reviews have synthesized findings in terms of methodologies and theories used and how they have contributed to building theories on IS business value. Coherent methodology and theories (or at least propositions) are regarded the essential "ingredients" of research manuscripts in general [12] and literature reviews in particular [11; 13-15]. The particular importance of theory building is stressed by Sutton and Staw [12, p. 380], who believe that *"[w]ithout constant pressure for theory building, the field would surely slide to its natural resting place in dust-bowl empiricism."* Sutton and Staw also highlight the importance of theory and methods.

In this paper, I conduct the aforementioned analysis by investigating 18 literature reviews on IS business value, which were published in pertinent academic outlets, such as MISQ, ISR, JMIS, EJIS, ICIS, CACM, JAIS, and ACM Computing Surveys, during the past 20 years. From a research methodological point of view, this paper is thus a meta review. Its main goals are to provide insights about how literature reviews on IS business value are performed within IS research, and to provide suggestions on how to overcome deficiencies in methodology.

The rest of this paper is structured as follows: Section 2 provides the background of the "ingredients" of my research, more specifically "IS and IS business value", "theories", and "literature review methodology". In Section 3, the research methodology of this study is presented. Section 4 analyzes the literature reviews regarding their applied methodologies and theories. Section 5 discusses the findings and draws a picture of how literature reviews influenced their successors in terms of theory use and theory building. Finally, Section 6 concludes this article and highlights major findings.

2 Background

2.1 IS and IS Business Value

The academic field of IS is terminologically pervaded by the use of syntactically similar notions, such as "information system (IS)", "information technology (IT)" and "information and communication technology (ICT)". However, these notions often lack any precise definition and differentiation, and they are often also based on different understandings of various authors. Reviewing articles published in "Information Systems Research", [16] find that the "IT artifact" has not been theorized and is widely interpreted depending on the specific research context. Having reviewed more than 200 papers related to IS business value, I find that this problem still exists. The notional fuzziness and heterogeneous semantics in literature is not surprising, because the IS discipline does not yet provide a broadly-accepted or even standardized ontology. For example, there are only few glossaries available, which even differ in their definitions of "IS" or "IT". In this paper, I adopt the "holistic" view on IS, as described in the ATIS Telecom Glossary [17, option 3]: *"The entire infrastructure, organization, personnel, and components for the collection, processing, storage, transmission, display, dissemination, and disposition of information."* Consequently, I consider literature reviews on the technological, organizational and/or personnel facet of IS.

The literature on the economic value of IS is extensive and, unsurprisingly, reveals different understandings of what IS business value is or can be. Understandings (can) differ in terms of notion and scope and in terms of the level, object and time of evaluation.

Notion and scope: The abundance of economic articles on IS offers a variety of notions and semantics. For example, early works use the notions "value", "benefit", "outcome" or "worth" [18; 19], Melville et al. [20] investigate "organizational performance", and Kohli and Grover [21] refer to value as "economic impact". This variety in terminology does not only mirror notional inconsistencies, it also reflects different understandings (semantics) of how to operationalize the economic impact of IS. For example, a large subset of empirical studies apply econometric approaches by analyzing the relationship between IS investments and economic variables, such as productivity [5], "Return on Sales" [21], or Tobin's q [22]. This view is accompanied by the widely adopted classification into process performance and organizational/firm performance measures [20; 23; 24]. Other studies stress that, beyond financial and non-financial measures, intangible assets can be affected by IS investments, such as organizational capabilities [9] or the strategic position [25].

Level of evaluation: The literature suggests different levels for the examination of the economic impact of IS. A widely used classification distinguishes individual level, firm level, industry level and economy level [26-30]. In addition, research can also focus on consumer surplus [26; 28; 29].

Object of evaluation: Consistent with the holistic definition of IS adopted in this paper, I address the economic impact of investments in information technology (hardware, software, technological infrastructure), in organizational assets (e.g. creation of a CIO position), and in personnel (e.g. improvement of employees' IS skills).

Time of evaluation: As Kohli and Grover [9] stress, research on IS value can be of "ex ante" and "ex post" nature. While "ex ante" research is closely related to decision making, "ex post" research is dedicated to the control of past expenses.

2.2 Theories

Because theories are an important concept in literature research methodology (see next subsection), I briefly introduce the concept of theories here. The first and probably most important question is what theory is. Although the notion of "theory" is widely used in many academic disciplines, there is a *"[...] lack of consensus what exactly theory is [...]"*, as [12, p. 371] remark. Based on the work of Dubin [31], Whetten [32] argues that a theory has four constituent elements: While factors (variables, constructs, concepts) and the relationship between them constitute the subject of a theory (what and how elements), the underlying dynamics that justify the selection of factors and the proposed causal relationships constitute the theoretical glue that welds the model together (why element). It should be noticed that [31; 32] do not distinguish between a "model" and a "theory"; Sutton and Staw [12] note in their introduction that *"[...] [t] here is a lack of agreement whether a model and a theory can be distinguished"*. Whetten [32] even uses the expression "theoretical model" to refer to the fourth element of a theory, the who, where and when conditions. They place limitations on the propositions generated from a theoretical model and need to be discovered through tests of the rudimentary theoretical statement. The inclusion of the why element is consistent with the view of Sutton and Staw [12], who require a theory to have logic included and who state (subsection "Lists of Variables or Constructs Are Not Theory") that *"[a] theory must also explain why variables or constructs come about or why they are connected"*.

According to Gregor [33], the consideration of explanations as a constituent element of theory is based on a specific perspective on theories. Other perspectives also allow for non-explaining theories. Gregor [33] suggests as components common to all theories "means of representation" (physical representation by words, logic, diagrams, tables etc.), "constructs" (phenomena of interest), "statements of relationship", and "scope" (degree of generality of the statements of relationships). She also proposes a taxonomy of theory types (analysis, explanation, prediction, explanation and prediction, design and action) in IS research. It should be noticed that, in contrast to [12; 31; 32], [33] does not require a theory to contain an explanatory component.

As this work is not about defining or building a theory, I will not discuss to what extent concepts proposed as theories – be they rooted in IS or in other disciplines – match different understandings; for a list of theories that are widely used in IS research see [34].

Although the aforementioned works are milestones in theory literature, it remains the question of how to resolve different understandings in the context of this paper, IS theories that are used or developed in literature reviews. I find the approach of Sutton and Staw [12] useful, who argue in their introduction that *"[...] though there is conflict about what theory is and should be, there is more consensus about what theory is not."* More specifically, the authors explicitly refer to references, data, lists of variables or constructs, diagrams, propositions, and hypotheses as concepts that are not theory (albeit they may be useful tools to build or describe a theory). In this paper, I consider theories used or developed in literature reviews through the lens of [12], which consequently means that I regard an explanatory component a mandatory feature of any theory.

2.3 Review Methodology

"Literature review" is an established research methodology [35; 36] and important for IS research, as stressed by Webster and Watson [11, p. xiii f), who argue that the literature review *"[...] facilitates theory development, closes areas where a plethora of research exists, and uncovers areas where research is needed. [...][T]he literature review represents the foundation for research in IS. As such, review articles are critical to strengthening IS as a field of study."* The relevance of literature reviews has also been addressed by editors of renowned IS journals. For example, several years ago "MIS Quarterly" launched its "MISQ Review Department", a unit dedicated to the publication of literature reviews that was later renamed "MISQ Theory and Review Department". The "European Journal of Information System" and the "Journal of Management Information Systems" are further examples of renowned journals that explicitly include review papers and surveys in their scope of invited contributions. Apparently, literature reviews are deemed an important methodology in IS research to preserve domain knowledge.

The particular challenge to write good reviews is stressed in the description of the objectives of the MISQ Theory and Review Department (http://www.misq.org/misreview/MISQTRObjectives.html). We better understand what this means when we read the paper of Webster and Watson [11]. They provide a guide for writing a literature review that recommends using four key methodological components: (1) the systematic identification of relevant literature, (2) the structuring of the literature review by a coherent concept, (3) the development or the extension of a theory and (4) the evaluation of this theory (extension). I briefly discuss these steps, which are shown in Figure 1, by linking steps 2-4 to the understanding of theories as discussed above:

1. The authors recommend a structured approach that includes scanning table of contents, querying journal databases, and viewing selected conference proceedings. They further recommend to conduct a backward search (following references of identified papers) and a forward search (e.g. by using Web of Science) to find articles that cite relevant works. The requirement to conduct a

literature search that is systematic and comprehensive is also stressed by Zorn and Campbell [14, p. 174].
2. The authors recommend a structured approach that includes scanning table of contents, querying journal databases, and viewing selected conference proceedings. They further recommend to conduct a backward search (following references of identified papers) and a forward search (e.g. by using Web of Science) to find articles that cite relevant works. The requirement to conduct a literature search that is systematic and comprehensive is also stressed by Zorn and Campbell [14, p. 174].
3. The presentation of literature findings needs to be structured by using a coherent concept [11, p. xiv; 13, p. 233; 14, p. 175]. Webster and Watson [11] cite Bem [15, p. 172]: *"A coherent review emerges only from a coherent conceptual structuring of the topic itself. For most reviews, this requires a guiding theory, a set of competing models, or a point of view about the phenomenon under discussion."* As this part of a review is dedicated to preserve past literature findings, presumably those theories are particularly relevant that are classified in [33] as "analysis theory" or "explanation theory". According to the understanding of Webster and Watson [11] and Bem [15], the usage of a theory is not regarded mandatory.
4. Literature reviews should not only synthesize prior research, but also identify critical knowledge gaps and motivate researchers to close this breach. In order to making a chart for further research, Webster and Watson [11] propose to develop a theory or to extend a current theory. However, their understanding of "theory" includes models, propositions, and justifications, although they refer to Sutton and Staw [12] by saying that *"[m]odels and propositions capture relationships between variables, but do not, on their own, represent theory."* (p. xix). As mentioned in the previous subsection, I follow the understanding of [12] and distinguish between theories and propositions.
5. The evaluation of theories or propositions is described as "difficult and nebulous" by Webster and Watson [11]. In the light of the above discussion of theories, this phase can be aligned to working out what Dubin [31] considers as "who, where and when conditions" of a theory.

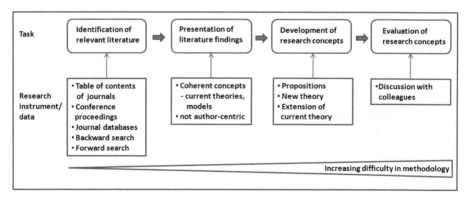

Fig. 1. Key tasks and research instruments in literature reviews, as suggested in [11]

3 Research Methodology

In order to achieve the goal of this paper, the identification of methodological and theory-related weaknesses of literature reviews, I first conducted a comprehensive literature search for reviews on IS business value. I used the research instruments for the identification of relevant literature, as described above. More specifically, I performed a title search in pertinent journal databases, namely Business Source Premier, MLA International Bibliography, EconLit, ScienceDirect, IEEE Xplore, The ACM Digital Library, and Web of Science. The logical search string was: ("IT" OR "information technology" OR "IS" OR "information systems") AND ("value" OR "investment" OR "productivity" OR "competitive" OR "performance" OR "measurement" OR "evaluation" OR "profit" OR "efficiency"). I did not limit my search to any specific time period. The last update of my search was conducted on 1 June 2008. In order to assure that no studies published in one of the most important IS journals are overlooked, I further scanned the table of contents of the following journals:

- MIS Quarterly, Communications of the ACM, Information Systems Research, Management Science, and Journal of Management Information Systems: These journals were classified as the five leading journals in the latest MIS journal ranking [37].
- European Journal of Information Systems, Information Systems Journal, and Journal of AIS: These journals are included in the more recent AIS list entitled "Senior Scholars' Basket of Journals" (http://home.aisnet.org/displaycommon.cfm?an=1&subarticlenbr=346).
- Academy of Management Review, ACM Transactions on Information Systems, American Economic Review: Reviewing many references provided in the literature, I found these journals appropriate candidates for containing valuable articles on IS business value. However, this selection mirrors the subjective opinion of the author. The time period under consideration was January 1995 until May 2008.

I also scanned the conference proceedings of the International Conference on Information Systems (1994-2008) using the AIS Electronic Library (AISeL).

I identified 18 literature reviews, which are listed in chronological order in Table 1. The model shown in Figure 1 is used to analyze these literature reviews in order to identify methodological and theory-related weaknesses. More specifically, the reviews are analyzed with regard to the identification of considered literature, the presentation of literature findings, the development of research concepts, and the evaluation of research concepts. Additionally, I apply a cross-review analysis in order to investigate the coherence of the literature review landscape in terms of whether literature reviews have considered each other and have jointly contributed to theory building in IS business value research.

4 Analysis

Table 2 (see Appendix) provides for each literature review a description of the considered literature and the identification procedure, the presentation of literature findings, the development of research concepts and the evaluation of research concepts. The following subsections describe the results and refer to the studies by their abbreviations as given in Tables 1 and 2.

Table 1. Investigated literature reviews

Year	Authors	Publication outlet
1989	Kauffman and Weill (KW) [27]	International Conference on Information Systems
1992	DeLone and Mclean (DM) [38]	Information Systems Research
1993	Brynjolfsson (Br) [39]	Communications of the ACM
1995	Soh and Markus (SM) [40]	International Conference on Information Systems
1996	Brynjolfsson and Yang (BY) [28]	Advances in Computers
1998	Sircar et al. (Si) [41]	The Journal of Engineering Valuation and Cost Analysis
1999	Seddon et al. (Se) [42]	Communications of the AIS
2000	Bannister and Remenyi (BR) [3]	Journal of Information Technology
2000	Chan (Ch) [43]	Journal of Management Information Systems
2000	Devaraj and Kohli (DK) [29]	Journal of Management Information Systems
2002	Dehning and Richardson (DR) [24]	Journal of Information Systems
2002	Irani and Love (IL) [44]	European Journal of Information Systems
2002	Sylla and Wen (SW) [45]	International Journal of Technology Management
2003	Dedrick et al. (De) [46]	ACM Computing Surveys
2004	Melville et al. (Me) [20]	MIS Quarterly
2007	Chau et al. (Chau) [30]	European Journal of Information Systems
2007	Wan et al. (Wa) [47]	Americas Conference on Information Systems
2008	Kohli and Grover (KG) [9]	Journal of the AIS

4.1 Considered Literature

Seven reviews (KW, Si, BR, DK, IL, SW, KG) do not describe how they identify relevant literature, the others provide a description that includes the period and/or the academic journals and conference proceedings selected. Only one study (Me) describes the selection procedure in detail. One study (SM) differs from all others in that it considers five other works and describes them in much detail.

4.2 Presentation of Literature Findings

Most reviews (KW, DM, Br, BY, Si, Se, BR, Ch, DK, IL, SW, Chau, Wa) apply a taxonomy/classification to structure the presentation of literature findings. One review (SM) analyzes five other theoretical models in detail; another review (KG) unfolds literature findings along research statements. Three reviews (DR, De, Me) propose and apply a research framework (I require a framework to contain at least what and how elements). One of these reviews (DR) lacks an explanatory component so that the framework is not regarded a theory in this paper. In contrast, the production system framework of (De) is explained and motivated, likewise the "IT Business Value Model "of (Me). Thus, I regard both frameworks as theories in the sense of Sutton and Staw [12].

4.3 Development of Research Concepts

While five reviews (Br, Si, Se, IL, Chau) do not develop any research concepts, six reviews (KW, BY, Ch, DR, De, Wa) provide informal research recommendations, three reviews (DK, Me, KG) provide concrete research propositions (KG even provide a detailed research agenda in their work, which is both a review and an essay), one review (SW) develops a formal decision model, one review (BR) suggests a process model (without explanatory component), and two reviews (DM, SM) propose theories (IS success model/theory and process theory, respectively).

4.4 Evaluation of Research Concepts

Only one work (DK) performs an evaluation of the research concept (propositions) through empirical study in health care industry. However, this study is not a designed as "pure" literature review, although it contains a comprehensive review component.

4.5 Cross-Review Analysis

An overview of the relationships between the 18 literature reviews shows Figure 2, which distinguishes between three types of relationships: a methodological or theoretical impact is indicated by a bold arrow, a (weaker) consideration of a work and inclusion in the list of references is indicated by a dashed arrow, and a dotted arrow symbolizes an indirect consideration through the citation of the work of Seddon [48], who extends the model of DeLone and McLean [38].

The IS success model/theory developed by (DM) is used by (Chau) in order to define the IS value dimension of their taxonomy. Although (Se) also rely on the work of (DM), (Se) do not use the model/theory of (DM), they only follow the research methodology of (SM) to test the generality of their proposed matrix.

The review of (Br) is used by the same author (and a new co-author) to present a revised and extended version. The work of (Br) is also used by (Wa), who code input and output variables for each empirical study, as (Br) argues that the definition and measurement of input and output may explain different results of firm productivity. (Wa) also analyze studies with regard to deficiencies in measurement and methodology, as identified by (Br).

The process theory proposed by (SM) is only used in one review (Si), which classifies studies according to whether they are supported by variance theory or by process theory.

The taxonomy applied by (Se) to structure their review is used by (Chau) in order to define one dimension, which accounts for stakeholders, types of system, units of analysis, types of data, and research methods.

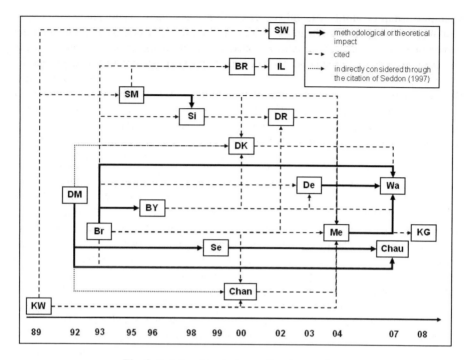

Fig. 2. Relationships between literature reviews

The theories of (De) and (Me) are used in only one review (Wa) to define their taxonomy.

5 Discussion

About one third of all reviews do not explicitly describe how the authors identified relevant literature and which criteria they used to select studies. This phenomenon is neither limited to specific outlets nor to specific time periods. Although this lack in description does not mean that the authors did not apply an appropriate procedure, but the reader is not informed about it. This limitation in transparency has at least two consequences: a) readers do not know whether the results of the review draw a representative picture of the literature, b) authors of future reviews have difficulties in identifying complementary literature search spaces, which still need to be explored. While consequence a) limits the informative value for the community and for those who doubt the economic value of IS, b) hampers progress in reviewing the literature. In cases where authors have already applied a systematic literature search, it is not laborious to describe the procedure, and they should do so. In other cases, authors should start to apply (and finally describe) their systematic literature search.

The presentation of literature findings is methodologically dominated by the application of a taxonomy/classification, which can regarded as research concept in the sense of Webster and Watson [11]. Only three reviews use a framework, with two of them also providing an explanatory component, and thus a theory. Overall, this picture is not surprising, as it is more challenging to present and to use a theory in the presentation of literature findings than to use a taxonomy. However, this result is sobering at the same time, as the application of a theory bears the potential for its validation. What we need is more reviews that are theory-based. Excellent examples and guides for future literature reviewers are the reviews of (Me) and (De).

The development of research concepts, including the development of theories is probably even more challenging than applying an existing concept or theory to structure the presentation of literature findings. This difficulty is mirrored in the investigated reviews: Those reviews that provide concepts for further research mainly use informal research recommendations or research propositions. Only two works (DM, SM) spare no efforts to propose a new theory for IS business value (IS success theory and process theory, respectively). They are most valuable for making a chart for further research. However, the history of literature reviews shows how difficult it is to propose new theories. The examples of (DM) and (SM) provide good examples of how to accomplish this task.

The evaluation of research concepts and proposed theories is the most disregarded task. Only one review (DK) tests its propositions through an empirical study. However, although the work of (DK) provides a good literate review, it was primarily not designed to synthesize findings, but to test propositions in the health care industry. However, in the contemporaneous presence of excellent reviews and absence of the evaluation of research concepts in all reviews but one, the question rises of whether we require reviews to provide too much. Some of the investigated literature reviews provide examples of how laborious it is to sufficiently accomplish the other three tasks. In order to make literature reviews more manageable, I therefore argue to regard the evaluation task as an optional part of a review.

The analysis of the relationships between reviews shows that only five reviews (Se, BY, Si, Wa, Chau) use prior reviews as methodological or theoretic input. Only one of these reviews (Se) is used by another review: however, the reviews (Chau) and (Wa) were published only two years ago (2007) so that their reuse cannot be reliably assessed currently. I found six reviews that impact other reviews. Interestingly, four of them (DM, SM, De, Me) use or propose theories. In other words, each review based on a theory is reused by at least another one. Apparently, it is the theory-based reviews that determine large parts of the relationships between reviews. However, the overall linkage of reviews is weak in terms of quantity and quality (progress in theory development through chains of reviews). One might argue that this phenomenon mirrors diversity in research and is therefore valuable. On the other hand, we see almost no progress in theory development and advancement, which are valuable, if not essential, for the identification and presentation of the economic value of IS.

6 Summary and Conclusions

As it is argued in the literature that researchers have not fully managed to identify and to explain the economic relevance of IS, this paper assumes that literature reviews, which represent the most powerful instrument for the identification and synthesis of knowledge, have not been conducted effectively due to deficiencies in methodology.

The analysis presented in this paper investigates 18 literature reviews published in pertinent academic outlets during the past 20 years, is based on the methodological framework proposed by Webster and Watson [11], and shows the following weaknesses of past literature reviews on IS business value:

- About one third of all reviews do not explicitly describe how the authors identified relevant literature and which criteria they used to select studies. This limitation in transparency should be avoided in further literature reviews on IS business value by applying systematic literature search and by also describing it explicitly. The review of Melville et al. [20] provides an excellent example.
- The presentation of literature findings very rarely contains an explanatory component, which is regarded as a mandatory component of a theory [12; 31; 32]. Thus, I suggest drawing on theories in future literature reviews more thoroughly. A good overview of theories already applied in IS business value research is provided in [20], which presents approaches based on microeconomic theory, industrial organization theory, and resource-based view, amongst others. The application of a theory in a literature review on IS business value is very well demonstrated in [20;46].
- Only two reviews [38;40] propose a new theory for IS business value, which is certainly one of the most challenging tasks in a literature review, but which is also valuable, if not necessary, for making a chart for further research. While it is one option (and probably the most challenging one) to develop a new theory from scratch, others are the adoption of theories from disciplines other than the IS discipline, and the extension or modification of theories already used in the IS business value literature. The latter option includes the adoption of theories used in literature reviews on IS business value. However, my analysis shows that only five literature reviews used prior reviews as methodological or theoretic input. Thus, I also suggest drawing on (theories used in) existing literature reviews on IS business value.
- The evaluation of research concepts and proposed theories has been the most disregarded task in literature reviews on IS business value. However, in the contemporaneous presence of excellent reviews and the absence of the evaluation of research concepts in all reviews but one, the question rises of whether we require reviews to provide too much. Thus, I argue to regard the evaluation task as an optional part of a review in order to make literature reviews more manageable. A valuable methodological contribution of further research would be the suggestion and demonstration of guidelines for the evaluation of research concepts and theories, which is still "difficult and nebulous" [11].

It should be emphasized that the identified weaknesses in the analyzed reviews are not necessarily due to methodological decisions of the respective authors. An alternative explanation would be that in some cases authors needed to consider (well-founded) demands from journal reviewers and editors. However, respective information has not been available (to the author).

Acknowledgement

I appreciate the critical and helpful remarks of three anonymous reviewers.

References

1. Carr, N.G.: IT Doesn't Matter. Harvard Business Review 81(5), 41–49 (2003)
2. WITSA, Global ICT Spending Tops $3.5 Trillion: Industry Experiences Subdued Spending Growth (2008),
   http://www.witsa.org/press/Digital_Planet_Release_final.doc
3. Bannister, F., Remenyi, D.: Acts of faith: instinct, value and IT investment decisions. Journal of Information Technology 15(3), 231–241 (2000)
4. West, L.A., Courtney, J.F.: The Information Problems in Organizations – A Research Model for the Value of Information and Information Systems. Decision Sciences 24(2), 229–251 (1993)
5. Hitt, L.M., Brynjolfsson, E.: Productivity, Business Profitability, and Consumer Surplus: Three Different Measures of Information Technology Value. MIS Quarterly 20(2), 121–142 (1996)
6. Stiroh, K., Botsch, M.: Information Technology and Productivity Growth in the 2000s. German Economic Review 8(2), 255–280 (2007)
7. Im, K.S., Dow, K.E., Grover, V.: A Reexamination of IT Investment and the Market Value of the Firm – An Event Study Methodology. Information Systems Research 12(1), 103–117 (2001)
8. Dehning, B., Stratopoulos, T.: Dupont Analysis of an IT-Enabled Competitive Advantage. The International Journal of Accounting Information Systems 3(3), 165–176 (2002)
9. Kohli, R., Grover, V.: Business value of IT: An essay on expanding research directions to keep up with the times. Journal of the Association for Information Systems 9(1), 23–39 (2008)
10. Agarwal, R., Lucas, H.C.: The Information Systems Identity Crisis: Focusing on High-Visibility and High-Impact Research. MIS Quarterly 29(3), 381–398 (2005)
11. Webster, J., Watson, R.T.: Analyzing the past to prepare for the future: Writing a literature review. MIS Quarterly 26(2), xiii–xxiii (2002)
12. Sutton, R.I., Staw, B.M.: What Theory Is Not. Administrative Science Quarterly 40(3), 371–384 (1995)
13. Baker, M.J.: Writing a Literature Review. The Marketing Review 1, 219–247
14. Zorn, T., Campbell, N.: Improving the Writing of Literature Reviews Through a Literature Integration Exercise. Business Communication Quarterly 69(2), 172–183 (2006)
15. Bem, D.J.: Writing a Review for Psychological Bulletin. Psychological Bulletin 118(2), 172–177 (1995)
16. Orlikowski, W.J., Iacono, C.S.: Desperately Seeking the 'IT' in IT Research. A Call to Theorizing the IT Artifact. Information Systems Research 12(2), 121–134 (2001)
17. ATIS, ATIS Telecom Glossary 2007 (2007), http://www.atis.org/glossary/
18. Wiseman, D.: Information Economics: a practical approach to valuing information systems. Journal of Information Technology 7(3), 169–176 (1992)
19. Berghout, E., Renkema, T.: Evaluating information systems investment proposals: a comparative review of current methodologies. Information and Software Technology 37(1), 1–13 (1997)

20. Melville, N., Kraemer, K., Gurbaxani, V.: Review: Information technology and organizational performance: An integrative model of IT business value. MIS Quarterly 28(2), 283–322 (2004)
21. Bharadwaj, A.S.: A resource-based perspective on information technology capability and firm performance: An empirical investigation. MIS Quarterly 24(1), 169–196 (2000)
22. Brynjolfsson, E., Yang, S.: The intangible costs and benefits of computer investments: Evidence from the financial markets. In: Proceedings of the International Conference on Information Systems, Atlanta, Georgia (1999)
23. Barua, A., Kriebel, C.H., Mukhopadhyay, T.: Information technologies and business value – an analytical and empirical investigation. Information Systems Research 6(1), 3–23 (1995)
24. Dehning, B., Richardson, V.J.: Returns on Investments in Information Technology: A Research Synthesis. Journal of Information Systems 16(1), 7–30 (2002)
25. Irani, Z.: Information systems evaluation – navigating through the problem domain. Information & Management 40(1), 11–24 (2002)
26. Bakos, J.Y.: Dependent Variables for the Study of Firm and Industry-Level Impacts of Information Technology. In: Proceedings of the International Conference on Information Systems, Pittsburgh, Pennsylvania, USA (1987)
27. Kauffman, R.J., Weill, P.: An Evaluative Framework for Research on the Performance Effects of Information Technology Investment. In: Proceedings of the International Conference on Information Systems, Boston, Massachusetts, USA, pp. 377–388 (1989)
28. Brynjolfsson, E., Yang, S.: Information Technology and Productivity: A Review of the Literature. Advances in Computers 43, 179–215 (1996)
29. Devaraj, S., Kohli, R.: Information technology payoff in the health-care industry: A longitudinal study. Journal of Management Information Systems 16(4), 41–67 (2000)
30. Chau, P.Y.K., Kuan, K.K.Y., Liang, T.P.: Research on IT value: what we have done in Asia and Europe. European Journal of Information Systems 16(3), 196–201 (2007)
31. Dubin, R.: Theory development. Free Press, New York (1978)
32. Whetten, D.A.: What constitutes a theoretical contribution? Academy of Management Review 14(4), 490–495 (1989)
33. Gregor, S.: The Nature of Theory in Information Systems. MIS Quarterly 30(3), 611–642 (2006)
34. York University, Theories Used in IS Research Wiki (2009), http://www.fsc.yorku.ca/york/istheory/wiki/index.php/Main_Page
35. Salipante, P., Notz, W., Bigelow, J.: A Matrix Approach to Literature Reviews. In: Staw, B.M., Cummings, L.L. (eds.) Research in Organizational Behavior, pp. 321–348. JAI Press, Greenwich (1982)
36. Cooper, H.M.: Synthesizing research - a guide for literature reviews, 3rd edn. Sage Publications, Thousand Oaks (1998)
37. Rainer, K., Miller, M.: Examining differences across journal rankings. Communications of the ACM 48(2), 91–94 (2005)
38. DeLone, W.H., McLean, E.R.: Measuring e-commerce success: Applying the DeLone & McLean information systems success model. International Journal of Electronic Commerce 9(1), 31–47 (2004)
39. Brynjolfsson, E.: The productivity paradox of information technology. Communications of the ACM 36(12), 66–77 (1993)

40. Soh, C., Markus, M.L.: How IT Creates Business Value: A Process Theory Synthesis. In: Proceedings of the 16th International Conference on Information Systems, Amsterdam, The Netherlands (1995)
41. Sircar, S., Turnbow, J.L., Bordoloi, B.: The impact of information technology investments on firm performance: a review of the literature. The Journal of Engineering Valuation and Cost Analysis 1(3), 171–181 (1998)
42. Seddon, P.B., Patnayakuni, R., Bowtell, M.: Dimensions of information systems success. Communications of the AIS 2(3), 1–61 (1999)
43. Chan, Y.E.: IT value: The great divide between qualitative and quantitative and individual and organizational measures. Journal of Management Information Systems 16(4), 225–261 (2000)
44. Irani, Z., Love, P.E.D.: Developing a frame of reference for ex-ante IT/IS investment evaluation. European Journal of Information Systems 11(1), 74–82 (2002)
45. Sylla, C., Wen, H.J.: A conceptual framework for evaluation of information technology investments. International Journal of Technology Management 24(2-3), 236–261 (2002)
46. Dedrick, J., Gurbaxani, V., Kraemer, K.L.: Information technology and economic performance: A critical review of the empirical evidence. ACM Computing Surveys 35(1), 1–28 (2003)
47. Wan, Z., Fang, Y., Wade, M.: The Ten-Year Odyssey of the IS Productivity Paradoxon – A Citation Analysis (1996-2006). In: Proceedings of the Americas Conference on Information Systems, Keystone, CO, USA (2007)
48. Seddon, P.B.: A respecification and extension of the DeLone and McLean model of IS success. Information Systems Research 8(3), 240–253 (1997)
49. Mason, R.O.: Measuring Information Output: A Communication Systems Approach. Information & Management 1(5), 219–234 (1978)
50. Shannon, C.E., Weaver, W.: The Mathematical Theory of Communication. University of Illinois Press, Urbana (1949)

Appendix

Table 2. Methodology of literature reviews

Review	Considered literature and identification procedure	Presentation of literature findings	Development of research concepts	Evaluation of research concepts
Kauffmann and Weill 1989 (KW)	13 empirical studies; selection driven by authors' preferences	Classification of studies according to methodology, focus, and caveats for measurement	Recommendations for research	--
DeLone and McLean 1992 (DM)	Conceptual contributions and 100 empirical studies; 01/81-01/88; 6 journals and one conference	Taxonomy with six dimensions of IS success (dependent variable): system quality, information quality, information use, user satisfaction, individual impact, and organizational impact; taxonomy influenced by communication theory [49; 50]	IS Success Model with categories of IS success, their relationships, and explanatory component (theory)	--
Brynjolfsson 1993 (Br)	Articles on productivity and IT, 30 leading journals in IS and economics	No research framework used; presentation of studies according to three categories: general studies, studies of IT in manufacturing, studies of IT in services; identification of deficiencies in measurement and methodology	--	--
Soh and Markus 1995 (SM)	Five theoretical process models	Each theoretical model is described in detail	Proposition of a process theory	--
Brynjolfsson and Yang 1996 (BY)	About 150 articles; selection based on studies considered in eight prior research studies, incl. Brynjolfsson 1993	No research framework used; presentation of studies according to five categories: general studies, economy-wide studies, industry-level studies, firm-level studies, studies on consumer surplus and economic growth; identification of deficiencies in measurement and methodology	Recommendations for further research	--
Sircar et al. 1998 (Si)	Productivity-related literature; selection of literature is not explained	Description of studies according to whether they are supported by variance theory or process theory	--	--
Seddon et al. 1999 (Se)	186 empirical papers that have been published in ISR, MISQ, or JMIS	Two-dimensional classification of IS effectiveness measures, with the type of system and the stakeholder being the dimensions	--	--
Bannister and Remenyi 2000 (BR)	Selection of literature is not explained	Taxonomy of techniques ("fundamental", "composite" and "meta model" techniques) for classifying evaluation techniques	Proposition of a decision process model; no explanatory component	--
Chan 2000 (Ch)	Articles published in CACM, ISR, JMIS, or MISQ; 1993-1998	Classification of contributions according to research methodology, measures used, and levels of analysis	Recommendations for research and management	--

Table 2. (*continued*)

Review	Considered literature and identification procedure	Presentation of literature findings	Development of research concepts	Evaluation of research concepts
Devaraj and Kohli 2000 (DK)	Selected studies; selection of studies is not explained in detail	Classification of research papers according to their level of study (economy, industry, firm) and the variables and measures used	Research propositions	Test of propositions through empirical study in health care industry
Dehning and Richardson 2002 (DR)	Classification of 31 empirical studies; 1997-2001; studies in leading journals and conferences and listed in Sircar et al. (1998)	Research framework that includes information technology measures, process measures, firm performance measures and contextual factors	Recommendations for further research	--
Irani and Love 2002 (IL)	Analysis of 36 studies on investment appraisal techniques; selection of literature is not explained	Classification of investment appraisal techniques in six categories	--	--
Sylla and Wen 2002 (SW)	Selection of literature not explained	Classification of IT evaluation techniques into those addressing tangible benefits, intangible benefits, or risk	Proposition of a formal decision model	--
Dedrick et al. 2003 (De)	Analysis of more than 50 empirical studies on productivity, 1985-2002; leading academic journals	Production system framework and classification into country, industry and firm level are used to organize the presentation of literature findings	Recommendations for future research	--
Melville et al. 2004 (Me)	Analysis of more than 200 articles; selection procedure adopted from [11]	Development and application of a descriptive model of the value generating process; model based on the resource-based view, microeconomics and industrial organization; use of the model to develop research questions, which are finally used to unfold literature findings	Development of research proposition	--
Chau et al. 2007 (Chau)	Analysis of articles published either at PACIS (1993-2005) or at ECIS (2000-2005)	Taxonomy (level of value, stakeholder, type of system, unit of analysis, type of data, and research method) for classifying research papers	--	--
Wan et al. 2007 (Wa)	Analysis of 150 articles (1996-2006) influenced by productivity paradox (Brynjolfsson & Hitt 1996); selection procedure described in detail	Classification of empirical research by their results (i.e., positive, negative, no effect, or contingent), research methods, and the input and output variables used	Recommendations for future research	--
Kohli and Grover 2008 (KG)	Selection of literature not explained	Research findings are summarized along seven statements	Proposition of a detailed research agenda	--

Author Index

Aanestad, Margunn 111
Adisa, Femi 34

Bødker, Keld 1
Bygstad, Bendik 50

Damsgaard, Jan 127

Ellingsen, Gunnar 93

Hanseth, Ole 50

Kaapu, Taina 18

Larsen, Eli 93
Lyytinen, Kalle 127

Madsen, Sabine 1

Pries-Heje, Lene 79

Salmela, Sari T. 65
Schryen, Guido 139
Schubert, Petra 34
Skorve, Espen 111
Sudzina, Frantisek 34
Syrjänen, Anna-Liisa 65

Tiainen, Tarja 18

Printing: Mercedes-Druck, Berlin
Binding: Stein+Lehmann, Berlin

Lecture Notes
in Business Information Processing 60

Series Editors

Wil van der Aalst
 Eindhoven Technical University, The Netherlands
John Mylopoulos
 University of Trento, Italy
Michael Rosemann
 Queensland University of Technology, Brisbane, Qld, Australia
Michael J. Shaw
 University of Illinois, Urbana-Champaign, IL, USA
Clemens Szyperski
 Microsoft Research, Redmond, WA, USA